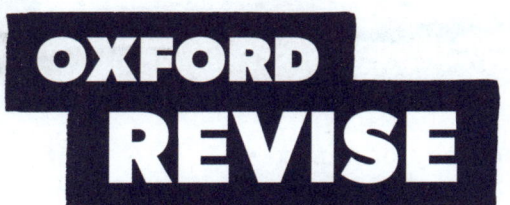

Edexcel GCSE
ENGLISH Language

COMPLETE REVISION AND PRACTICE

Series Editor: Jennifer Webb

Steve Eddy

Contents

 Shade in each level of the circle as you feel more confident and ready for your exam.

| How to use this book | iv |

| **Concept Knowledge** | **2-63** |

The key knowledge and concepts you need to know for the Edexcel GCSE English Language exam.

1 Texts and their meaning — 2
- Knowledge ⊖
- Retrieval ⊖

2 Figurative language — 10
- Knowledge ⊖
- Retrieval ⊖

3 Rhetorical language — 18
- Knowledge ⊖
- Retrieval ⊖

4 Characterisation, setting, and mood — 26
- Knowledge ⊖
- Retrieval ⊖

5 Ideas and perspectives — 34
- Knowledge ⊖
- Retrieval ⊖

6 Sentence forms — 42
- Knowledge ⊖
- Retrieval ⊖

7 Narrative structure — 48
- Knowledge ⊖
- Retrieval ⊖

8 Structuring an argument — 56
- Knowledge ⊖
- Retrieval ⊖

| **Exam Knowledge** | **64-213** |

The key requirements of the exam and revision guidance for each question.

Paper 1 Overview — 64

Question 1 — 66
- Knowledge ⊖
- Retrieval ⊖
- Practice ⊖

Question 2 — 72
- Knowledge ⊖
- Retrieval ⊖
- Practice ⊖

ii

Question 3	78
⚙ Knowledge ⊖	
⮂ Retrieval ⊖	
✏ Practice ⊖	

Question 4	88
⚙ Knowledge ⊖	
⮂ Retrieval ⊖	
✏ Practice ⊖	

Question 5/6	102
⚙ Knowledge ⊖	
⮂ Retrieval ⊖	
✏ Practice ⊖	

Paper 2 Overview — 118

Question 1	122
⚙ Knowledge ⊖	
⮂ Retrieval ⊖	
✏ Practice ⊖	

Question 2	128
⚙ Knowledge ⊖	
⮂ Retrieval ⊖	
✏ Practice ⊖	

Question 3	134
⚙ Knowledge ⊖	
⮂ Retrieval ⊖	
✏ Practice ⊖	

Question 4/5	146
⚙ Knowledge ⊖	
⮂ Retrieval ⊖	
✏ Practice ⊖	

Question 6	152
⚙ Knowledge ⊖	
⮂ Retrieval ⊖	
✏ Practice ⊖	

Question 7a	164
⚙ Knowledge ⊖	
⮂ Retrieval ⊖	
✏ Practice ⊖	

Question 7b	182
⚙ Knowledge ⊖	
⮂ Retrieval ⊖	
✏ Practice ⊖	

Question 8/9	200
⚙ Knowledge ⊖	
⮂ Retrieval ⊖	
✏ Practice ⊖	

Source banks — 214

Paper structure — 233

How to use this book

Oxford Revise Edexcel GCSE English Language is divided into two parts:

1 Concept Knowledge
2 Exam Knowledge

Part 1: Concept Knowledge

This section covers the key concepts and devices that you need to revise going into your exams.

Each topic includes Knowledge Organisers and Retrieval questions to support you to revise effectively.

The topics covered in this section include: texts and their meaning, figurative language, rhetorical language, character, setting, and mood, attitudes and perspectives, sentence forms, narrative structure, and structuring an argument.

Part 2: Exam Knowledge

This section takes you through all the questions you will encounter in Paper 1 and Paper 2 of your Edexcel GCSE English Language exam, following the Knowledge, Retrieval, Practice approach. It includes an overview of each paper, with guidance on each question and sample questions and answers. You will then check your knowledge through the Retrieval questions before moving onto the Practice exam-style questions.

The exam will measure how you have achieved against assessment objectives (AOs). In the Paper overview spreads in the Exam Knowledge section, you will see which AOs are tested in each question.

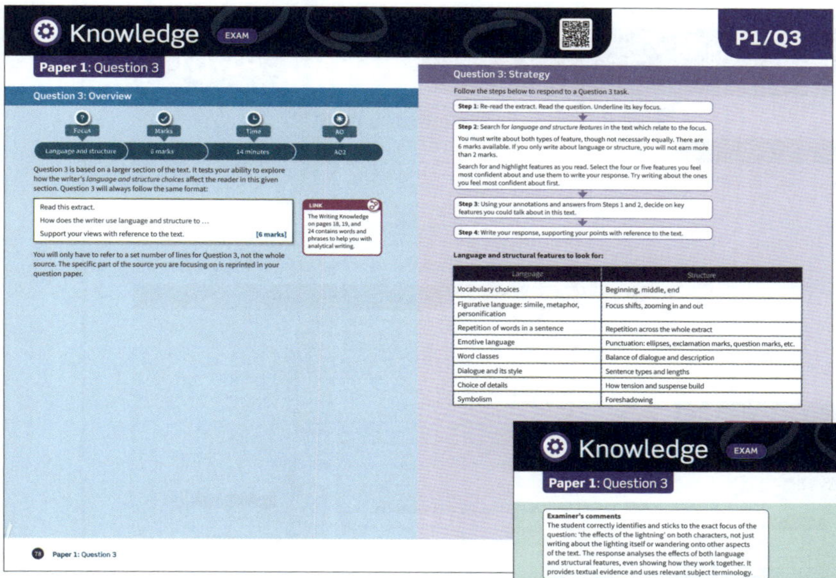

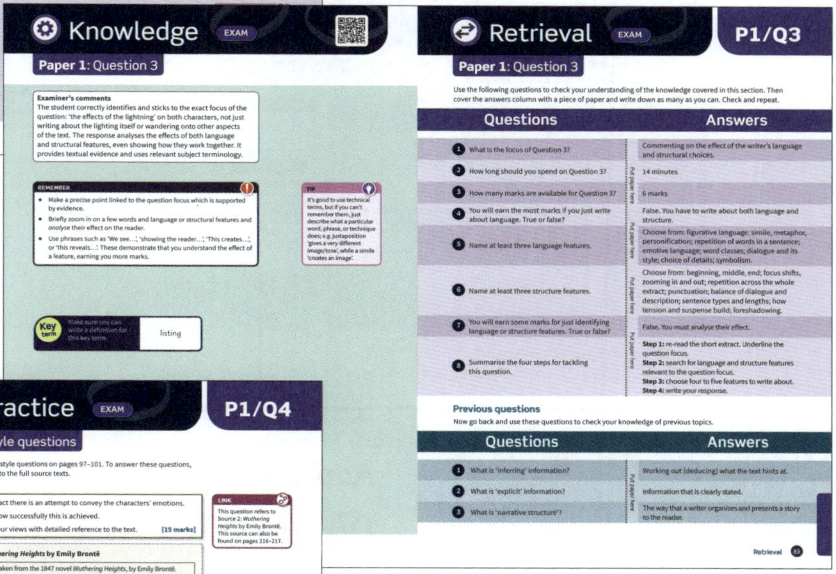

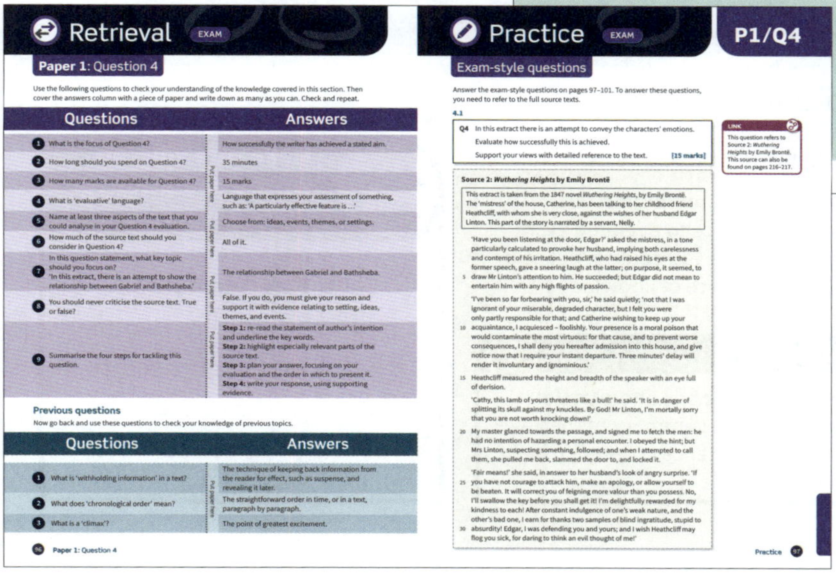

A Source Bank at the end of the book provides the source texts in the style of the exam and they are explored in questions in the Practice section.

On the following page, you will learn more about the Oxford Revise three-step approach to revision: Knowledge, Retrieval and Practice.

How to use this book

This book uses a three-step approach to revision: **Knowledge**, **Retrieval**, and **Practice**.
It is important that you do all three; they work together to make your revision effective.

 Knowledge

Knowledge comes first. Each chapter starts with a **Knowledge Organiser**. These are clear, easy-to-understand, concise summaries of the content that you need to know for your exam. The information is organised to show how one idea flows into the next so you can learn how everything is tied together.

> **LINK**
> The **Link** box offers a reference to a related topic or piece of knowledge that you could refer to for an exam question.

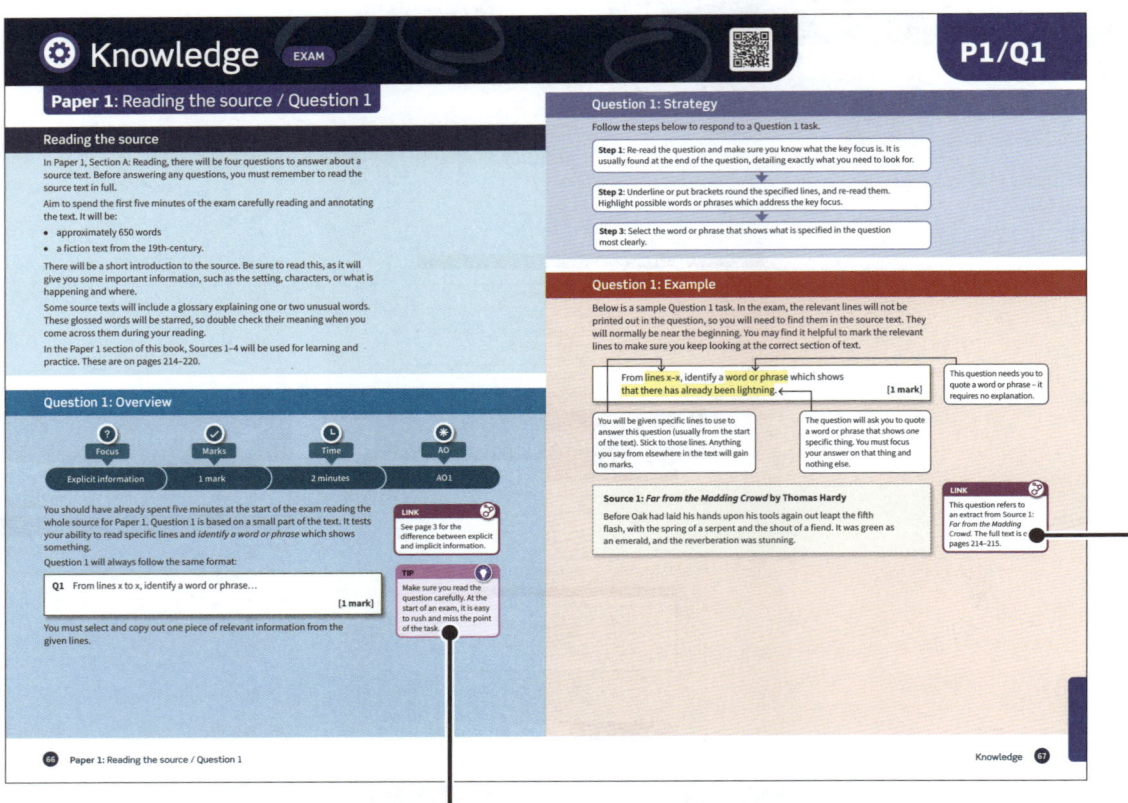

TIP
The **Tip** box offers you helpful advice and guidance to aid your revision and help you to understand key concepts and question requirements.

Additional features

> **QUESTION CONNECTION**
> The **Question Connection** box offers a reference to a related exam question where you could practise or include that piece of knowledge.

> **REMEMBER**
> The **Remember** box offers useful guidance and a summary of the key points and guidance covered in each exam unit.

> **Key terms** — Make sure you can write a definition for these key terms
>
> The **Key terms** box highlights the key words and phrases you need to know, remember, and be able to use confidently.

Retrieval

The **Retrieval questions** help you learn and quickly recall the information you've acquired. These are short questions and answers about the content in the Knowledge Organiser you have just revised. Cover up the answers with some paper and write down as many answers as you can from memory. Check back to the Knowledge Organiser for any you got wrong, then cover the answers and attempt all the questions again until you can answer *all* the questions correctly.

Make sure you revisit the Retrieval questions on different days to help them stick in your memory. You need to write down the answers each time, or say them out loud, for your revision to be effective.

Previous questions

Each chapter also has some **Retrieval questions** from **previous chapters**. Answer these to see if you can remember the content from the earlier chapters. If you get the answers wrong, go back and do the Retrieval questions for the earlier chapters again.

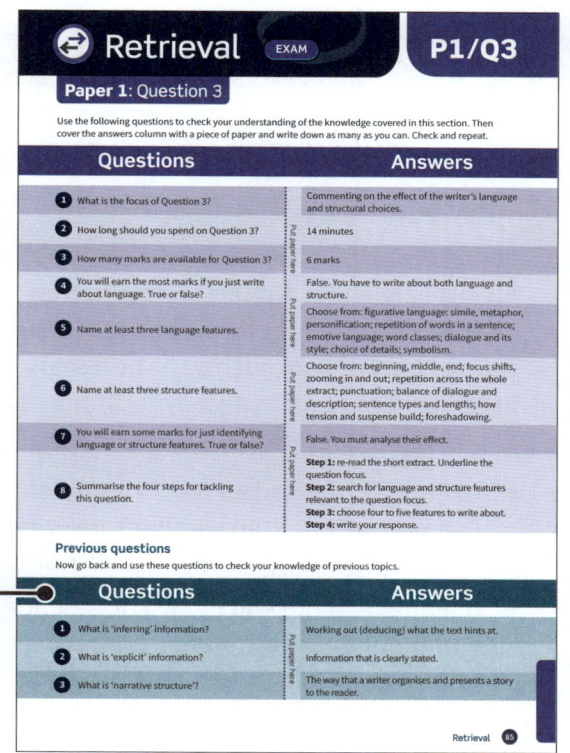

Practice

Once you are confident with the Knowledge Organiser and Retrieval questions, you can move on to the final stage: **Practice**.

Each chapter has **exam-style questions** to help you apply all the knowledge you have learnt.

Answers and Glossary

You can scan the QR code at any time to access sample answers and mark schemes for the exam-style questions, a glossary containing definitions of the key terms, as well as further revision support at go.oup.com/OR/GCSE/Ed/EngLang

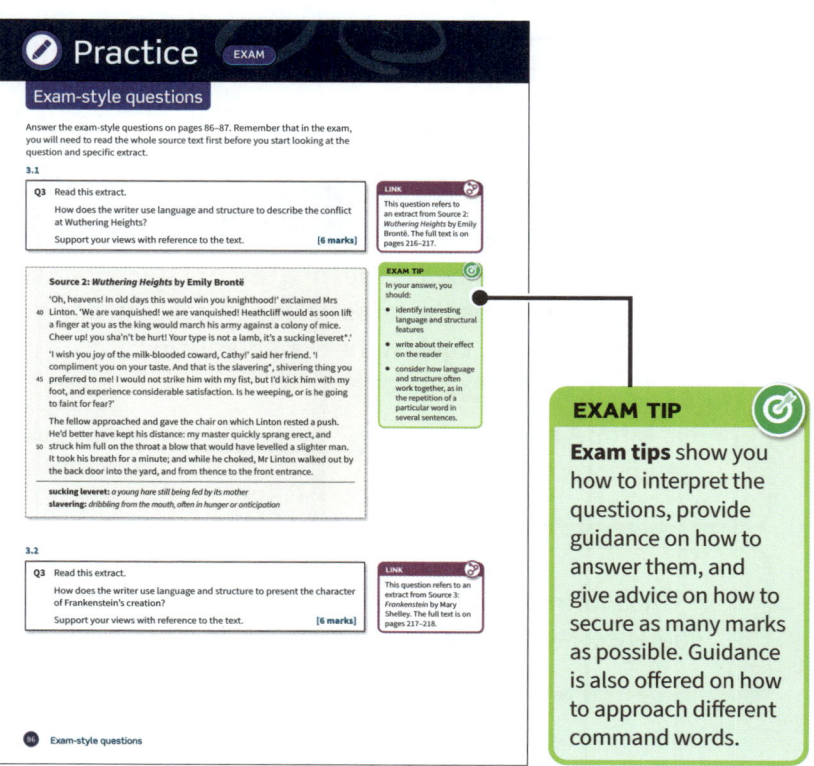

vii

Knowledge   CONCEPT

1 Texts and their meaning

What are texts and how do they create meaning?

It is important to establish the **text form**, **audience**, and **purpose** of any text, as these will influence the language, style, and structure.

Text forms

All texts are either **fiction** or **non-fiction** and they can be further divided into different forms of text. The text form refers to the style or type of text, such as a short story or speech. You will be asked to comment on and write a range of text forms in your English Language exam.

> **QUESTION CONNECTION**
>
> You could comment on text form in Paper 2 Questions 3 and 6.

- In Paper 1, the source text to comment on will be prose fiction (a story written from a writer's imagination). The text you will write will be fiction (either a description or narrative).
- In Paper 2, there will be two non-fiction source texts to comment on. They might include one or more of the following forms:

| articles | reports | autobiographies | accounts |
| letters | diaries | speeches | travel writing |

The text you will write in Paper 2 will be one of the following forms:

| letter | speech | article | review | section for leaflet/guidebook |

Audience

The audience is the intended reader of a text or listener of a speech. Who the audience is will shape the text's language, content, and the way it is presented to the reader. Look at the examples below.

Text form: A personal letter
Audience: One person
← This is likely to have a relaxed tone, mentioning details known only to the writer and the reader.

Text form: A speech
Audience: Multiple people
← This is likely to be more formal and well presented. However, the language used in a speech for children would be different to the language used in a speech for MPs, so it is important to establish the specific audience.

1

Purpose

The purpose of a text is the reason it is written, based on what the writer wants to achieve. It will also influence its content and how it is presented and written. One of the primary purposes of fiction is to engage readers in the characters and their story. Some of the purposes of non-fiction are below.

QUESTION CONNECTION

When writing a response to Paper 2 Question 8 or 9, give careful thought to the purpose of the text, as this will shape the language, content, and structure of your writing.

- to inform
- to instruct
- to argue a case
- to persuade
- to advise
- to entertain

Explicit meaning

This refers to information that is openly and clearly stated. The reader does not have to work it out or interpret it in any way.

> Toby was frightened of the dark.

QUESTION CONNECTION

The exam section explains how you will need to find explicit meaning for Paper 1 Question 1 (see pages 66–71) and Paper 2 Question 1 (see pages 122–127) and both *explicit* and *implicit* meaning for Paper 1 Question 2 (see pages 72–77) and Paper 2 Question 2 (see pages 128–133).

This sentence is a clear statement. The information is **explicit**.

Implicit meaning

This refers to information that must be deduced from clues in the text. The writer could be implying, hinting, or suggesting something. The reader must pick up on those clues, make conclusions, and work out what the **inference** is.

> 'Could you leave a light on?' said Toby nervously.

In this sentence, the reader can work out that Toby is scared of the dark, as he wants the light on and is nervous. The information is **implicit**.

Connotation

A **connotation** is a common association or link that a word or phrase might carry, in addition to its main explicit meaning.

> As they approached the house, night suddenly fell and the moon appeared.

The ideas of dark nights and moonlight have connotations of uncertainty and danger because of links with gothic stories.

1 Knowledge   3

Knowledge — CONCEPT

1 Texts and their meaning

What effects do writers create in different texts?

The text below is non-fiction. It is a piece of travel writing, which might be included as a source text in Paper 2. The purpose of travel writing is typically to engage and entertain an audience who are keen to share the writer's experiences of the place described.

Notice how the writer conveys information both explicitly and implicitly, using connotations to add subtle suggestions.

❶ Connotation
The colour of the train sounds happy and positive: bright yellow has connotations of sunshine or a new day to begin the journey.

❸ Implicit meaning
This suggests that the journey will be at a continuous pace, *implying* that it will be easy and relaxing from this point.

❺ Connotation
Rockets taking off have connotations of other worlds.

Extract 1: 'Through the Pyrenees on the little yellow train' by Gavin Bell

This extract below is one of a series of newspaper articles published in *The Telegraph* about rail journeys. The writer describes travelling through the mountains of France.

The train I board has a choice of four closed and two open-air carriages, all painted bright yellow, ❶ and as the sun is beaming from clear blue skies I opt for one of the latter. With a shrill whistle we are off, ❷ quickly
5   reaching our cruising ❸ speed of about 15mph as we rock and roll past Vauban's battlements.

This is the way to travel through tumultuous scenery, at a gentle pace with time to gaze on fast flowing streams, deep forests, and dizzying gorges. Mountain villages are
10   etched on the skyline, clinging to impossible slopes ❹, their church towers like rockets poised to take off ❺ for the heavens.

The eyes are constantly drawn upwards to forests in the sky, and convoluted valleys snaking up to barren
15   peaks, ❻ a grand, sweeping symphony of nature. At times the railway seems to defy gravity, and when we halt there is no rumbling of diesel engines, only silence broken by the rushing of a river below.

❷ Explicit meaning
An *explicit* statement. The use of an adjective to describe the whistle as 'shrill' and the short phrase 'we are off' reflects how the train leaves the station quickly.

❹ Implicit meaning
This implies that houses are built on steep slopes, but by describing them as being 'etched on the skyline', it suggests first that they look beautiful rather than being unsafe.

❻ Implicit meaning
These details *imply* that there is a lot to look at in the mountains, both high and low, as eyes are being drawn to look.

Another form of text that might be included in Paper 2 is a news article. Whereas a news *report* is likely to focus mainly on explicit facts and information, the purpose of a news *article* is to convey the writer's own opinions and ideas.

In the news article below, the writer expresses an opinion about the constant updates he has to download to his new smartphone. He presents his ideas and feelings in a humorous way, using vivid imagery to convey meaning and to entertain his readers. The writer also uses both implicit and explicit meaning to express his point of view.

Extract 2: 'Apple's software updates are like changing the water in a fish tank. I'd rather let the fish die' by Charlie Brooker

This extract is an article from *The Guardian* about one person's view of software updates.

> Updates are awful. ❶ All you want to do is watch TV and rot in your own filth. ❷ Instead you spend the evening backing up your phone, downloading a gigantic file and sitting around while your phone undergoes an
> 5 intense psychological makeover, ❸ at the end of which it may or may not function. Often, it takes an hour or more. Fiddly, time-consuming admin – it's like having to change the water in a fish tank. … it's why I don't have an aquarium. I'd rather let the fish die. ❹

❶ Explicit meaning
An *explicit* statement. It shows his opinion of updates clearly.

❸ Implicit meaning
For comic effect, this *implies* that the phone has feelings, and that the update is unnecessary.

❷ A direct address encourages readers to identify with the writer. This also includes exaggeration for comic purposes.

❹ Exaggerated comic comparison and humorous confession.

TIP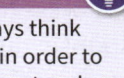
When you are reading any non-fiction text, always think about what effects the writer is trying to create in order to fulfil the purpose of the text and to make it relevant and appealing to a specific audience.

1 Knowledge

Knowledge

CONCEPT

1 Texts and their meaning

How can I write about different types of text?

When writing about a fiction text for Paper 1 Question 3, think carefully about its **genre**. There are many different genres, such as: horror, romance, fantasy, science-fiction, mystery, thriller. Some stories are more than one genre. The genre of the text will help you to identify the type of effects that the writer is trying to create.

In fiction, writers often convey implicit information ('showing' the reader) rather than explicit information ('telling' the reader). Look at the dialogue below from the novel: *The Unlikely Pilgrimage of Harold Fry* by Rachel Joyce.

Extract 3: *The Unlikely Pilgrimage of Harold Fry* by Rachel Joyce

This extract is from a novel, and is about Maureen and her husband, Harold, as they eat breakfast. Harold has received a letter.

'Well?' said Maureen again.
'Good lord. It's from Queenie Hennessy.'
Maureen speared a nugget of butter with her knife and flattened it the length of her toast. 'Queenie who?'
5 'She worked at the brewery. Years ago. Don't you remember?'
Maureen shrugged. 'I don't see why I should. I don't know why I'd remember someone from years ago. Could you pass the jam?'
'She was in finances. She was very good.'
'That's the marmalade, Harold. Jam is red. If you look at things before you pick
10 them up, you'll find it helps.'

If you were asked how the writer presents the character of Maureen, a sample response might be like the one below. Notice how this focuses on implicit meaning to suggest Maureen's mood and character, rather than explicit meaning.

TIP
Try to keep your quotations short and embed them within your sentences, rather than copying out large chunks of text.

Maureen speaks abruptly to her husband, indicating her impatience with him: 'Well?', 'Queenie who?' ❶ The use of the verb 'shrugged' implies her lack of interest ❷ in something that seems important to him, implied by his exclamation 'Good lord'. The description of Maureen's actions also portrays her as angry and perhaps aggressive. ❸ She 'spears' the butter and 'flattened' it, bringing in connotations of war and weapons. ❹ This impression is strengthened by her sarcastically stating the obvious — that 'jam is red', and advising Harold ironically that 'you'll find it helps'. This creates tension between the characters, and leaves the reader unsure of what caused this. ❺

❶ Analysis of what is *implied*, followed by evidence.

❷ Focuses on what one word *implies*.

❸ Statement leads on to another aspect of the dialogue.

❹ Evidence followed by what it *implies*.

❺ Summarises the effect.

1

When writing about a non-fiction source text, especially when answering Paper 2 Questions 3 and 7(b), think carefully about the writer's purpose and the effects they are aiming to create for the reader. Then look closely at *how* exactly the writer conveys meaning. You may wish to draw out what is explicitly stated and what the reader can **infer** (work out).

For example, for Extract 1 on page 4, if you had to explore how the writer makes his train travel through the mountains of France sound appealing, you could focus on the details and language in the text. A sample response might be like the one below. As well as entertaining the reader, the writer is giving detailed information to convey the positive experience he felt as a traveller. This creates a powerful effect for the reader.

❶ Introduces the idea of a new day with embedded quotations.

❷ Includes a quotation and an explicit statement.

❸ Shows how the sense of old-fashioned, traditional travel is introduced and continued through the passage.

❹ The reader infers information from descriptions.

❺ Builds up to an inference that nature is beautiful in an otherworldly way.

> The author creates a cheerful impression of the train, with bright yellow 'open-air carriages' reinforced by the 'clear blue skies', suggesting the start of a new day. ❶ He explicitly states that 'with a shrill whistle, we are off', which suggests quick, easy, and exciting travel, as the sentence is short and the whistle is 'shrill'. ❷ A train whistle also implies old-fashioned train travelling, giving a sense of comfort and familiarity, which is reinforced by words such as 'cruising' and 'gentle pace' to describe the journey. ❸ The writer describes the view as a 'sweeping symphony of nature', looking up at 'barren peaks' and down at 'convoluted valleys'. This implies that the view is going up and down, and is beautiful, like different notes of music that create a symphony. ❹ This is reinforced as the railway seems to 'defy gravity' and towers are 'like rockets poised to take off', implying the beauty is otherworldly, in the same way space is. ❺

1 Knowledge 7

Knowledge CONCEPT

1 Texts and their meaning

How can I write in a particular text form?

In Paper 1 Question 5 or 6, you will write a fictional text of your own (a description or a narrative). In Paper 2 Question 8 or 9, you will write a non-fiction text, such as a speech, article, or letter.

Newspaper or magazine articles

You might be given the readership of your article. It could be 'for your school magazine', in which case you would need to appeal to teenagers but without alienating adult readers. This means writing in a slightly informal way, with some direct address to teenagers.

TIP
Remember that an article has to be engaging and can include personal opinions.

Letters

A letter might, for example, be addressed to the head teacher and argue a case. Think carefully about how you open the letter, how you structure the paragraphs, and the most appropriate way of signing off.

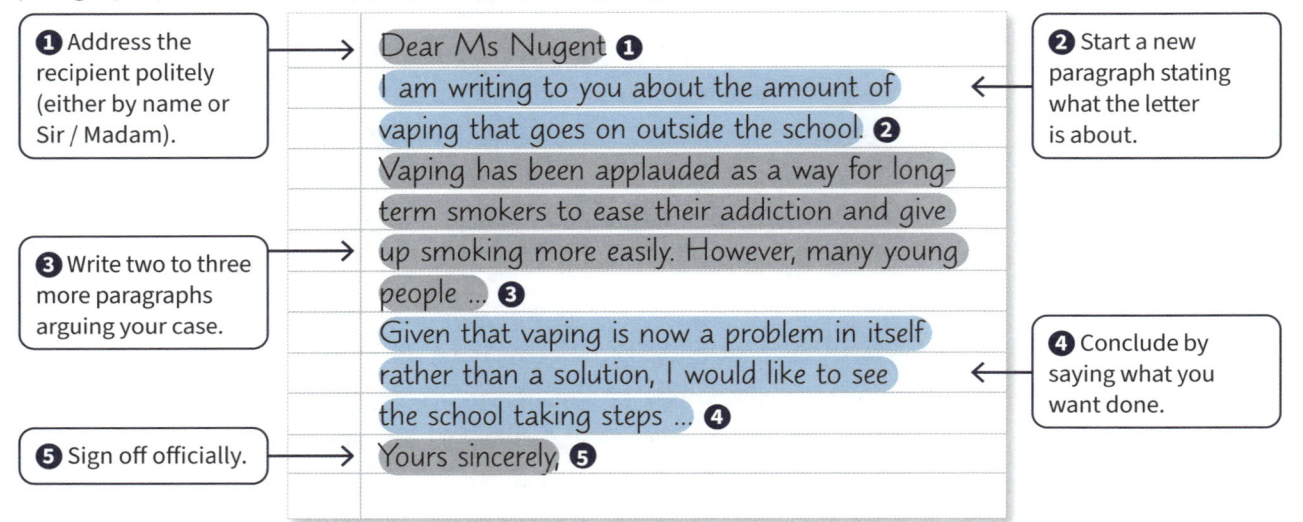

❶ Address the recipient politely (either by name or Sir / Madam).

❷ Start a new paragraph stating what the letter is about.

❸ Write two to three more paragraphs arguing your case.

❹ Conclude by saying what you want done.

❺ Sign off officially.

Dear Ms Nugent ❶
I am writing to you about the amount of vaping that goes on outside the school. ❷
Vaping has been applauded as a way for long-term smokers to ease their addiction and give up smoking more easily. However, many young people … ❸
Given that vaping is now a problem in itself rather than a solution, I would like to see the school taking steps … ❹
Yours sincerely, ❺

Speeches

A speech could be aimed at a particular audience. It should be fairly formal and polite but could still include some humour and **anecdotes** (short stories about personal experiences). It could use personal pronouns to include the audience.

I'm delighted to see you all here. I'll be talking about a subject that affects us all, but especially young people: the environment.

Key terms Make sure you can write a definition for these key terms

anecdote   audience
connotation   direct address
explicit   fiction   genre
implicit   infer   inference
non-fiction   purpose   text form

8   1 Texts and their meaning

Retrieval — CONCEPT 1

Use the following questions to check your understanding of the knowledge covered in this section. Then cover the answers column with a piece of paper and write down as many as you can. Check and repeat.

Questions | Answers

#	Question	Answer
1	All texts are either fiction or non-fiction. True or false?	True
2	What type of source text will you be given to read and comment on in Paper 1?	Prose fiction – an extract from a novel or short story.
3	Name at least four different types of non-fiction text forms that you might be given to read and comment on in Paper 2.	Possible answers include: report; travel writing; biography or autobiography; diary; speech; letter; review; article.
4	Name at least four different genres of fiction.	Possible answers include: science fiction; fantasy; romance; historical fiction; thriller; mystery; horror.
5	What are the three key features to identify in a text, and why are they important?	Text form, audience, purpose. They strongly influence the structure, language, and style of a text.
6	Name at least four possible purposes of a non-fiction text.	Possible answers include: to inform; to entertain; to persuade; to instruct; to argue; to explain.
7	What is explicit information?	Information that is clearly stated. The reader does not have to infer the meaning.
8	Which of these sentences contains an implicit meaning, and what is that meaning? (a) Cricket: just when you think the game has to be nearly over, it goes on – and on, and on. (b) Rugby is a contact sport.	Sentence (a): it implies that cricket is boring.
9	What does *infer* mean?	To work out meaning that is only hinted at, rather than explicitly stated.
10	Why is it important to think about audience when writing a text?	The audience are the people you hope will read your text or listen to your speech. You need to write in a way that is appropriate and appealing to your audience.
11	What is the connotation of a word or phrase?	It is the additional meaning that it commonly carries, as well as its main, explicit meaning.
12	What might be an appropriate way of signing off a letter to a head teacher or school governor?	Yours sincerely; Kind regards; Regards.

1 Retrieval

Knowledge CONCEPT

2 Figurative language

What is figurative language?

Figurative language uses descriptive words and phrases, such as **similes** and **metaphors**, to convey meaning imaginatively rather than just literally. While this section focuses on language, in Question 3 of both papers, you will have to write about both language and structure.

> **QUESTION CONNECTION**
>
> You will have to comment on the effect of language features, including figurative language in Paper 1 Question 3 and Paper 2 Question 3. You may also use figurative language in the writing tasks in Paper 1 Question 5 or 6, and Paper 2 Question 8 or 9.
>
> You might also comment on language when analysing setting, incidents / issues, themes, and events in Paper 1 Question 4, and Paper 2 Question 6.

Simile

Similes create an image in the reader's mind by directly comparing something with something else that it somehow resembles. They always use comparison words, such as 'like', 'as', 'as if' or 'than'.

| The child wriggled like a worm. | Her smile was as wide as the desert sky. | He ran desperately, as if pursued by a pack of wolves. |

Metaphor

Metaphors, like similes, compare two or more things. However, instead of using comparison words, such as 'like' or 'as', they describe things as if they actually *are* something else.

| The road was a ribbon of moonlight. | He barked a command and they all stood to attention. | The dark pathway snakes into the distance. |

A metaphor (or simile) may create meaning in more than one way. A 'dark pathway' that 'snakes' could be long and winding, like the body of a snake. It could also be secretive and unpredictable like a snake. Both ideas imply a sense of danger and uncertainty in where the path might be heading.

Extended metaphor

Extended metaphors takes the comparison of two ideas a step further, creating further similarities. They can use the same idea several times in a sentence, in a paragraph, or across a text.

| The company's mountain of debt proved too steep to climb. | Swept along on the tide of her enthusiasm, I found myself washed up on strange shores. | Life is a long and twisting road. Sometimes the going is rough, sometimes easy, and sometimes you get to a crossroads where you don't know which way to go. |

10 2 Figurative language

Symbolism

Symbolism is the use of a simple image to represent something more than its literal meaning. Symbols usually represent a complex or abstract idea. Many symbols can represent more than one idea, like the eagle example below.

> A rose with thorns is often used to symbolise love, but also the pain it can bring.

> An eagle soaring high could either symbolise freedom, as it flies free, or power and dominance, as it preys on other animals.

Personification

Personification is when something non-human or abstract is described as if it has human qualities.

> The house scowled unwelcomingly on all who approached it.

> The sun smiled through the stormy clouds.

> Love comes to your door when you've given up waiting.

Pathetic fallacy

Pathetic fallacy is when something non-human (often in the natural world) is given human emotions or feelings.

> Furious waves tossed our little boat without mercy.

> Mount Everest jealously guards its summit from the unprepared.

> The storm raged around the house, determined to do damage.

2 Knowledge

# Knowledge

CONCEPT

2 Figurative language

What are the effects of figurative language?

Figurative language describes something imaginatively by drawing on its similarities with something else. It is important when analysing figurative language to focus on what the imagery has in common with the thing it is describing, and what the effect of that is.

Writers often use figurative language to create an overall impression, for example of a setting or person.

Read the extracts and annotations on these pages, which highlight the writers' use of figurative language in the texts. The first extract uses figurative language when describing how tractors are demolishing farmland.

TIP
When writing about the writer's use of figurative language in the exam, you must do more than just 'spot' examples. Explain how it affects the reader and how each example suggests further qualities or ideas.

❶ Metaphor and simile

'Crawlers' and 'crawled' metaphorically describe the tractors as being animal or insect-like, which is reinforced by the simile 'like insects'. This makes them seem relentless and lacking in human sympathy.

❸ Metaphor

The words 'snub-nosed' and 'sticking their snouts into it' are features and images of pigs, digging down into the earth and searching in the soil for food, which suggests the tractors are greedy, only focusing on getting the crops and making money.

Extract 1: *The Grapes of Wrath* by John Steinbeck

This extract is from a novel set in America during the Great Depression and focuses on the poverty of farmers. It describes how tractors are demolishing the farmland.

> The tractors came over the roads and into the fields, great crawlers moving like insects, having the incredible strength of insects. They crawled ❶ over the ground, laying the track and rolling on it and picking it up. Diesel
> 5 tractors, puttering while they stood idle; they thundered when they moved, ❷ and then settled down to a droning roar. Snub-nosed monsters, raising the dust and sticking their snouts into it, ❸ straight down the country, across the country, through fences, through
> 10 dooryards, in and out of gullies in straight lines.

❷ Personification

The verb 'thundered' implies the tractors are loud, powerful, and threatening. The phrase 'they thundered when they moved' implies that they have minds, but still no concern for the farms and features of the landscape that they destroy.

The figurative language in the extract suggests that the tractors represent a powerful, greedy, inhuman force that does not consider the natural environment. The writer does this by comparing the movement of the mechanical tractors to the relentless, single-minded activity of insects or animals that destroy and devour the landscape as they look for food.

12 2 Figurative language

The next extract is from *Great Expectations* and describes a strange, unwelcoming room in Miss Havisham's house. The writer uses figurative language to show the gloomy, desolate atmosphere of the room, focusing on the fire and tablecloth.

Extract 2: *Great Expectations* by Charles Dickens

> A young boy, Pip, is visiting the unwelcoming home of the elderly Miss Havisham. He describes the visit years later from the perspective of his adult self.

A fire had been lately kindled in the damp old-fashioned grate, and it was more disposed to go out than to burn up, ❶ and the reluctant ❷ smoke which hung in the room seemed colder than the clearer air – like our own
5 marsh mist. Certain wintry branches of candles ❸ on the high chimney-piece faintly lighted the chamber; or it would be more expressive to say, faintly troubled its darkness. ❹

[*There is a table in the centre of the room.*]

10 … it was so heavily overhung with cobwebs that its form was quite undistinguishable; and, as I looked along the yellow expanse out of which I remember its seeming to grow, like a black fungus, ❺ I saw speckle-legged spiders with blotchy bodies running home to it, and
15 running out from it, as if some circumstances of the greatest public importance had just transpired in the spider community. ❻

❶ Pathetic fallacy
The fire is 'more disposed to' (meaning more willing to) go out rather than burn. It suggests the fire has feelings.

❸ Metaphor
The candles in the candelabra are described as 'wintry branches' (i.e. bare branches). This description contributes to the unwelcoming atmosphere, as wintry branches give the impression of cold discomfort outside, rather than the warmth we would expect in a house.

❺ Simile
Describing the centrepiece as 'like a black fungus' makes it seem as if there is something rotten and unhealthy about the room.

❷ Pathetic fallacy
The 'reluctant' smoke also seems to have feelings. This builds on the idea of the fire wanting to go out.

❹ Pathetic fallacy
For the darkness to be 'troubled' it must have feelings.

❻ Simile
This suggests that the spiders are hurrying in and out, which seems a little threatening. However, the idea of a 'spider community' is comical. Dickens seems to want the reader to be both disgusted and fascinated.

The figurative language in this extract makes the room seem unwelcoming and inhospitable. The writer does this by using pathetic fallacy to show the mood of the room: the fire is reluctant to burn and gives little warmth or light to the room or any visitors. This suggests to the reader that it is an unwelcoming and even threatening place to visit for the narrator. The language seems to build up to the climax of the spiders rushing in and out for comical and repulsive effect.

2 Knowledge

Knowledge CONCEPT

2 Figurative language

How can I write about figurative language?

In order to write about language in a text, including figurative language, you must identify the techniques the writer uses and analyse their effects and how these are achieved.

If writing about Extract 1 (on page 12), you could begin with a *statement*, such as:

> The writer uses metaphors, similes, and personification to portray the tractors as powerful, inhuman, and unconcerned about what they destroy …

You also need *evidence*. You could continue the first sentence:

> … describing them as crawling 'like insects', as 'monsters', and as animals 'sticking their snouts' into the dust.

TIP
Your evidence can be a direct quotation from the text itself, such as a word or phrase, or a reference to a specific part of the text, such as 'In the first sentence' or 'in line 10'.

Finally, you need to *analyse the effects in detail* of this evidence on the reader:

> This implies that the tractors lack any human feeling about what they are destroying. The machines are like greedy pigs, aggressively feeding on the land.

When analysing the effects of figurative language, you may find it helpful to use sentence stems such as those below.

| This implies that … | This creates a sense of … | This gives the reader the impression that … | Using this comparison suggests that … |

When writing about figurative language and its effects, try to include some subject terminology and to comment in detail on the overall effects of the language, as well as individual examples. Develop your interpretation in as much detail as possible.

You could improve this answer by using terminology and suggesting further interpretation:

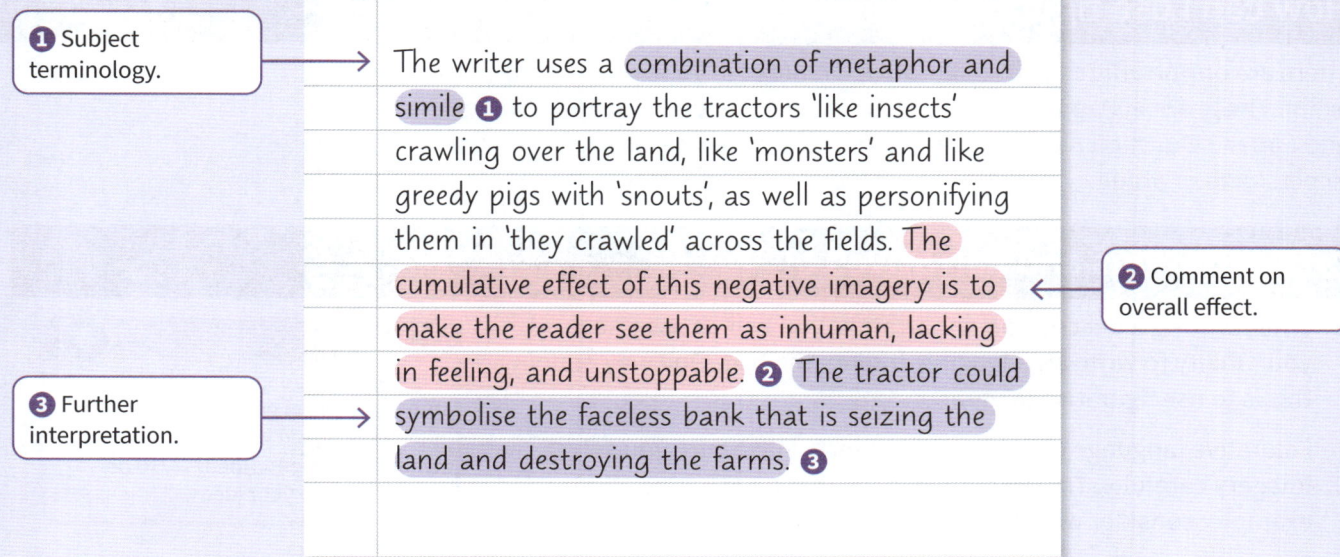

- ① Subject terminology.
- ② Comment on overall effect.
- ③ Further interpretation.

> The writer uses a **combination of metaphor and simile** ① to portray the tractors 'like insects' crawling over the land, like 'monsters' and like greedy pigs with 'snouts', as well as personifying them in 'they crawled' across the fields. The **cumulative effect of this negative imagery is to make the reader see them as inhuman, lacking in feeling, and unstoppable.** ② The tractor could **symbolise the faceless bank that is seizing the land and destroying the farms.** ③

For Extract 2 (on page 13), you could focus on how the figurative language creates an overall impression. The example below explores a number of different language devices to show how the author uses them to create a powerful effect for the reader. This example would be part of a longer Paper 1 Question 3 answer.

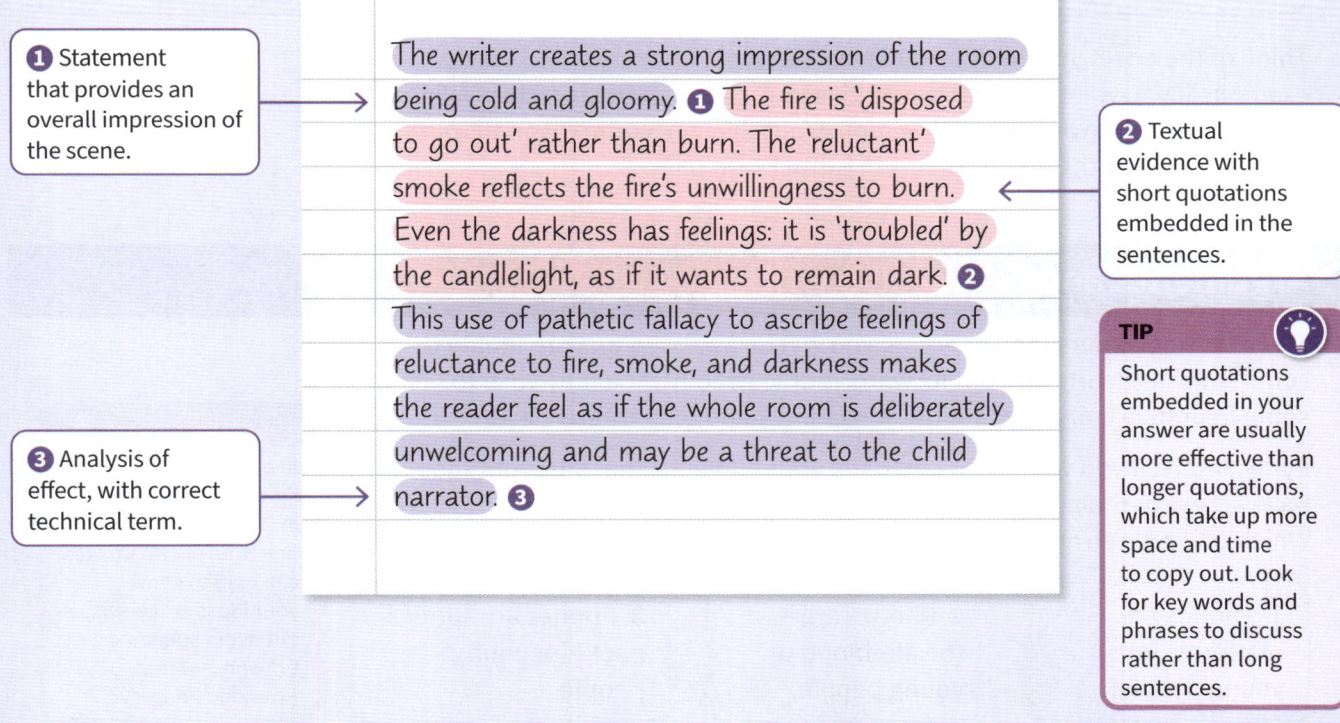

- ① Statement that provides an overall impression of the scene.
- ② Textual evidence with short quotations embedded in the sentences.
- ③ Analysis of effect, with correct technical term.

> The writer creates a strong impression of the room being cold and gloomy. ① The fire is 'disposed to go out' rather than burn. The 'reluctant' smoke reflects the fire's unwillingness to burn. Even the darkness has feelings: it is 'troubled' by the candlelight, as if it wants to remain dark. ② This use of pathetic fallacy to ascribe feelings of reluctance to fire, smoke, and darkness makes the reader feel as if the whole room is deliberately unwelcoming and may be a threat to the child narrator. ③

TIP

Short quotations embedded in your answer are usually more effective than longer quotations, which take up more space and time to copy out. Look for key words and phrases to discuss rather than long sentences.

2 Knowledge

Knowledge CONCEPT

2 Figurative language

How can I use figurative language in my own writing?

There are opportunities to use figurative language in your own writing in the exam. These are in Paper 1 Question 5 or 6 in a description or narrative text and Paper 2 Question 8 or 9 in a non-fiction text for a specific purpose such as to persuade or argue.

Descriptions and narratives

When writing a description or narrative, you will be assessed on your ability to write an engaging, interesting text. One way of doing this is to use figurative language.

Figurative language compares two things. Make sure you select imagery carefully. Try to create images that have impact. For example, consider which of these three similes works best.

TIP
Figurative language works best if the comparison gives the reader powerful, varied ideas about what is being described. Try to be imaginative in your ideas.

1. The train hurtled past like a fast car.	2. The train hurtled past like a big bird.	3. The train hurtled past like a raging bull.
Simile 1 is weak because a train is too similar to a car.	Simile 2 is better: a train resembles a bird slightly.	Simile 3 is best, because a raging bull, like a train, is fast, powerful, and unstoppable.

Think of the effect you want to achieve, then what imagery could create it. For example, if you want to create a negative impression of tractors destroying farms, compare it with something monstrous, like the comparison to thunder and animals that the writer selects in Extract 1 on page 12.

Arguments and persuasive writing

When writing to persuade or argue, you will be assessed on your ability to communicate clearly and put forward your viewpoint. You may wish to include some figurative language, but use it sparingly and only when relevant.

For example, if you wanted to persuade your audience that students should have access to their phones during the school day, you might use a metaphor. Which of the three metaphors below do you think is most effective?

TIP
Avoid overusing figurative language in Paper 2 Question 8 or 9. One or two images can help to convey your ideas and views, but avoid spending time on creating extended imagery.

1. Phones are platforms for young people.	2. Phones are the life-blood of young people.	3. Phones are survival packs for young people.

Key terms — Make sure you can write a definition for each of these key terms.

extended metaphor   figurative language   metaphor
pathetic fallacy   personification   simile   symbolism

2 Figurative language

Retrieval   CONCEPT   2

Use the following questions to check your understanding of the knowledge covered in this section. Then cover the answers column with a piece of paper and write down as many as you can. Check and repeat.

Questions | Answers

#	Question	Answer
1	What two words are typically used in similes?	Like, as
2	How is a metaphor different from a simile?	It describes a thing as if it is something else, without using 'like' or 'as'.
3	Explain how the sentence 'The train rocketed past' is more effective than 'The train rushed past like a rocket'?	The word 'rocketed' already conveys the idea of speed, so 'rushed' is unnecessary.
4	What technique is used here, and what is its effect? *The students swarmed into the dining hall.*	Metaphor. It suggests that a crowd of students moves quickly and all at once, like swarming insects.
5	What technique is used in this sentence, and what is its effect? *The pen resisted the urge to keep writing.*	Personification. It suggests that the pen has thoughts and feelings, like a person.
6	What is pathetic fallacy?	A figurative language technique that gives human emotion to something non-human (usually something in the natural world).
7	Is the following an example of pathetic fallacy or personification, and why? *Time waits for no one.*	This is personification because it makes time sound like a person but does not describe it as having any human emotion.

Previous questions

Now go back and use these questions to check your knowledge of previous topics.

Questions | Answers

#	Question	Answer
1	What is explicit information?	Information that is clearly stated. The reader does not have to work it out.
2	What does *infer* mean?	To work out meaning that is only hinted at, rather than explicitly stated.

Knowledge

CONCEPT

3 Rhetorical language

What is rhetorical language?

Rhetorical language can be used in speeches or in written texts. It aims to persuade, motivate or inspire people. It uses techniques (devices) that help to impress ideas on the audience, emphasising the ideas and making them persuasive and memorable.

> **QUESTION CONNECTION**
> You may have to analyse rhetorical language features alongside structure in Paper 2 Question 3. You could use rhetorical language when writing your response to Paper 2 Question 8 or 9.

Repetition

Writers often use **repetition** of words or phrases to emphasise them and to help secure ideas in the audience's mind.

| We must fight for <u>freedom</u> to speak, <u>freedom</u> to go where we want, <u>freedom</u> to live as we want. | Exercise will help you build a <u>stronger</u> body and a <u>stronger</u> mind. | <u>We need</u> access to clean water. <u>We need</u> a market for our crops. |

Emotive language

Emotive language aims to make readers respond emotionally – for example, with sympathy or outrage.

| Lucy spent last Christmas shivering in a shop doorway. Will you provide her with warmth and comfort this year? | Precious rainforest is being devoured by monstrous machinery. | Our beautiful river is dying – poisoned by chemicals, choked by algae. |

Rhetorical questions

Rhetorical questions are asked to challenge the listener or reader, but without expecting answers.

| Should people who've worked hard all their lives be left in poverty when they retire? | Do you really expect people to put up with this? | Is it right that young people have nowhere to meet but street corners? |

> **TIP**
> When writing about rhetorical features, explain why the writer has used them and what effect they create. Do not just name the feature. Also, make what you say relevant to any focus given to you in the exam question.

Tricolons (triples)

Tricolons, or triples, are lists of three connected things. Often, the third one is the most powerful, and sometimes it is expressed in more words.

> People are tired of empty promises; they're tired of the same old lies; and they're tired of being told that everything is wonderful when clearly it isn't!

> Thousands are dying from ignorance, greed, and cynical indifference.

> There are people who don't know, people who don't care, and people who care but don't act.

Direct address

When a writer or speaker makes a direct address to a reader or audience, using the pronouns 'you' or 'we', it makes the audience feel personally involved and included. The use of 'we' gives a sense of unity and common purpose.

> You've worked for your exams, and now you expect a job that rewards your efforts.

> We all want our efforts to be appreciated.

> If, like me, you want our children to have a planet to live on …

Hyperbole

Hyperbole is **exaggeration** used to emphasise a point, either for humorous effect or to ensure a strong impact on the reader.

> I'm so hungry, I could eat a horse!

> When it comes to prisoner rehabilitation, we're still in the Middle Ages!

> You might as well look for a phone box on Mars as on the streets of London nowadays.

Juxtaposition

Juxtaposition means presenting two ideas or objects alongside each other in order to highlight their differences, make a point or create a literary effect.

> We will turn the darkness of despair into the light of hope.

> Some are born into wealth and privilege, others into poverty and disadvantage.

> A good result could mean fame and fortune; a bad one will mean disappointment and relegation.

Anecdotes

Anecdotes are short, personal stories of a few lines that illustrate a point.

> I was walking up the high street the other day when a car sped past me …

> The other day I saw a group of students at a bus stop – all on their phones.

> Last summer I took my family to the seaside, hoping for a good day out …

Knowledge

CONCEPT

3 Rhetorical language

What are the effects of rhetorical language?

Rhetorical language can be used in many ways, but it works particularly well in texts that aim to persuade the audience or argue a point of view, such as speeches or articles.

In the extract below, President Obama reflects on the history of the presidential oath and how it has served America well and should continue to do so, even though the country is facing many challenges. Notice how he uses rhetorical features to reinforce his argument.

TIP

A persuasive text must have a clear, strong argument running through it. Rhetorical language can help to reinforce that argument, simplifying and summarising ideas and making them memorable.

Extract 1: President Obama's Inaugural Address, calling for 'a new era of responsibility'

This extract is from President Obama's inauguration speech, the first speech he gave after becoming President.

Forty-four Americans have now taken the presidential oath. The words have been spoken during rising tides of prosperity and the still waters of peace. ❶ Yet, every so often the oath is taken amidst gathering clouds
5 and raging storms. ❷ At these moments, America has carried on not simply because of the skill or vision of those in high office, but because We the People ❸ have remained faithful to the ideals of our ❸ forebears, and true to our ❸ founding documents.
10 So it has been. So it must be ❹ with this generation of Americans.

That we are in the midst of crisis is now well understood. Our nation is at war, ❺ against a far-reaching network of violence and hatred. Our economy
15 is badly weakened, a consequence of greed and irresponsibility on the part of some, but also our collective failure to make hard choices and prepare the nation for a new age. Homes have been lost; jobs shed; businesses shuttered. ❻ Our healthcare is too costly;
20 our schools fail too many; and each day brings further evidence that the ways we use energy strengthen our adversaries and threaten our planet. ❼

❶ Juxtaposition
The two images of 'rising tides' and 'still waters' reflect positive periods in American history.

❸ Direct address
The words 'we' and 'our' create a sense of unity with the audience.

❺ Hyperbole
The 'war' is not literal, but refers to the fight against terrorism.

❼ Tricolon
Three more items in the list of challenges, building up to a climax, with the longest and most serious item last.

❷ Juxtaposition
Weather metaphors for social upheaval contrast strikingly with previous metaphors for prosperity and peace.

❹ Repetition
This reinforces a sense of continuity.

❻ Tricolon
Three items give a concise, powerful summary of the difficulties faced by many Americans.

The rhetorical language in the extract above helps to impress strong ideas and images in the audience's mind: the importance of the principles that America was founded upon; the responsibility of current Americans to uphold those principles; the extent of the challenges that they all face. The words and images conveyed through the language are powerful and memorable.

3

Rhetorical language can be used to make the audience think carefully about an issue and stir up an emotional response to make them act, or make them agree with the argument.

In the article below, the writer uses rhetorical language to reinforce her argument against trophy hunting (hunting wild animals for pleasure). Notice how she uses rhetorical language to engage the reader and provide memorable images.

Extract 2: 'The hunter who killed Cecil the lion doesn't deserve our empathy' by Rose George, 29 July 2015

This extract is from an article in the *Guardian* and shows the writer's view of a trophy hunter killing a famous lion in Zimbabwe.

Trophy hunters like Walter J. Palmer shouldn't receive death threats – but there is no excuse for their argument that hunting serves conservation.

We love a good fight, don't we? ❶ Enter Walter J. Palmer,
5 a tanned dentist from Minnesota, with a bow and arrow. Along comes Cecil the lion, the alpha male of his pride, minding his own business being the best-known and most beloved lion in Zimbabwe if not in Africa, as well as the subject of an Oxford University study. ❷ Then Cecil
10 is shot with a bow and arrow, taking 40 hours to die, ❸ all because Palmer thought killing a magnificent animal was sporty.

I read the story of Cecil's killing and my education and intellect deserted me for a minute. I felt only
15 disgust and rage, somewhat inarticulately. I feel no calmness about big-game hunters. I am not persuaded by their justifications, which can be easily punctured with buckshot. ❹ Trophy hunting contributes to conservation, they say: when the Dallas Safari Club
20 auctioned the right to kill an endangered Namibian black rhino, it said the $350,000 winning bounty – they called it a "bid" – went towards conservation efforts in Namibia.

Elephants, leopards, polar bears and giraffes are all hunted for "sport" too. Shooting an endangered species
25 and calling it sustainable is like waving a fan and thinking you're helping to stop global warming. ❺

❶ Rhetorical question and direct address

The question challenges the reader to think about the issue. The use of 'we' creates a bond between the writer and the reader.

❸ Emotive detail

Stimulates the reader's awareness of the extent of Cecil's suffering.

❺ Hyperbole

Using a comparison to demonstrate how nonsensical this idea is.

TIP

Emotive language doesn't have to shock; it can be more subtle. Look out for any language that might create an emotional response in the reader.

❷ Emotive language

Empathy for the lion is created by naming him, making him sound majestic ('alpha male'), innocent, and widely loved – a celebrity.

❹ Imagery

An appropriate hunting metaphor adds colour and wit to the writing.

The rhetorical language in the extract helps to engage the reader, challenging them to think carefully about the issue, and stirring up their emotions. The imagery, humour, and exaggeration help to reinforce the argument, making it powerful and memorable.

3 Knowledge 21

Knowledge **CONCEPT**

3 Rhetorical language

How can I write about rhetorical language?

In order to write about rhetorical language, you must identify the techniques the writer uses and analyse how their effects are achieved. It might be tempting to simply 'spot' devices, but you must focus on the effect of individual devices and on their cumulative effect throughout a source text.

> **TIP**
> Think about the writer's or speaker's purpose. What are they trying to achieve by using rhetorical language? For example, are they trying to inspire the public or promote a viewpoint or argument?

Re-read the first paragraph of Extract 1 on page 20. In analysing this paragraph, you could write about the rhetorical language and its effects like this:

> The purpose of the speech is to inspire and reassure Americans, **①** so the speaker uses a variety of rhetorical devices to help do this.
>
> First he uses juxtaposition to establish two images of prosperity and peace: 'rising tides' and 'still waters'. **②** Then he contrasts these two positive images with two metaphors for troubled times 'gathering clouds' and 'raging storms'. As dark clouds suggest a storm is coming, this has connotations that something else negative could happen, such as national threat or economic difficulty. **③**
>
> These contrasts reinforce the idea that the presidency always survives change. **④** The speaker also congratulates Americans, personified collectively as 'America', for remaining 'faithful' to national ideals. This encourages a sense of national solidarity, reinforced by the inclusive use of pronouns and determiners in 'We the People', 'our forebears', and 'our founding documents'. **⑤**

① Identifies the purpose and audience.

② Explains how the juxtaposition works with embedded quotations.

③ Identifies connotations and how they link to the context of the speech.

④ Focuses on the broad effects of the contrasts.

⑤ Analyses the direct address and inclusive language.

> **TIP**
> When analysing the use of any language feature, remember to make a point, use evidence from the text, and explain the effect it creates for the audience.

22 3 Rhetorical language

3

Now re-read the first two paragraphs of Extract 2 on page 21. Here is how you could write about these paragraphs:

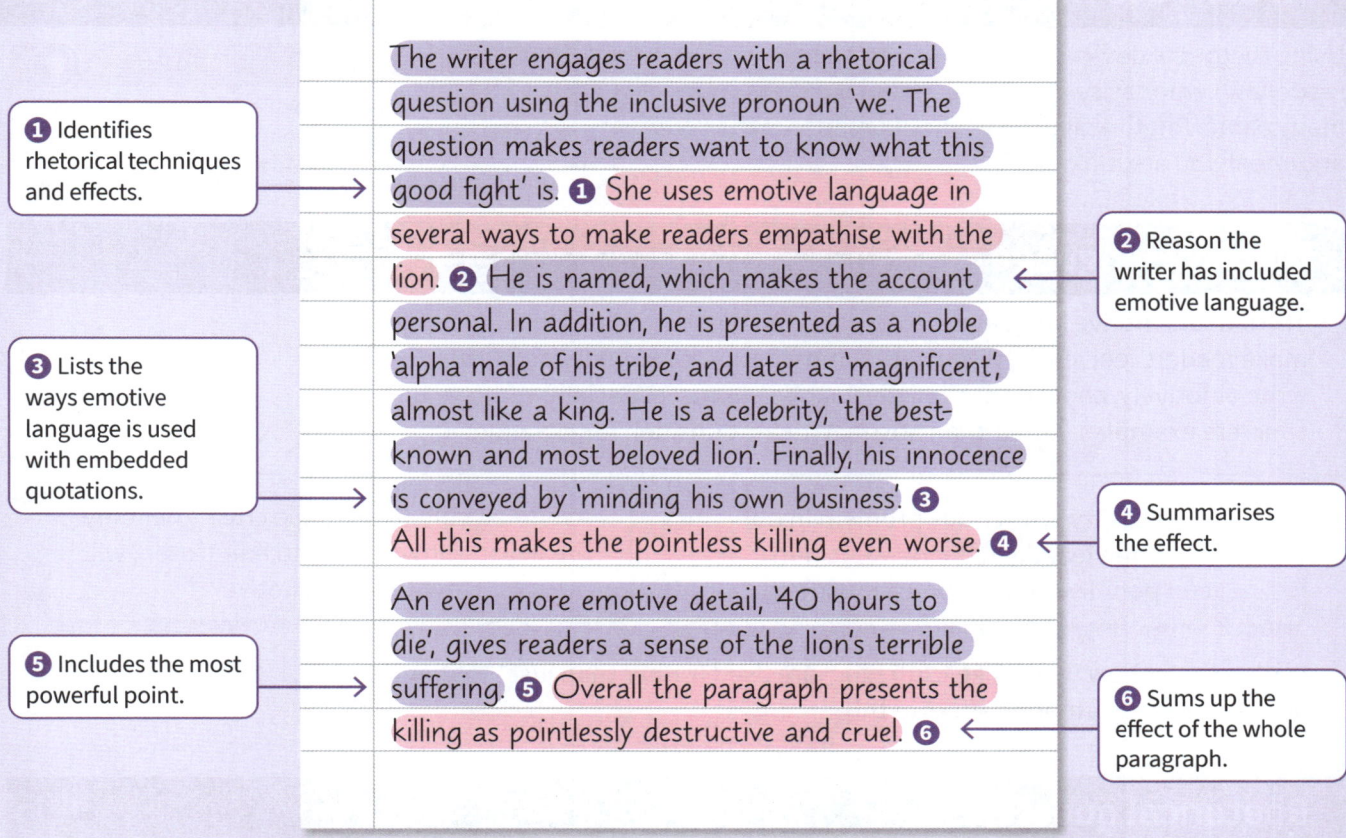

❶ Identifies rhetorical techniques and effects.

❷ Reason the writer has included emotive language.

❸ Lists the ways emotive language is used with embedded quotations.

❹ Summarises the effect.

❺ Includes the most powerful point.

❻ Sums up the effect of the whole paragraph.

Notice how this student varies the way in which they identify rhetorical language and explain its effects. They use words and phrases to link their ideas together fluently. You may find some of the following useful in your own work.

The writer engages …	The writer encourages readers …	… to make readers empathise
In addition …	… is conveyed by …	The paragraph presents …
The overall effect …		

3 Knowledge   23

Knowledge CONCEPT

3 Rhetorical language

How can I use rhetorical language in my own writing?

Using rhetorical devices will help you to engage your reader and emphasise your ideas and make them memorable. Rhetorical devices should reinforce the core argument you are making.

TIP
Whichever effect you want to achieve, don't overdo it. If readers feel you are trying to manipulate them, or if what you say is too horrifying, you will just turn them off.

Emotive language

The aim of emotive language is to produce an emotional response. You might make readers feel angry, disgusted, sympathetic – even guilty or fearful. To write emotively, choose emotionally 'loaded' words, especially verbs, and concrete examples, rather than abstract ideas. Consider, for example:

> Child poverty is a serious problem in our society, often leading to inadequate nutrition and poor living conditions. (Abstract)

> A toddler, clutching a stale crust – her only breakfast – unwashed and half-frozen, will not thrive. (Emotive)

Look again at how words like 'clutching' are used (rather than just 'holding') and consider the emotive effect of this.

Rhetorical questions

Use rhetorical questions sparingly to give them maximum effect. If arguing against a ban on risky sports, you might write:

> Is it right to ban the very spirit of adventure that is at the heart of human progress?

Juxtaposition

Juxtaposing images or ideas can create contrast or balance. Think carefully about the effect you want to create. Avoid placing images or ideas next to each other without a specific purpose.

TIP
Check your exam response to make sure you haven't overused any one rhetorical technique.

Direct address and anecdotes

By directly addressing your audience and recounting anecdotes, you may find that you create more of a bond with your listeners or readers, as you are making your argument more personal and appealing. People are more likely to agree with someone whom they like.

Key terms — Make sure you can write a definition for each of these key terms.

emotive language   exaggeration   juxtaposition
repetition   rhetorical questions   tricolons

3 Rhetorical language

Retrieval — CONCEPT 3

Use the following questions to check your understanding of the knowledge covered in this section. Then cover the answers column with a piece of paper and write down as many as you can. Check and repeat.

Questions / Answers

1 What is emotive language? Choose from:
- Language describing movement.
- Language aiming for an emotional response.
- Language with a purpose.

Language aiming for an emotional response.

2 Which of these is a rhetorical question, and what is its effect?
- What is the capital of Wales?
- Have you bought the train tickets?
- Do you think I was born yesterday?

Do you think I was born yesterday? The speaker means he or she is not easily fooled, like a newborn baby.

3 What technique is used here, and what is the effect?
We're tired, we're hungry, and we want to go home.

Tricolon (triple). Having three items makes the list more powerfully persuasive. Here, the final item is the most important.

4 What technique is used here, and what is the effect?
We all want to do well in our exams.

Use of the first person plural pronoun (we) and determiner (our) makes readers feel included in the statement.

5 What is juxtaposition, and what is its effect?

It is placing two ideas or images near each other to create a sense of balance or contrast.

6 Rhetorical language is only found in speeches. True or false?

False

7 Rhetorical language can influence the way people think and what they do. True or false?

True

8 You should aim to include as many rhetorical features in your writing as possible. True or false?

False

Previous questions

Now go back and use these questions to check your knowledge of previous topics.

Questions / Answers

1 What two words are typically used in similes?

Like, as

2 How is a metaphor different from a simile?

It describes a thing as if it is something else, without using 'like' or 'as'.

3 Retrieval 25

Knowledge — CONCEPT

4 Characterisation, setting, and mood

What are characterisation, setting, and mood?

A fiction writer creates different characters, settings, and moods to convey stories to the reader. All these elements build a context for the plot to develop, taking the reader into the writer's imaginative world.

> **QUESTION CONNECTION**
> You will comment on setting, ideas, themes, and events when responding to Paper 1 Question 4. Paper 1 Questions 1, 2, and 3 might also focus on characters or mood in some way. You will also need to use your knowledge of these aspects when writing your own text in Paper 1 Question 5 or 6.

Characterisation

A writer can portray character through explicit information, by telling the reader directly about how the character looks. This might include their features, clothes, and other aspects of their physical appearance.

> Under the brim of an immaculate top hat, her smiling eyes reflected the green of her waistcoat.

As well as direct information about the character's clothes, the 'smiling eyes' suggest a cheerful, friendly character.

> **LINK**
> See more about explicit and implicit meaning on page 3.

> **TIP**
> Remember that characters are not real people. Also, the views they express may not be the same as the views of the writer. Writers make deliberate choices about how they portray their characters in order to influence the way that readers will respond.

Writers also convey character through implicit information. The writer *shows* the reader what the character is like through:

- their actions – incidents in the narrative
- what they say – speech, which can move the narrative on
- how they interact with other characters.

For example, this character's *actions* show his concern and sense of responsibility for his younger siblings, implying that he is kind and mature:

> Before they embarked on their journey, Sameer checked that his younger brothers had their warm coats and comfortable shoes.

Look at the **dialogue** below. The *speech* and *interaction* between these two characters suggest, in this situation, that Maureen is domineering, while Zoe is sensitive and trusting:

> 'I don't want to hear any more about it,' Maureen said.
>
> Zoe blinked back tears. 'But you promised,' she sobbed. 'And now everyone knows.'

When drawing conclusions about characters, it is important to consider the context of the situation and infer why characters might be acting in certain ways.

Setting

Setting gives an overall context for the story. The setting is when and where the action occurs: the time and place. Time might be:

- a historical period, such as medieval times or in the future
- a season, such as autumn or summer
- a particular month or celebration, such as Ramadan, Diwali or Christmas
- a time during the day, for example at dawn, at midday, or in the evening.

Setting also covers place, which could refer to a particular town or country, to a building like a theme hotel, to scenery like the desert, or to a fantasy world. Writers often use setting as a device to establish the **mood** of the text, set the scene, and reflect the themes and characters. Look at an example below.

> The planet's third moon was just rising as Thar stepped out of the silver pod onto the dusty yellow soil. She was surrounded by a random scattering of jagged rocks, each with its own moon shadow pooling from beneath it. The faint breeze carried a distinct smell of sulphur.

Mood

A good writer will choose language to describe events, characters, and setting to create a mood. Mood is the overall emotion and atmosphere that the writer wants the reader to feel when reading a story. For example, notice how in the extract below the writer uses the setting of a 'cold and gloomy room' and a locked door to create a mood of fear and danger:

> As Marek stepped into the cold and gloomy room, a deeper darkness detached itself from the shadows and began to creep steadily towards him. He fumbled for the door behind him. It was locked.

TIP

Notice the setting of the text extract from Paper 1 Section A. It may help you think about language and structure for Question 3 and make a judgement about the writer's success for Question 4.

Mood can also be created by descriptions of weather. The weather can be used to echo the feelings of the characters or to enhance dramatic effects. For example, a hot, sultry day might echo the idleness or boredom of a character; the gathering clouds of a storm might echo tension building up between characters before an argument.

> The day of the wedding dawned unpromisingly. Dark clouds loomed, and a sharp north wind lifted and scattered the dead leaves across the road like ghostly confetti. She looked uncertainly out of her window and shivered.

4 Knowledge

Knowledge CONCEPT

4 Characterisation, setting, and mood

What are the effects of characterisation, setting, and mood?

Characters are often established at the start of a novel or story. As you read through a source text, think about why the writer has made the choices they have.

- What effects have they tried to create for the reader?
- Why have they chosen to use certain language?
- What is being implied about the character?
- What is being suggested, beyond the direct information we are given?

Read the extract below. The annotations focus on how the writer presents the character of Mr Knoppert and the effects they create.

① The use of his full name and title makes him sound rather formal and distant, and therefore unsympathetic.

③ The word 'repellent' strongly suggests their negative reaction. His pleasure in this makes him seem strange as a character.

⑤ His words make him seem mysterious, as he has not previously cared about nature but finds snails beautiful – unlike most people.

Extract 1: 'The Snail Watcher' by Patricia Highsmith

This extract from a short story is about Mr Knoppert and his hobby of snail watching.

When Mr Peter Knoppert ① began to make a hobby of snail-watching, he had no idea that his handful of specimens would become hundreds in no time. Only two months after the original snails were carried up
5 to the Knoppert study, some thirty glass tanks and bowls, all teeming with snails, lined the walls, rested on the desk and windowsills, and were beginning even to cover the floor. ② Mrs Knoppert disapproved strongly, and would no longer enter the room. It smelled, she
10 said, and besides she had once stepped on a snail by accident, a horrible sensation she would never forget. But the more his wife and friends deplored his unusual and vaguely repellent pastime, the more pleasure Mr Knoppert seemed to find in it. ③
15 'I never cared for nature before in my life,' Mr Knoppert often remarked – he was a partner in a brokerage* firm, a man who had devoted all his life to the science of finance ④ – 'but snails have opened my eyes to the beauty of the animal world.' ⑤
20 If his friends commented that snails were not really animals, and their slimy habitats hardly the best example of the beauty of nature, Mr Knoppert would tell them with a superior smile that they simply didn't know all that he knew about snails. ⑥

brokerage: *buying and selling stocks and shares*

---

② For most readers, the character's fascination with snails would make him seem unpleasant. The use of 'teeming' might make readers feel uncomfortable with this environment, and therefore with the character.

④ The use of 'science' implies that Knoppert also has a scientific interest in snails.

⑥ His 'superior smile' and the mysterious way he presents his knowledge suggests that he feels he is better than other people.

The writer uses language to present Mr Knoppert as a mysterious man with an unusual interest in snails. The effects of this language will make the reader curious about him, therefore likely to pay attention to him when they continue to read.

28 4 Characterisation, setting, and mood

Writers also use language to create a setting and a particular mood in a story. As you read a source text, ask yourself:

- What is being implied?
- What is the effect of any figurative language?
- What sort of mood do certain words and phrases create?

It is important that you can comment on the language choices a writer makes, explaining the effects they create for the reader.

Read the extract below. The annotations focus on how the writer builds up a particular sense of place and mood.

> **TIP**
>
> You should assume that any setting described in the exam source text is intended to create a particular mood. You need to explain what this is. Do not just write: 'The author describes the setting so that you can really imagine being there.'

❶ Glass and steel are cold, hard materials, reflecting the **narrator's** experience of the setting in which she finds herself.

❸ The woman is raised up and very visible, and even her desk is made of glass. This makes her seem vulnerable and visible in a way that Nazneen herself would hate.

❺ These statements are not literally true. They imply that this is a world of impersonal, unsympathetic corporate power.

❼ The men are part of the setting. The phrases 'trotted briskly', 'barked', normally apply to horses and dogs, so this world seems inhuman. There is also a sense of them being on important business from which Nazneen is excluded.

Extract 2: *Brick Lane* by Monica Ali

This extract is from a novel, and is from the point of view of Nazneen, who has recently arrived in London from Bangladesh, and is walking in a business district in London.

She looked up at a building as she passed. It was constructed almost entirely of glass, with a few thin rivets of steel holding it together. The entrance was like a glass fan, ❶ rotating slowly, sucking people in,
5 wafting others out. ❷ Inside, on a raised dais, a woman behind a glass desk ❸ crossed and uncrossed her thin legs. She wedged a telephone receiver between her ear and shoulder and chewed on a fingernail. Nazneen craned her head back and saw that the glass
10 above became dark as a night pond. ❹ The building was without end. Above, somewhere, it crushed the clouds. ❺ The next building and the one opposite were white stone palaces. There were steps up to the entrances and colonnades* across the front. ❻ Men in
15 dark suits trotted briskly up and down the steps, in pairs or in threes. They barked to each other and nodded sombrely. ❼

colonnades: *rows of columns, as in ancient Greek architecture*

❷ The entrance, personified as 'sucking people in', implies that the institution the building represents devours people, ignoring their individuality.

❹ Nazneen craning her head back suggest that she is awed by the huge impersonal nature of the building. The 'night pond' simile is an image from nature, suggesting the less urban world that Nazneen may come from.

❻ They are not really 'palaces', but the word implies how much wealth has gone into building them.

Overall, the writer presents Nazneen's perception of the setting as being huge, hard, and cold. This shows the reader how alienated she feels in this environment, surrounded by corporate wealth and power rather than comfort. Through the mood of these descriptions, the writer suggests that there is nothing that the narrator can relate to.

4 Knowledge 29

Knowledge CONCEPT

4 Characterisation, setting, and mood

How can I write about characterisation, setting, and mood?

When you are commenting on how the writer creates **characterisation**, setting, and mood, remember to refer to words or phrases in the text, then explain the effects that the language creates for the reader. You might find some of the words and sentence stems below helpful in your commentary.

> ...portrays...   ...conveys a sense of...   ...implies that...
> ...creates an impression of...   ...focuses attention on...

TIP
Character, setting, and mood are often conveyed through language and structure. You could analyse these for Paper 1 Question 3. You could also evaluate the writer's success in conveying them in Paper 1 Question 4.

Writing about characterisation

When writing about characterisation, consider the explicit information that the writer gives you and also the implicit information that you can gain from the way a character acts, speaks, and interacts with others.

Imagine you have been given Extract 1 (page 28) and that the question asks:

> How does the writer use language and structure to convey Mr Knoppert's attitude towards his hobby?

Read one student's partial response below, considering how the language reveals more about Mr Knoppert's character.

TIP
Focus on what the question asks you. Here the focus is on *Mr Knoppert's attitude towards his hobby* – not just 'his character' or 'how the snails are presented'. You will need to tie the evidence you select to the specific focus of the question. For Paper 1 Question 3 this will relate to the writer's use of language and structure. For Question 4 you will have to evaluate how successfully an effect is achieved.

❶ Analyses language closely, linking word choice to information given later.

→ Mr Knoppert's 'hobby of snail-watching' sounds casual, but 'specimens' implies a more scientific approach that reflects his previous devotion to the 'science of finance'. ❶ The author's language suggests Mr Knoppert's growing obsession by creating an impression of the huge number of snails that he quickly acquires. The structure of the first paragraph underlines this growth, showing how a 'handful of specimens' became 'hundreds', and eventually 'thirty glass tanks and bowls, all teeming with snails'. This creates a sense of his hobby getting out of control. ❷ A tricolon emphasises how they fill his study, on the 'walls', 'desk', and 'windowsills' and even 'the floor'. This makes him seem disturbingly eccentric. ❸

The negative verb 'deplored' and the description 'vaguely repellent' convey how his wife and friends react to his hobby. He seems to take 'pleasure' in their response, as if he enjoys their disgust. ❹

❷ Analyses how the structure creates a sense of his hobby growing.

❸ Supports the point with precise evidence and sums up the effect.

❹ Explains, with evidence, how his attitude to their reaction reveals his own character.

30 4 Characterisation, setting, and mood

Writing about setting and mood

The creation of character, setting, and mood are usually closely interlinked, but an exam question might ask you to focus on just one aspect of a text. Take care to focus on exactly what is asked.

Imagine you have been given Extract 2 (page 29) and the question:

> In this extract, there is an attempt to create a sense of Nazneen's reaction to her surroundings.
>
> Evaluate how successfully this is achieved.

TIP

For Paper 1 Question 4, focus closely on the effect of just one or two words from the source text at a time. You will have more than enough to write about, so be selective.

Read one student's response below. The annotations focus on how the student structures their response, keeping their focus clearly on Nazneen's reaction to her surroundings.

❶ A clear statement about the link between setting and character.

❸ Makes a point, gives evidence, and analyses it.

❺ Comments on how the description of the setting reflects Nazneen's feelings in this section of the text.

> The writer creates a strong sense of Nazneen's reaction by presenting the setting through Nazneen's eyes. ❶ The fact that she notices the construction of the buildings, even making an effort by craning her head back to see one, implies that they are strange to her. ❷ It seems extraordinary to her that one is 'constructed almost entirely of glass, with a few thin rivets of steel'. It seems both hard and improbably flimsy. ❸
>
> The writer uses the symbol of glass very effectively. It is everywhere. The entrance is 'like a glass fan', and the woman sits 'behind a glass desk'. Glass and steel are cold, hard materials, reflecting Nazneen's experience of this world and creating a mood of unsympathetic alienation. The glass becomes 'dark as a night pond'. This simile from the natural world, applied to this very unnatural world, is effective in conveying Nazneen's sense of threat. ❹
>
> She sees the skyscraper as 'without end'. This, together with its violent 'crushing' of the clouds really creates a sense of how overwhelmed she feels. ❺

❷ Works out implied meaning through the writer's word choice.

❹ Focuses on one important feature, analysing how it shows Nazneen's mood.

If a question asks you to focus on particular aspects of a text, you should make explicit reference to these aspects in your response. Note that the student response above mentions both 'setting' and 'mood' in relation to the specific question focus.

4 Knowledge

Knowledge — CONCEPT

4 Characterisation, setting, and mood

How can I use characterisation, setting, and mood in my own writing?

Characterisation

If you are writing a story in the exam, it is best to focus on just two or three characters so that you have time to develop them properly. The diagram below shows what to consider for each character.

Character
- Gender and approximate age?
- How might looks and clothing suggest character?
- How do they speak? What is a typical line they might say?
- What problem(s) or fears do they have?
- What motivates them? What do they want?
- How could their behaviour or manner suggest character?

TIP

Remember, as a writer, you can portray characters through explicit information, *telling* the reader directly about the character, or through implicit information, through their actions.

In your writing, consider:

- the reason for including that particular character
- how that links to the impact you want your text to have
- what are characters' intentions
- how they are feeling in the context they are in.

Setting and mood

A story or description works best if it has a clear sense of where and when it takes place. This provides a background for the action in a story or a clear context for more detailed description.

Think about what mood you want to create. What type of emotional world will you take your reader into? It might be one of the following:

- joyful
- sinister
- melancholy
- relaxed
- tense
- romantic

You can create mood by the details and language you use to describe the setting. For example:

> Summer is truly over. The swallows have abandoned us. Bees no longer buzz through the flowers and a moaning wind has swept upon us.

Notice how this student has conveyed a depressed mood through careful, vivid description of the setting. A moaning wind has replaced the buzz of bees, suggesting a change to a more unpleasant environment.

Key terms: Make sure you can write a definition for each of these key terms.

characterisation   dialogue   mood   narrator

Retrieval **CONCEPT** 4

Use the following questions to check your understanding of the knowledge covered in this section. Then cover the answers column with a piece of paper and write down as many as you can. Check and repeat.

Questions / Answers

#	Questions	Answers
1	Writers create characters only by describing their appearance. True or false?	False
2	How else can writers convey information about their characters?	Through a character's actions, words, and relationships with other characters.
3	Setting just refers to time. True or false?	False: it also includes place.
4	What sort of timing could be included in a setting?	Historical time, time of day or night, season, yearly or monthly festival or celebration.
5	What is the 'mood' of a text?	The atmosphere created in the text and the emotional response in the reader, created by the writer.
6	What mood is created by the following description? *It was a warm spring morning and the garden was coming into bloom. Early birds sang brightly, and cherry blossom waved in a kindly breeze.*	Happy, optimistic
7	How can a description of weather help to create mood?	It can reflect the feelings of a character, or the situation they are in.

Previous questions

Now go back and use these questions to check your knowledge of previous topics.

#	Questions	Answers
1	What is emotive language?	Language aiming for an emotional response.
2	What is juxtaposition, and what is its effect?	It is placing two ideas or images near each other to create a sense of balance or contrast.

4 Retrieval   33

Knowledge   CONCEPT

5 Ideas and perspectives

What are ideas and perspectives?

Ideas

The **ideas** in a text are made up of its topics (subject matter) and its themes and issues (questions raised and explored). For example:

- A text might look at the *topic* of education.
- It might explore the *theme* of education being socially useful.
- It could raise the *issue* of whether art and science are equally valuable subjects.

Perspective

The **perspective** in a text is the view that the writer has taken on a topic. The writer will decide their perspective, based on what they want to convey and their purpose.

A perspective is revealed through what the writer says – their **attitude**, opinions, thoughts and feelings. It's conveyed in what they say and how they say it. It's revealed through voice, **tone**, **register** and other methods, including:

- viewpoint and mood
- word classes, such as verbs, adjectives, and adverbs
- figurative, emotive, or sensory language
- structural elements, such as repetition of key ideas.

> **QUESTION CONNECTION**
>
> You should comment on ideas and perspectives in Paper 2 Question 7(b) when comparing the topics and themes in two source texts and the writers' views on them. Tone is also relevant to language comments for Paper 1 Question 3 and Paper 2 Question 3.

Tone

The tone of a text reveals a writer's attitude towards a topic and also the type of relationship they want to establish with their reader. They might create a serious, angry tone to shock and engage the reader:

> We are frustrated by the same old excuses!

Or a light-hearted, friendly tone to bond with the reader:

> If you're like me, you probably like to put your feet up at the end of the day.

There are a variety of tones that writers might choose to create, for example:

irritated   thoughtful   humorous   sarcastic   encouraging

sympathetic   detached   comic   judgemental

> **TIP**
>
> A tone can vary throughout a text, varying in intensity from mildly annoyed, for example, to furious ranting.

Register

Register is the way a writer, or speaker, uses language differently in different circumstances and for different audiences. For example, think of how you would speak differently to your friends and to your head teacher or older members of your family.

Register can refer to the level of formality in a text or speech. For a formal register, a writer will choose serious language, as well as longer and more complex sentences. A formal register is appropriate for texts such as legal reports, NHS health leaflets or letters to your MP. An informal register uses simpler, more **colloquial language**.

> Temperatures are predicted to be high today. (Formal register)
> I reckon it's gonna be a right scorcher. (Informal register)

Standard and non-standard English

Standard English is a widely recognised formal version of English not linked to any region, but used in schools, books, official publications, and public announcements. Standard English uses standard grammar and vocabulary. It can be spoken in any accent.

Non-Standard English is a more informal version of English, and can include **dialect** (words and grammar used only in one region), colloquial words and expressions, and slang.

> **TIP**
> You should use Standard English in your exam question responses (unless you choose not to for a purpose in the writing questions).

> The potatoes were delicious. (Standard English)
> Them tatties were yummy. (Non-Standard English)

Viewpoint

The viewpoint (or narrative viewpoint) is the point of view from which a text is written or narrated.

An article in a magazine might use a **first-person viewpoint**, using the pronouns 'I' and 'we' as they offer an opinion on a current event or issue.

> I've always loved watching films, so the controversy about film ratings has made me think about the influence films can have.

A news report is likely to be written with a **third-person viewpoint**, giving facts and recounting events using the pronouns 'he', 'she', 'it', and 'they'.

> The storm caused damage to towns on the coast. It also swept a man into the sea as he walked along a beach.

Knowledge CONCEPT

5 Ideas and perspectives

How do writer's methods convey ideas and perspectives?

You would expect certain types of text to be in a very formal register so that their meaning is clear and they are taken seriously. One such text type is a presidential speech. Look at the perspective of the speaker: he is critical of what has come before him and motivated for a new beginning. These are conveyed through methods in the speech.

LINK
The context of this speech and the rhetorical devices included are explored in more detail on page 20.

Extract 1: President Obama's Inaugural Address, calling for 'a new era of responsibility'

This extract is from President Obama's inauguration speech, the first speech he gave after becoming President.

> That we are in the midst of crisis is now well understood. ❶ Our nation is at war, against a far-reaching network of violence and hatred. Our economy is badly weakened, a consequence of greed and
> 5 irresponsibility on the part of some, but also our collective failure to make hard choices and prepare the nation for a new age. ❷ Homes have been lost; jobs shed; businesses shuttered. ❸ Our healthcare
> 10 is too costly; our schools fail too many; and each day brings further evidence that the ways we use energy strengthen our adversaries and threaten our planet. ❹

❶ Formal wording conveys a serious tone. The first-person plural perspective ('we') includes himself with all Americans.

❷ Long, complex sentence with the formal 'on the part of some' showing he wants to indicate that some people have been greedy, but without naming any particular group. First-person plural perspective ('Our') has been included to be as one with the audience.

❸ Three examples convey a regretful tone that people have suffered these losses.

❹ Formal register expresses his deep concern. The words 'adversaries' and 'threaten', together with the use of 'we' and 'our', imply a caring attitude and a sense of unity.

The overall effect is to command respect, and to convey his attitude of concern for the serious problems all Americans face, without apportioning blame. He also expresses a sympathetic tone for people's personal losses and implies a sense of unity in that he and all Americans are facing these problems together.

To understand the formality of this language, consider what Obama says above alongside possible informal versions.

Formal	Informal
That we are in the midst of crisis is now well understood.	Everyone knows we're in a mess.
a consequence of greed and irresponsibility on the part of some	because of a few greedy, irresponsible people
Homes have been lost	People have got nowhere to go / are on the streets
brings further evidence that the ways we use energy strengthen our adversaries	shows more and more that our energy use helps our enemies

The formal language conveys a more serious tone, reflecting the concern and determination in the speaker's attitude towards the country's situation.

A magazine or newspaper article may seek to convey a humorous tone if the purpose is to entertain the reader.

Look again at this extract from an article in the *Guardian* by Charlie Brooker, in which he shares his perspective on updating his smartphone. Notice how it differs from the President Obama speech. The writer knows that exaggerating his attitude for comic effect, while still making a point about the modern world, will be successful with his audience.

LINK
The context of this article is explored in more detail on page 5.

❶ Simple sentence, showing a negative attitude.

❸ Casual expression implying impatience: the update is a waste of his time. The register is informal and annoyed.

❺ Colloquial word 'fiddly' reveals his attitude: the update is not hugely important, but it's annoying – and probably pointless.

Extract 2: 'Apple's software updates are like changing the water in a fish tank. I'd rather let the fish die' by Charlie Brooker

> This extract is an article from the *Guardian* about one person's view of software updates.

Updates are awful. ❶ All you want to do is watch TV and rot in your own filth. ❷ Instead you spend the evening backing up your phone, downloading a gigantic file and sitting around ❸ while your phone undergoes
5 an intense psychological makeover, ❹ at the end of which it may or may not function. Often, it takes an hour or more. Fiddly, time-consuming admin ❺ – it's like having to change the water in a fish tank. … it's why I don't have an aquarium. I'd rather let the fish die. ❻

❷ Direct address 'you' and a casual, humorous expression reflect his perspective that he would rather waste time in his own chosen way.

❹ Humorous exaggeration shows an exasperated attitude to what he thinks is an unnecessary procedure.

❻ Exaggerated humour shows his quirky view that both things are equally tedious.

The overall effect of this informal register and humorous tone is to make readers identify with the writer. It also entertains them, as the writer comically expresses his negative, critical attitude towards wasting time updating his phone.

5 Knowledge

Knowledge

CONCEPT

5 Ideas and perspectives

How can I write about ideas and perspectives?

Identifying the writer's perspective and ideas is key, so make sure you explicitly state this in your answer. You can then explore the reason that this idea or perspective is formed or taken, and through what language or structural devices.

You should now be able to identify:

- ways in which writers reveal their attitude towards a subject
- typical differences between a formal and an informal register
- what types of text are more likely to use a formal or informal register
- Standard and non-Standard English – an important element of register
- how writers create tone to help express their ideas
- the different perspectives that writers can use, depending on the type of text they are writing, its purpose and audience.

To comment on the attitudes in Extract 1 (page 36), you could write:

> The speaker wishes to outline his view that America has problems without blaming anyone in particular, and to present himself as a responsible and capable leader. **❶** He speaks in a formal register and a serious tone to express his perspective. **❷** The topic sentence at the start of the paragraph is formally impersonal: 'is now well understood'. His attitude is that everyone knows that America has problems. It also avoids saying exactly who understands this, as some listeners might disagree. **❸**
>
> The formal register is also shown in the long, complex sentence beginning, 'Our economy …', and in the impersonal 'on the part of some' that identifies a problem but avoids blaming anyone. The use of 'our' expresses his attitude that he and all Americans face these problems together. **❹** The language is also formal: 'the midst of crisis' rather than 'a mess', and 'adversaries' rather than 'enemies'. This shows that he takes America's problems, and his role, very seriously. **❺**

❶ Identifies context and aims and focuses on perspective, showing a specific attitude.

❷ Explains how Obama's perspective on America's problems influences register and tone.

❸ Gives evidence of attitude and analyses its effect.

❹ Gives grammatical evidence and analyses effect.

❺ Analyses formal language and effect, with examples.

QUESTION CONNECTION

It is essential that you identify perspectives and ideas that relate to the focus in the question in Paper 2 Question 7(b) and compare corresponding perspectives from both sources. This section looks at how to comment on texts individually. In Paper 2 Question 7(b) you will have to compare the attitudes and perspectives in two texts. See pages 182–189 for how to do this.

LINK

Learn more about topic sentences on page 57.

To comment on the ideas and perspectives in Extract 2 (page 37), you could write:

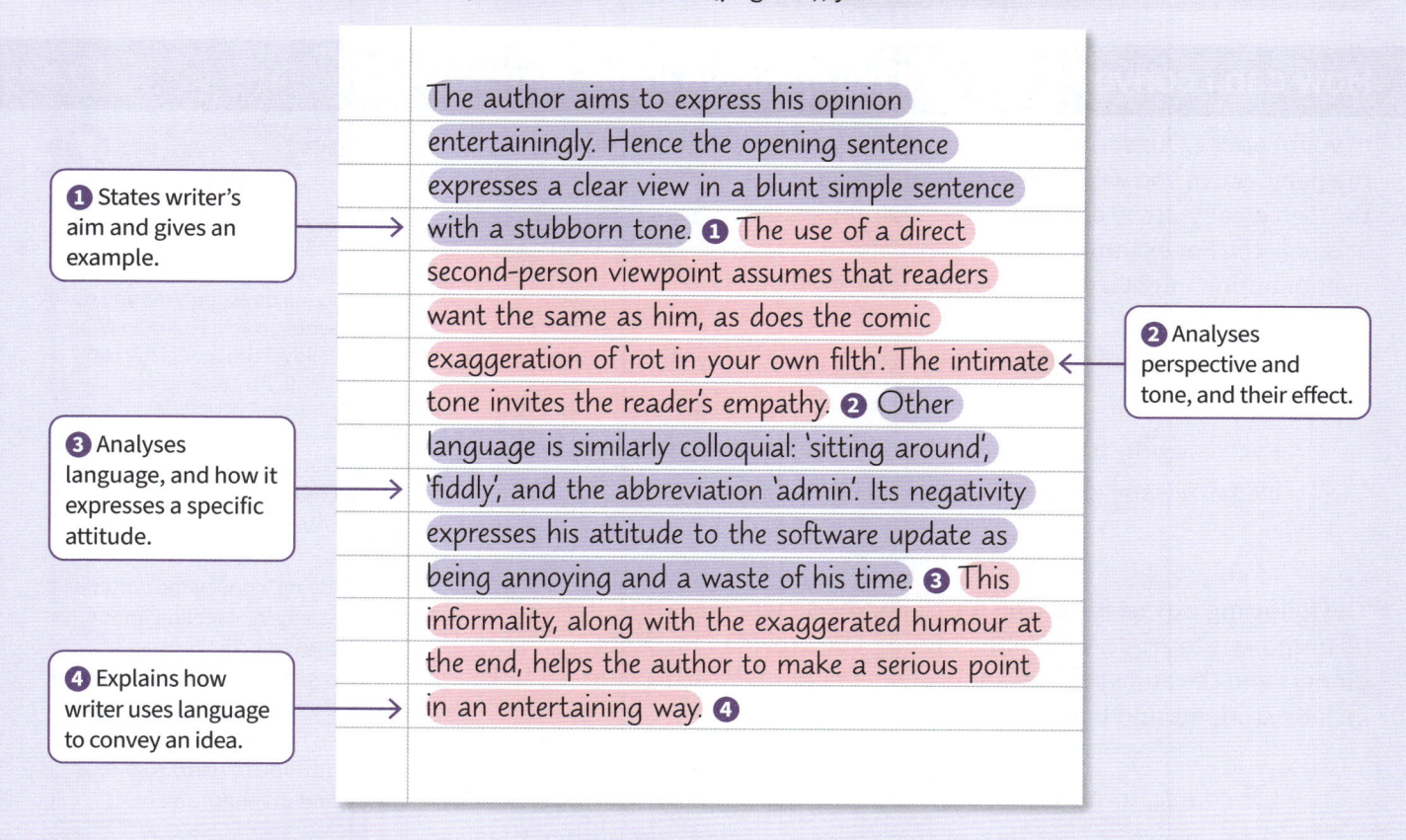

> The author aims to express his opinion entertainingly. Hence the opening sentence expresses a clear view in a blunt simple sentence with a stubborn tone. ❶ The use of a direct second-person viewpoint assumes that readers want the same as him, as does the comic exaggeration of 'rot in your own filth'. The intimate tone invites the reader's empathy. ❷ Other language is similarly colloquial: 'sitting around', 'fiddly', and the abbreviation 'admin'. Its negativity expresses his attitude to the software update as being annoying and a waste of his time. ❸ This informality, along with the exaggerated humour at the end, helps the author to make a serious point in an entertaining way. ❹

❶ States writer's aim and gives an example.

❷ Analyses perspective and tone, and their effect.

❸ Analyses language, and how it expresses a specific attitude.

❹ Explains how writer uses language to convey an idea.

The student identifies how register and tone combine to express the writer's attitude towards the update as being an annoying waste of his time – a view with which he assumes his readers will empathise.

> **TIP**
> When commenting on a source text, you should always write in Standard English. You should also use Standard English when writing your own text, unless you are writing dialogue between characters.

5 Knowledge 39

Knowledge

CONCEPT

5 Ideas and perspectives

How can I convey ideas and perspective in my own writing?

In your Paper 2 Question 8 or 9 writing task, you should decide on the perspective you will take on the subject, and convey that view through what you say and the relevant writer's methods, such as tone and register. For example, a letter conveying a critical perspective on river pollution might use a firm, angry tone:

> Environmental authorities whose responsibility it is to protect the river and how clean it is have consistently failed to do so. The river is dying from a lethal cocktail of agricultural phosphates, illegal sewage discharge, and chicken manure.

> **TIP**
> As a general rule, you should use a formal register in your exam responses. However, if an exam question asks you to write an article aimed at fellow teenagers, you can be slightly less formal.

> Notice how the tone is created by careful choice of vocabulary: words such as 'lethal' and 'dying' convey the writer's strength of feeling about the river. The formal register and serious tone ('consistently failed to do so') convey the writer's attitude towards a serious and urgent problem.

The following extract is from an article for the school magazine. Its purpose is to argue for healthier food to be provided for school dinners and the audience is readers of the magazine, which could include students and teachers.

> Of course, in an ideal world, teenagers should eat what's good for them, which means lots of fresh veg and salad, and dishes that are low-fat, low-sugar, and low-salt. This would probably improve their brain function (pass that maths test!) and their all-round health. It would also set up good habits which would stop them being prone to heart disease or diabetes later in life. However, the reality is that teenagers want tasty snacks, which wipes all that low-fat and low-sugar off the menu.

Notice how the register here is a little more informal ('lots of fresh veg', 'off the menu'). The tone is informative and helpful, but it aims to appeal to teenagers, as in the humour of 'pass that maths test!'. The writer's attitude is realistic, aware of health issues, but resigned to the fact of teenagers often liking unhealthy food.

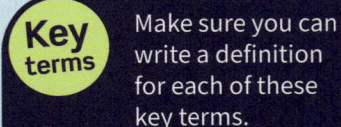

> **Key terms** Make sure you can write a definition for each of these key terms.
>
> attitude   colloquial language   dialect
> first-person viewpoint   non-Standard English
> perspective   register   second-person viewpoint
> Standard English   third-person viewpoint   tone

Retrieval CONCEPT 5

Use the following questions to check your understanding of the knowledge covered in this section. Then cover the answers column with a piece of paper and write down as many as you can. Check and repeat.

Questions / Answers

#	Question	Answer
1	A text that is written from a first-person viewpoint will use the pronouns 'I' and 'we'. True or false?	True
2	A text that is written from a third-person viewpoint uses the pronoun 'you'. True or false?	False. A text written from a third-person perspective would use the pronouns 'he', 'she', 'it', and 'they'.
3	A text that is written from a second-person viewpoint speaks directly to a reader or audience, addressing them as 'you'. True or false?	True
4	What is meant by the writer's ideas?	The topics, themes, and issues they are writing about.
5	How would you describe the tone of this sentence? *'Go home; I'm not going to listen to another word you say.'*	Possible answers include: assertive; aggressive; angry; decisive; determined; exasperated.
6	What is Standard English?	English that is widely accepted as appropriate formal English, following standard grammar rules, and used in schools and official publications.
7	What is colloquial language?	Conversational, casual language.
8	What is dialect?	A type of language that is spoken just in one area, rather than nationwide.
9	The register of your language will vary depending on who you are talking to and where. True or false?	True

Previous questions

Now go back and use these questions to check your knowledge of previous topics.

Questions / Answers

#	Question	Answer
1	What sort of timing could be included in a setting?	Historical time, time of day or night, season, yearly or monthly festival or celebration.
2	What is the 'mood' of a text?	The atmosphere created in the text and the emotional response in the reader, created by the writer.

5 Retrieval 41

Knowledge

CONCEPT

6 Sentence forms

What are sentence forms?

Writers organise words into sentences to convey meaning. Understanding different sentence forms will help you in your own writing.

> **QUESTION CONNECTION**
>
> You will use your knowledge of sentence forms in your own writing for Paper 1 Question 5 or 6, and Paper 2 Question 8 or 9. You may analyse sentence forms when commenting on structure, for Paper 1 Question 3 and Paper 2 Question 3.

Single-clause (simple) sentences

A **single-clause sentence** is a sentence that contains just one main clause. A main clause is a group of words that has a verb as its headword and a subject (either a noun, noun phrase, or pronoun).

It is important not to overuse simple sentences, and include a variety of sentence types in your writing.

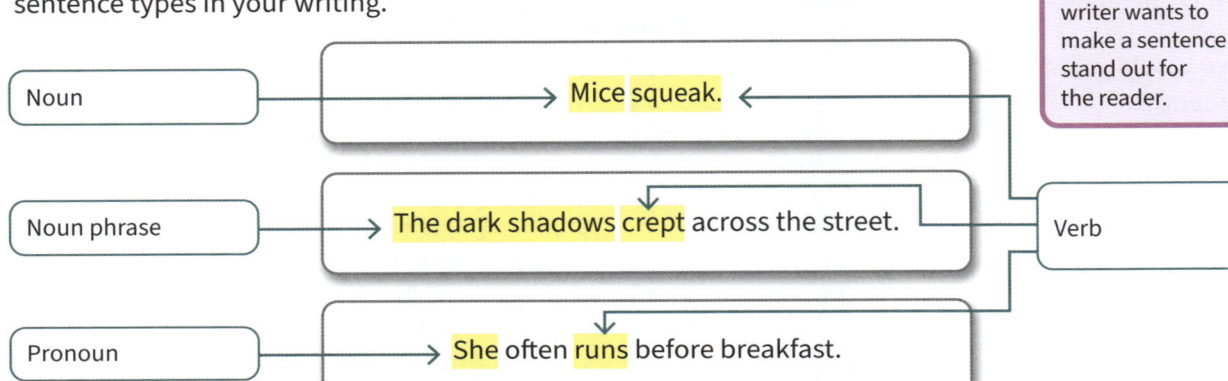

> **TIP**
>
> A single-clause sentence can stand alone as a paragraph if the writer wants to make a sentence stand out for the reader.

- Noun → **Mice** **squeak**.
- Noun phrase → **The dark shadows** **crept** across the street.
- Pronoun → **She** often **runs** before breakfast.

(Verb)

Minor sentences

These are short sentences. They might not contain a subject or a verb. A writer might use a **minor sentence** to emphasise a point. Note that the term 'minor sentence' does not mean they are unimportant. They can be used to express strong emotion or to draw attention to something.

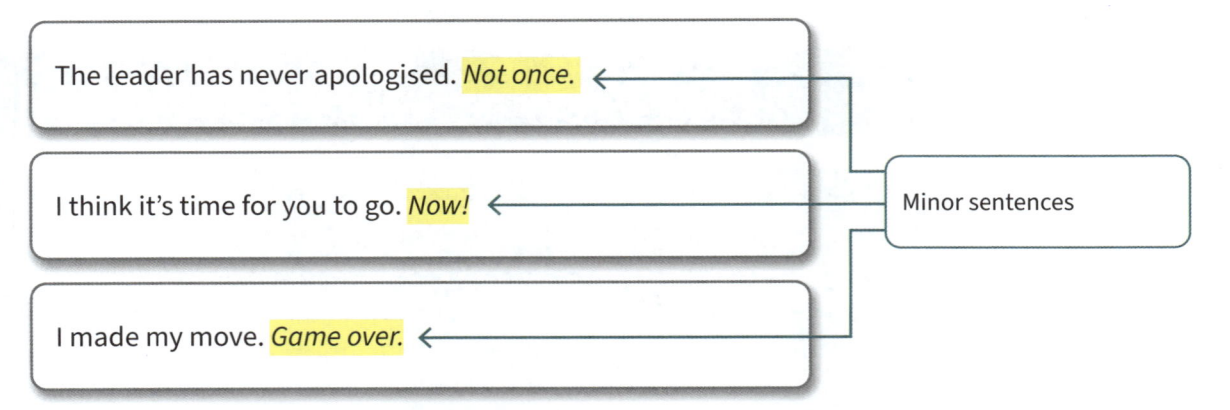

- The leader has never apologised. *Not once.*
- I think it's time for you to go. *Now!*
- I made my move. *Game over.*

(Minor sentences)

Multi-clause (compound) sentences

These combine two or more clauses, using a **coordinating conjunction**, such as 'and', 'but', or 'yet'.

Fish have to swim **and** bats have to fly.

Cats are independent, **but** some enjoy being stroked.

I looked through the window every day, **yet** I never saw the fox again.

Coordinating conjunctions. There are other examples you can use in your writing; these are just the most common.

Multi-clause (complex) sentences

These combine at least two clauses using a **subordinating conjunction**, such as 'despite', 'which' or 'because'. Complex sentences contain one main clause and one or more subordinate clauses (subordinate clauses can add detail to a main clause but can't work as a sentence on their own).

Aaron, **despite being a poor swimmer**, jumped in immediately to save his friend.

Subordinate clause adding information in mid-sentence, with a comma before and after.

Hamid apologised, **which is more than could be said for Elena**.

Subordinate clause adding information at the end of the sentence, preceded by a comma.

Subordinate clauses can be found at the beginning of a sentence, in the middle, or at the end and are usually separated from the main clause by a comma or commas. Writers often decide where to position the subordinate clause depending on what they want to draw the reader's attention to first.

Sentence types

There are four main types of sentences, each with a different purpose:

- **Statements** – state a fact: 'You're my best friend.'
- **Questions** – seek information: 'What's that?'
- **Imperatives** – give an order or instruction: 'Replace the lid.'
- **Exclamations** – express an emotion, such as surprise or disapproval: 'You've got to be kidding!'

> **TIP**
> Remember to check the punctuation of your sentences. This includes the correct use of commas, full stops, question marks, exclamation marks, apostrophes, and speech marks.

6 Knowledge

Knowledge   CONCEPT

6 Sentence forms

What are the effects of varying sentence forms?

Understanding how writers use different sentence forms can help you to vary them effectively in your own writing. Look at how the writer uses sentence structures in the extract below to help build up an argument. Note that the full text is on page 21.

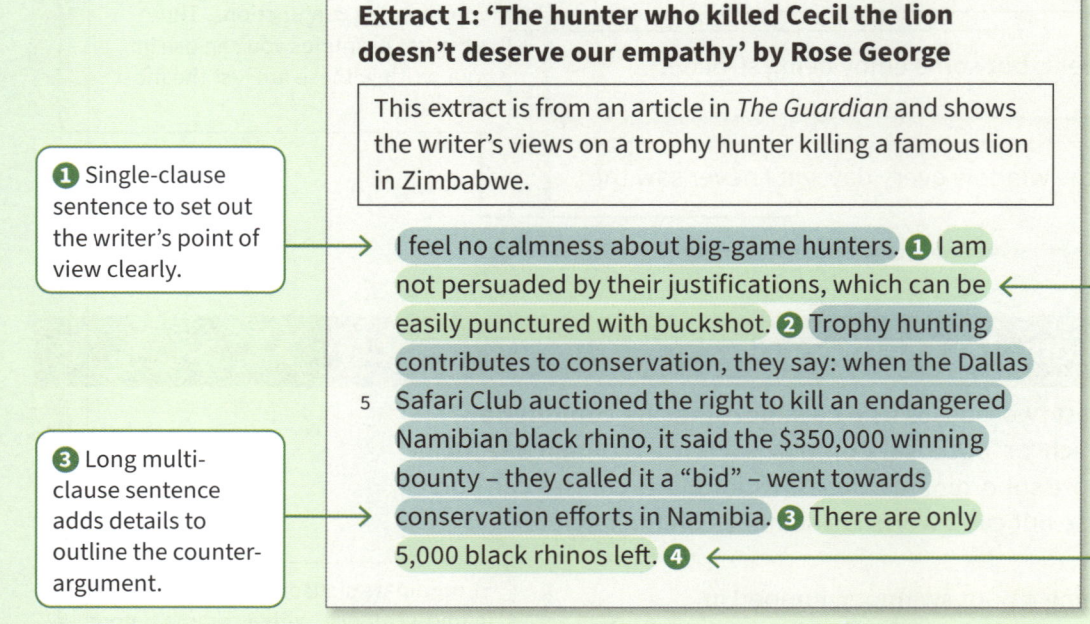

Extract 1: 'The hunter who killed Cecil the lion doesn't deserve our empathy' by Rose George

This extract is from an article in *The Guardian* and shows the writer's views on a trophy hunter killing a famous lion in Zimbabwe.

I feel no calmness about big-game hunters. ❶ I am not persuaded by their justifications, which can be easily punctured with buckshot. ❷ Trophy hunting contributes to conservation, they say: when the Dallas Safari Club auctioned the right to kill an endangered Namibian black rhino, it said the $350,000 winning bounty – they called it a "bid" – went towards conservation efforts in Namibia. ❸ There are only 5,000 black rhinos left. ❹

❶ Single-clause sentence to set out the writer's point of view clearly.

❷ Multi-clause sentence to provide additional detail.

❸ Long multi-clause sentence adds details to outline the counter-argument.

❹ Single-clause sentence simply to defeat the counter-argument and confirm the writer is correct.

Notice how the writer varies the sentence forms to introduce, explain, and then build up her argument. The final short sentence is an effective statement of fact that proves how hollow and misguided the big-game hunters' claims are.

How can I write about sentence forms?

It is not necessary to comment on sentence forms in your exam, as it is quite simple analysis and will receive few marks. The only time you might comment on sentences would be when they are used for specific effect. The paragraph below could be part of an answer on how the writer uses language and structure to convey their argument.

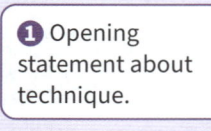

The author uses increasing sentence length and complexity to build a case. ❶ She begins with a simple sentence clearly stating her viewpoint and proceeds with a longer complex sentence about how hunters attempt to justify themselves, then builds to a climax with an even longer complex sentence putting forward the hunters' argument. ❷ Finally, this argument is punctured with the short simple statement that only 5,000 black rhinos are left. ❸

❶ Opening statement about technique.

❸ Uses discourse marker ('Finally') to introduce dismissal of the hunters' argument.

❷ Demonstrates how the climax is reached.

LINK
You can read more about using discourse markers to build an argument on page 57.

TIP
You could include sentence forms in your comments on structure for Question 3 of both papers.

44 6 Sentence forms

How can I vary sentence forms in my own writing?

In the Writing questions of the exam, you must vary your sentence structures effectively. This means knowing how to use different sentence structures to keep your reader engaged and following your narrative or argument closely.

> **QUESTION CONNECTION**
> In Paper 1 Question 5 or 6, and Paper 2 Question 8 or 9, you will be assessed on AO5 and AO6. AO6 states that you must use a range of sentence structures for clarity, purpose, and effect.

Sentence forms in fiction

In fiction, different sentence forms can help to convey the pace of action and the mood of a scene.

Look at how the sentence forms vary in the narrative extract below, reflecting the content of the narrative and breaking it up into logical snippets.

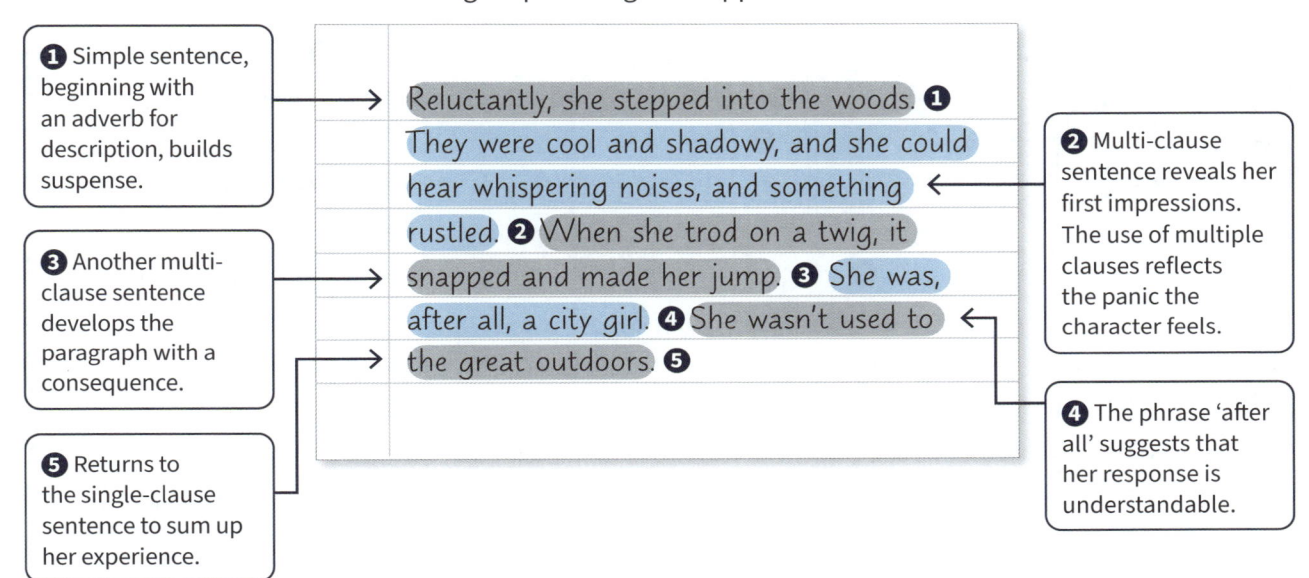

- ❶ Simple sentence, beginning with an adverb for description, builds suspense.
- ❸ Another multi-clause sentence develops the paragraph with a consequence.
- ❺ Returns to the single-clause sentence to sum up her experience.

> Reluctantly, she stepped into the woods. ❶ They were cool and shadowy, and she could hear whispering noises, and something rustled. ❷ When she trod on a twig, it snapped and made her jump. ❸ She was, after all, a city girl. ❹ She wasn't used to the great outdoors. ❺

- ❷ Multi-clause sentence reveals her first impressions. The use of multiple clauses reflects the panic the character feels.
- ❹ The phrase 'after all' suggests that her response is understandable.

Sparing use of simple and minor sentences can be effective when writing fiction.

Here the sentence variations are used to control the mood of the text and the effects on the reader.

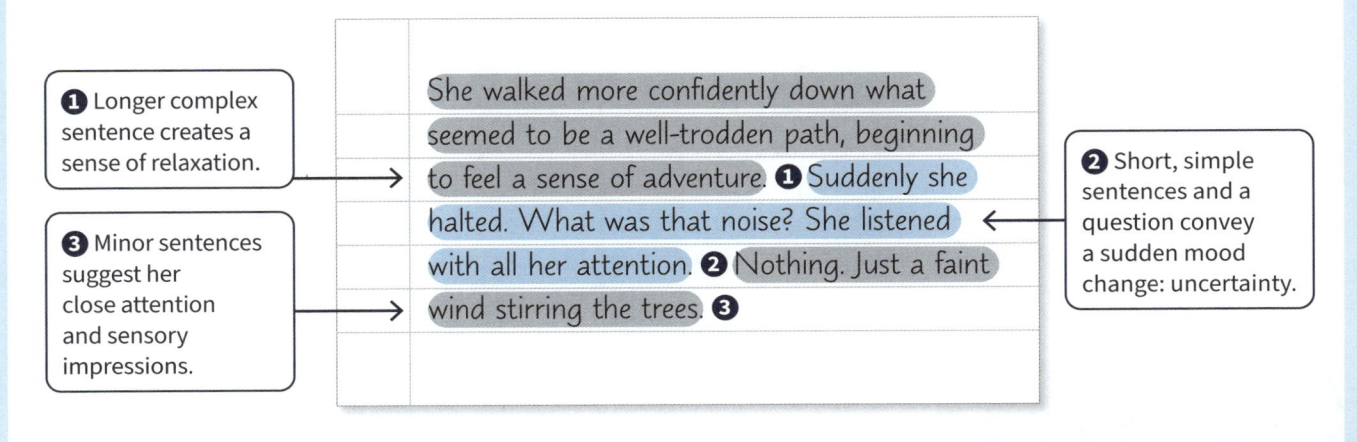

- ❶ Longer complex sentence creates a sense of relaxation.
- ❸ Minor sentences suggest her close attention and sensory impressions.

> She walked more confidently down what seemed to be a well-trodden path, beginning to feel a sense of adventure. ❶ Suddenly she halted. What was that noise? She listened with all her attention. ❷ Nothing. Just a faint wind stirring the trees. ❸

- ❷ Short, simple sentences and a question convey a sudden mood change: uncertainty.

6 Knowledge 45

Knowledge   CONCEPT

6 Sentence forms

Sentence forms in non-fiction

When writing a non-fiction text, such as presenting a viewpoint or argument, you will need to vary the sentence forms you use. This variety can be used to:

- emphasise important points
- add detailed information
- challenge your audience to consider issues and make memorable points
- generally strengthen the power of what you are saying.

See how the writing below uses a range of sentence forms to present an argument effectively.

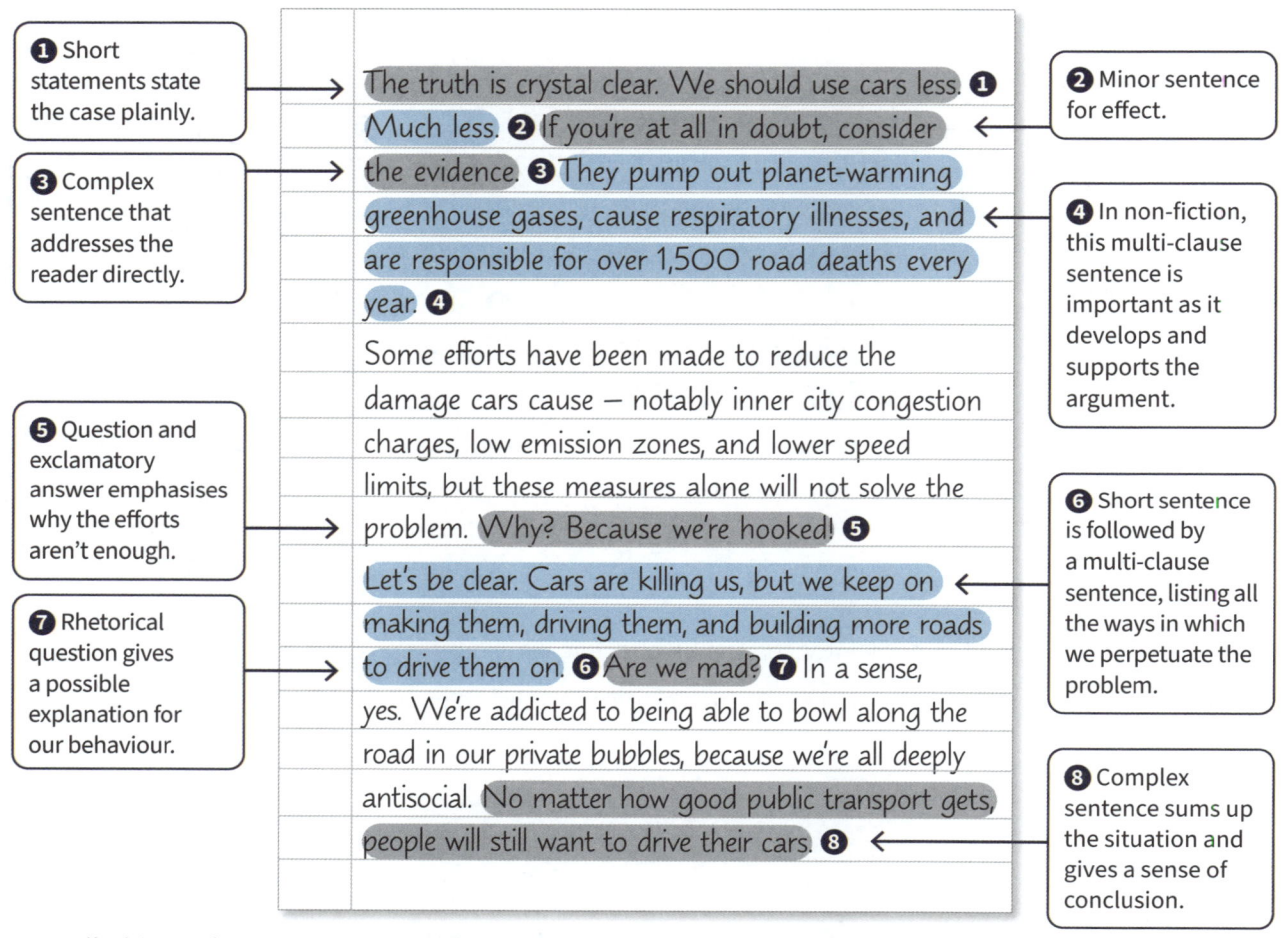

❶ Short statements state the case plainly.

❸ Complex sentence that addresses the reader directly.

❺ Question and exclamatory answer emphasises why the efforts aren't enough.

❼ Rhetorical question gives a possible explanation for our behaviour.

> The truth is crystal clear. We should use cars less. ❶ Much less. ❷ If you're at all in doubt, consider the evidence. ❸ They pump out planet-warming greenhouse gases, cause respiratory illnesses, and are responsible for over 1,500 road deaths every year. ❹
>
> Some efforts have been made to reduce the damage cars cause — notably inner city congestion charges, low emission zones, and lower speed limits, but these measures alone will not solve the problem. Why? Because we're hooked! ❺ Let's be clear. Cars are killing us, but we keep on making them, driving them, and building more roads to drive them on. ❻ Are we mad? ❼ In a sense, yes. We're addicted to being able to bowl along the road in our private bubbles, because we're all deeply antisocial. No matter how good public transport gets, people will still want to drive their cars. ❽

❷ Minor sentence for effect.

❹ In non-fiction, this multi-clause sentence is important as it develops and supports the argument.

❻ Short sentence is followed by a multi-clause sentence, listing all the ways in which we perpetuate the problem.

❽ Complex sentence sums up the situation and gives a sense of conclusion.

Overall, this student uses a variety of sentence forms to state the case clearly, create dramatic emphasis, and draw the reader into the issue. The sentences build up to state the problem, explain efforts to solve it, and analyse why these efforts may never work.

Key terms — Make sure you can write a definition for each of these key terms.

coordinating conjunction   exclamation   imperative
minor sentence   multi-clause sentence
single-clause sentence   statement   subordinating conjunction

Retrieval — CONCEPT — 6

Use the following questions to check your understanding of the knowledge covered in this section. Then cover the answers column with a piece of paper and write down as many as you can. Check and repeat.

Questions / Answers

#	Question	Answer
1	What is a clause?	A sentence or part of a sentence that includes a subject (noun, noun phrase, or pronoun) and a verb.
2	A multi-clause sentence can have more than two clauses in it. True or false?	True
3	A single-clause sentence is always very short. True or false?	False. For example: The young boy on the drums gave an incredible performance last night.
4	What kind of sentence is in italics below, and what is its effect? 'You mean everything to me. *Everything*.'	A minor sentence. Here it is used for emphasis and focus.
5	Turn the following into a multi-clause sentence. (You can add or take away words.) Abshir comes from Somalia. It is in Africa. Many African countries experience drought.	Answers may vary. For example: Abshir comes from Somalia, which is in Africa, where many countries experience drought.
6	You will gain marks by simply identifying sentence structures in a text. True or false?	False. Only identify sentence structures if there is a significant reason the writer has chosen them and explain the effect they create.
7	What is a statement?	A sentence that states a fact, such as: *Birds have wings*.
8	What are *imperative* sentences, and in what kind of text might you find them?	Sentences giving orders or instructions. You might find them in persuasive, advisory, or instructional texts.
9	What kind of sentence is this, and what is its effect? *'Don't tell me you forgot the marmalade!'*	Exclamative. It expresses an emotion such as shock, dismay, disbelief, or anger.

Previous questions

Now go back and use these questions to check your knowledge of previous topics.

#	Question	Answer
1	What is meant by the writer's ideas?	The topics, themes, and issues they are writing about.
2	What is colloquial language?	Informal language, as if in conversation.

Knowledge   CONCEPT

7 Narrative structure

What is narrative structure?

Narrative structure is the way in which a writer organises the sequence of events. It can be a fiction story or a sequence of events in a non-fiction text, such as a narrative which describes a journey in travel writing. Some of the key features of narrative structure can be found below.

> **QUESTION CONNECTION**
>
> You will have to comment on narrative structure in Paper 1 Questions 3 and possibly 4. Also in Paper 2 Questions 3 and possibly 7(b). You will have to create your own narrative structure in your writing when responding to Paper 1 Question 5 or 6.

Openings

Here are some of the ways a story may begin:

- In the middle of the action (this is known as *in media res*):

  > It was only half a mile to school. He'd probably make it if he pedalled fast.

- Describing a scene or setting:

  > It was a hot, cloudless, and almost windless day, and there was hardly an inch of bare sand left on Saltash Beach.

- Introducing a character:

  > Aisha viewed herself in the bathroom mirror: dark, thoughtful eyes in a rounded face.

Inciting incident

Near the start of a story, there is usually an **inciting incident** – a problem or event that sets off a sequence of events that drive the narrative of the story.

> Jamila was just checking her phone as she stepped off the kerb into the path of the pizza delivery bike.

Endings

Here are some of the ways a story may end:

- A resolution to a problem, bringing reconciliation between characters.
- A **cliffhanger** – a dramatic point in the story, leaving the reader wondering what will happen next.
- A return to the beginning of the story, or mirroring the start of the story in some way (a circular narrative).

Shifts in focus

The **focus** of a narrative is whatever the writer is concentrating on at any particular time. This focus will shift as the narrative develops. It may:

- move from one character to another
- move from one location to another
- shift between description and action or dialogue and internal thoughts
- zoom in or zoom out on aspects of the setting or character.

Writers often signal a change of focus with structural features, such as a **discourse marker** or new paragraph:

> Georgia steadied her feet as she walked out of the tube station.
>
> With a step forward, she became just one person in a sea of thousands. The buildings soared high, piercing the skyline.

This example begins with a zoom in on Georgia's emotions. A new paragraph then begins with a discourse marker to zoom out and shift the reader's focus to aspects of the setting.

Sequencing

A narrative may tell a story in **chronological** order – with a straightforward sequence of events each following on from the other, linked by cause and effect. It could also involve a shift backwards or forwards in time. The narrative could shift forwards to later that day, include a **flashback** (shifting backwards to the previous day or five years earlier) or **foreshadowing** (shifting forwards to a moment in the future).

TIP
It can work well to begin a story with an exciting problem and then flash back to what led up to it: 'Just a few hours earlier …'.

> She swung the axe until the tree was felled. The crash rippled through the forest.
> (A chronological sequence of events)
>
> Gazing at the river, all at once she was a child again, with her brother playing near the water – much too near the edge.
> (Flashback)
>
> If he had known then what he knew later, he might have paid more attention.
> (Foreshadowing)

Tension and suspense

A good writer considers how to create **tension** and **suspense** by making structural choices about their story, such as including flashbacks and foreshadowing. Structural features, such as withholding information and dropping hints will build suspense and tension with the reader. Tension builds up the reader's anticipation, and suspense creates a sense of danger or uncertainty.

Climax

The **climax** is the peak of excitement in a whole text; for example, when the hero confronts the villain and is in the greatest danger. The climax normally comes towards the end of the story structure, before the resolution. Some stories include a small **crisis** (before the main climax), but they usually build towards the main climax.

Knowledge

CONCEPT

7 Narrative structure

What are the effects of different narrative structural devices?

A writer organises narrative structure to lead the reader through the story, shifting focus to keep the reader engaged, revealing more details about setting and characters as the plot unfolds. This section focuses on structure, but in Question 3 of both papers, you will have to write about both language *and* structure.

Writers control levels of tension and suspense through their narrative structure. Sometimes information is withheld and only gradually revealed. Readers may enjoy guessing what the outcome may be.

In Extract 1 below, the writer creates a shift in focus by beginning with a description of a busy street scene and then zooming in on a hesitant, nervous character. The effect of this contrast is to concentrate the reader's attention on the character's emotional state. This builds up a sense of suspense before Arjun finally enters the building.

> **TIP**
> When reading a text, think about the story visually as it would be shown in a film. This will help you notice any shifts in the narrative focus, time or perspective.

① Topic sentence
This sums up what the writer is about to describe.

③ Focus shift
Contrasting Arjun with the crowd in his momentary stillness. Writer withholds why Arjun is 'consumed by hesitation', to keep the reader guessing.

⑤ Hint
Indicating the character's anxiety.

⑥ Focus shift
New paragraph marks focus shift. The discourse marker ('Finally') signals a shift in focus.

Extract 1: *Transmission* by Hari Kunzru

This extract is from a novel and is about a man trying to make a success in his career as a computer programmer.

Around him Connaught Place seethed with life. ① Office workers, foreign backpackers, messengers and lunching ladies all elbowed past the beggars, dodging traffic and running in and out of Palika Bazaar like
5 contestants in a game. ② For a moment Arjun Mehta, consumed by hesitation, was the only stationary figure in the crowd. He was visible from a distance, a skinny flagpole of a boy, hunching himself up to lose a few conspicuous inches before making his entrance. ③
10 The face fluttering on top wore an expression of mild confusion, partly obscured by metal-framed glasses whose lenses were blurred with fingerprints. Attempting to assert its authority over his top lip was a downy moustache. ④ As he fiddled with his collar, it twitched
15 nervously, a small mammal startled in a clearing. ⑤
Finally, ⑥ feeling himself as small as he would ever get, he clutched his folder of diplomas to his chest, stated his business to the chowkidar [watchman], and was waved up the steps into the air-conditioned cool of the
20 office lobby. ⑦

② Description of setting
Emphasis on the confusing, frenzied activity.

④ Zoom in
Focus on Arjun's face as a way of conveying character.

⑦ Focus shift
Arjun clutching folder, announcing himself, and his being 'waved up', prepare for a scene change. His 'diplomas' hint that he is going for a job.

In the extract below, the writer organises the narrative structure to build up tension and suspense, vividly conveying the sense of danger and desperation felt by the protagonist.

Extract 2: 'The Waste Land' by Alan Paton

In this short story, a man gets off a bus at night with his week's wages.

① Opening
Launches into the action ('*in media res*') but provides key information: a lone man at night is in danger from some young men.

The moment that the bus moved on he knew he was in danger, for by the lights of it he saw the figures of the young men waiting under the tree. ① That was the thing feared by all, to be waited for by young men. It was a thing he had talked about, now he was to see it for himself. ②

② Foreshadowing
He is about to experience his fear becoming reality.

③ Raises tension
He is now in a 'sea' of danger, with no help at hand.

It was too late to run after the bus; it went down the dark street like an island of safety in a sea of perils. ③ Though he had known of his danger only for a second, his mouth was already dry, his heart was pounding in his breast, ④ something within him was crying out in protest against the coming event. ⑤

④ Tension
His physical response raises tension even more.

⑤ Foreshadowing
Foreshadows (anticipates) the probable attack and his possible death.

[*He is chased through a dark wasteland. He knocks one man down with his stick.*]

Then he turned and began to run again, but ran first into the side of an old lorry, which sent him reeling. He lay there for a moment expecting the blow that would end him, but even then his wits came back to him, and he turned over twice and was under the lorry. ⑥ His very entrails seemed to be coming into his mouth, and his lips could taste sweat and blood. His heart was like a wild thing in his breast, and seemed to lift his whole body each time that it beat. ⑦ He tried to calm it down, thinking it might be heard, and tried to control the noise of his gasping breath, but he could not do either of these things. ⑧

⑥ Tension
Tension pauses as he finds a hiding place.

⑦ Tension
Extreme tension in his intense physical fear response. Beginning of climax.

⑧ Suspense
He is doomed if they hear him.

⑨ Focus shift
New paragraph signals focus shift and creates sense of drama for the moment of greatest suspense: will the young men look under the lorry?

Then suddenly against the dark sky he saw two of the young men. ⑨

TIP
In the exam, there will be an introduction at the top of the extract, which will give you a greater understanding of the extract and enable you to write about it with more insight.

Knowledge — CONCEPT

7 Narrative structure

How can I write about narrative structure?

When writing about the structure of a story, think carefully about what aspects of the narrative you are going to focus on and also how the writer takes the reader from one focus point to the next.

For example, if writing about the structure of Extract 1 (on page 50), you might start like this:

> **TIP**
> For Paper 1 Question 3, you will have to write about both structure and language, not just one or the other. You will also need to note the exact focus of the question.

① Introduces extract, with a link to place and character.

③ Notices how the pronoun shifts the focus.

⑤ Technical term correctly used, with note of effect ('intrigues').

> The text begins with a sentence that sets the scene, and introduces a place and a main character. ① It then shifts to lots of people who make up the 'seething' mass, and what they are doing: elbowing past beggars, 'dodging traffic', 'running in and out' of the bazaar. By describing the place as busy, 'seething', and zooming out to show multiple people 'around him', it highlights that the main character is feeling out of place. ② The focus then shifts back to the 'him' in the first line, as if zooming in. ③ His being a 'stationary figure', reinforces the idea of him standing out, anxious and not knowing where he is or what to do. ④ The author intrigues the reader by withholding information ⑤ about why Arjun is 'consumed by hesitation' and what 'entrance' he is about to make. The wording foreshadows the fact that he is about to do something important. ⑥

② Neatly leads on from the previous sentence to explain the focus shift.

④ Awareness of interplay between character and setting.

⑥ Comments on how wording relates to structure.

Structurally, Extract 2 (on page 51) is all about tension and suspense building to a climax. You could analyse the **opening** like this:

① Identifies the function and impact of the opening.

> The author engages the reader's interest immediately by launching straight into the action with the story's problem — a lone man getting off a bus at night to find menacing young men waiting for him. ① The author heightens the reader's anticipation by ensuring the reader is

7 Narrative structure

> with the main character as he gets off the bus, seeing the young men waiting in the distance at the same time. Therefore, the reader will empathise more with his situation. The writer also uses foreshadowing: 'now he was about to see it for himself'. This reveals that the story will be about whether the man survives. ❷ The reader sees, as the man does, the lights of the bus disappearing into the darkness, moving away from him and leaving him alone. The structural choice to position the reader with the character creates a more vivid or intense experience of the emotions of the character. ❸ The man's rapid physical fear reaction reinforces this tension. ❹ The author almost makes the man's fate seem inevitable in the foreshadowing of his 'protest against the coming event'. This makes the reader even more anxious for him, ❺ as the 'event' will be his being attacked, perhaps killed.

❷ Comments on the effect of the reader's position, time, and foreshadowing, with evidence.

❸ Explains the importance of the reader position and bus in raising tension and suspense.

❹ Comments on another means by which tension is increased.

❺ Explains what is foreshadowed.

A further paragraph could analyse how the author builds to a climax:

❶ Identifies structural development: the character's fear reaching its peak.

❸ Gives an opinion on how a key detail creates a sense of crisis.

❹ Identifies a structural climax.

> The passage develops towards a frightening climax with the man hiding under the lorry. ❶ The physicality of his fear is intense, with his guts seeming to fill his mouth, the taste of his own 'sweat and blood', and his hammering heart. This shift in focus to zoom in on his body makes the emotion much more believable to the reader. ❷ The sense of tension and crisis is perhaps strongest ❸ when he is unable to calm his heart or breathing and fears that his pursuers will hear. The suspense, however, reaches a peak with him seeing 'two of the young men'. ❹ The new paragraph, consisting of a single sentence, underlines what a moment of crisis this is. ❺

❷ Well-chosen evidence: reference and direct quotation.

❺ Explains how two structural features contribute to this.

TIP

When answering Paper 1 Question 3, remember to analyse both structure and language in your response to gain high marks.

7 Knowledge

Knowledge

CONCEPT

7 Narrative structure

How can I create narrative structure in my own writing?

To use narrative structure effectively, you need to plan your writing carefully. Consider the whole story or description that you intend to write, even if you're not sure of the details. Focus on the progression – how you will take the reader on a journey, start to finish.

> **QUESTION CONNECTION**
>
> In Paper 1 Question 5 or 6, you will be asked to write a narrative or a description. Whichever form you write, plan the structure before you start.

Planning a story

Consider:

- How will you begin? For example, you could begin in mid-flow, like Extract 2 in this unit. You could also begin with dialogue or a rhetorical question.
- Plan how you will move the story on stage by stage, through conflict to resolution. Begin each stage with a new paragraph.
- Decide where you will place the reader in relation to the action, and whether you will write in first, second, or third person.
- How will you include shifts in time or focus? Consider how you could use flashbacks or foreshadowing.
- How will you create tension or conflict? Without at least one of these, your story will not engage the reader. For example, an argument might trigger strong emotion or dramatic action.
- Think about how to *withhold* and *reveal* key information. Don't spill it all out at once.
- How will you end your writing? You might use a cliffhanger or reach a resolution.

Planning a description

Consider:

- How will you draw the reader in from the start? Perhaps with a surprising statement or a moment of intense emotion or drama.
- What will be the highlights of your description?
- How will you organise your description into sections that lead on from each other? For example, you could focus on a detail and then describe a wider perspective. Each section should begin with a new paragraph.
- Consider how you will set out different aspects of setting. Will you shift through place (location or view); or through time, describing the place at one point and then again later?
- Think carefully about how to use topic sentences and discourse markers to guide your reader through and across paragraphs.
- How will you bring your description to a satisfying conclusion?

> **TIP**
>
> As a writer, you can control the amount of information you give your reader. Sometimes, what you *don't* reveal or only reveal bit by bit, can help to create tension and suspense.

Key terms — Make sure you can write a definition for each of these key terms.

chronological   cliffhanger   climax   crisis   discourse marker
flashback   focus   foreshadowing   inciting incident
opening   suspense   tension

Retrieval **CONCEPT** 7

Use the following questions to check your understanding of the knowledge covered in this section. Then cover the answers column with a piece of paper and write down as many as you can. Check and repeat.

Questions / Answers

#	Question	Answer
1	Narrative structure is the way that a writer organises and presents a story to a reader. True or false?	True
2	Narrative structure can only be found in fiction texts. True or false?	False
3	What is meant by 'focus' in narrative structure?	What the writer is concentrating on at any particular time.
4	What structural devices can be used to signal a change of focus?	A new paragraph; discourse markers.
5	What is foreshadowing and what effect does it create for the reader?	Foreshadowing is a narrative device that suggests what is going to happen later on in the story. It helps the reader anticipate how the story might unfold.
6	What is a circular narrative?	A story that ends in the same or similar place to where it began.
7	What narrative devices might a writer use to create tension and suspense?	Withholding information or giving small clues to keep the reader guessing and anticipating what might happen next.
8	What term describes the peak of excitement in a narrative?	The climax
9	If a story starts *in media res*, what does this mean?	The story starts in the middle of the action. It then goes on to reveal what happened before and after this event.
10	What is a flashback, and why might a writer use it?	A shift back in time in a story. A writer might use this to explain why a character acts as they do, or why a situation has arisen.

Previous questions

Now go back and use these questions to check your knowledge of previous topics.

#	Question	Answer
1	What is a clause?	A sentence or part of a sentence that includes a subject (noun, noun phrase, or pronoun) and a verb.
2	What is a statement?	A sentence that states a fact, such as: *Birds have wings*.

Knowledge **CONCEPT**

8 Structuring an argument

What is an argument?

A written argument expresses an **opinion** and tries to persuade the reader to agree with it. It provides factual evidence and explains what, in the writer's view, this evidence proves.

An argument should:

- pick a point of view to argue, for example: the school day should be shorter
- argue consistently for it, giving reasons, for example: students learn more effectively in the morning
- address the opposite point of view to build your argument
- give your personal opinion, ensuring it contributes to a coherent argument.

An argument should be logical, but to be effective it also needs to be persuasive. This is why rhetorical language is used to express an argument.

> **QUESTION CONNECTION**
> Look at page 200 for the steps to follow to answer Paper 2 Question 8 or 9, which ask you to write a text to argue or persuade.

> **LINK**
> You can read more about rhetorical language on pages 18-25.

Fact and opinion

In order to write about authors' arguments, or write one yourself, you need to be clear about the difference between facts and opinions.

Fact	Opinion
What is it?	
A **fact** is something that can be proved to be true.	An opinion is someone's viewpoint or judgement.
How is it used?	
Facts can be used to: – build strong evidence to support your point – build an authoritative tone in your argument.	Opinions can be used to: – persuade the reader or listener, as they appeal to emotions.
What should I remember?	
Be accurate when using facts, to make them believable.	As opinions are often someone's viewpoint or judgement, use them to argue your point by suggesting that many others already agree with you.

Both facts and opinions are hugely valuable when writing about a topic and are best used in combination. By using both, you can build a cohesive argument.

> The Earth is spherical. (Fact)
> Students should be given more homework. (Opinion)
> Asia is the largest continent in the world. (Fact)
> Lions deserve to be saved more than rhinos. (Opinion)

Topic sentences

A **topic sentence** is a sentence, usually at the start of a paragraph, that prepares the reader for what is coming next – usually for the rest of the paragraph.

An effective written argument leads the reader carefully through a series of connected ideas. A topic sentence in effect tells the reader, 'Now we're going on to this next big idea, which will be developed in this paragraph.'

> There are many reasons why it is good to recycle clothes. The first reason is …

Discourse markers

Discourse markers are words or phrases that link ideas in a text. They show the relationship between one idea and the next and are especially important when writing an argumentative or persuasive text. They can be used to:

- point out the direction in which the text is heading
- refer back to ideas that have come earlier.

Discourse markers are usually used at the start of the sentence, but can be used mid-sentence.

Some discourse markers are:

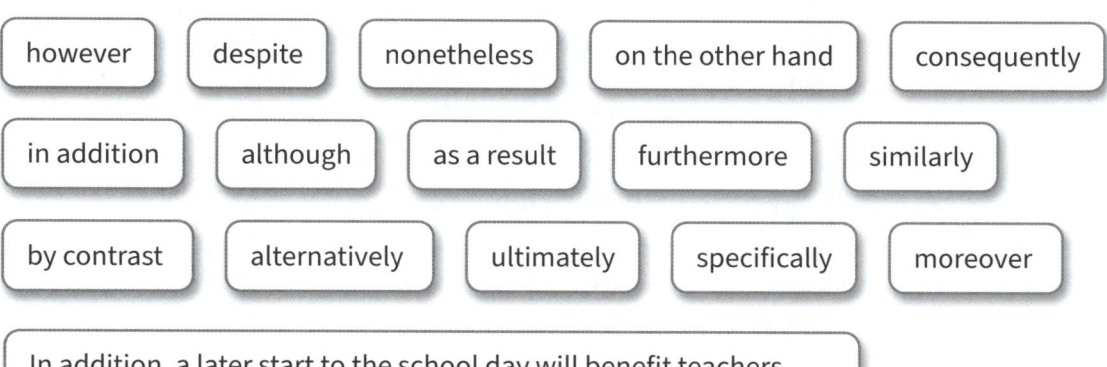

however	despite	nonetheless	on the other hand	consequently
in addition	although	as a result	furthermore	similarly
by contrast	alternatively	ultimately	specifically	moreover

> In addition, a later start to the school day will benefit teachers who need to plan the next school day.
>
> Similarly, students will be able to prepare for the next day as well.

8 Knowledge

Knowledge — CONCEPT

8 Structuring an argument

What are the devices used in a written argument?

When you read a written argument, for example in a persuasive newspaper editorial or magazine article, you will recognise some typical structural features.

- An introduction stating what the issue is in a way that readers can relate to and which will capture their interest (approximately one paragraph).
- A development explaining more about the problem or issue, often providing evidence, perhaps in the form of examples, case studies, facts or opinions (approximately two or three paragraphs).
- A **counter-argument** anticipating what those opposing the writer's views might say, and why the writer thinks they are wrong (approximately one paragraph).
- A conclusion bringing the strands of the argument together, and perhaps suggesting what might be done – often using the word 'should' (approximately one paragraph).

Look at how these features appear in the following newspaper article.

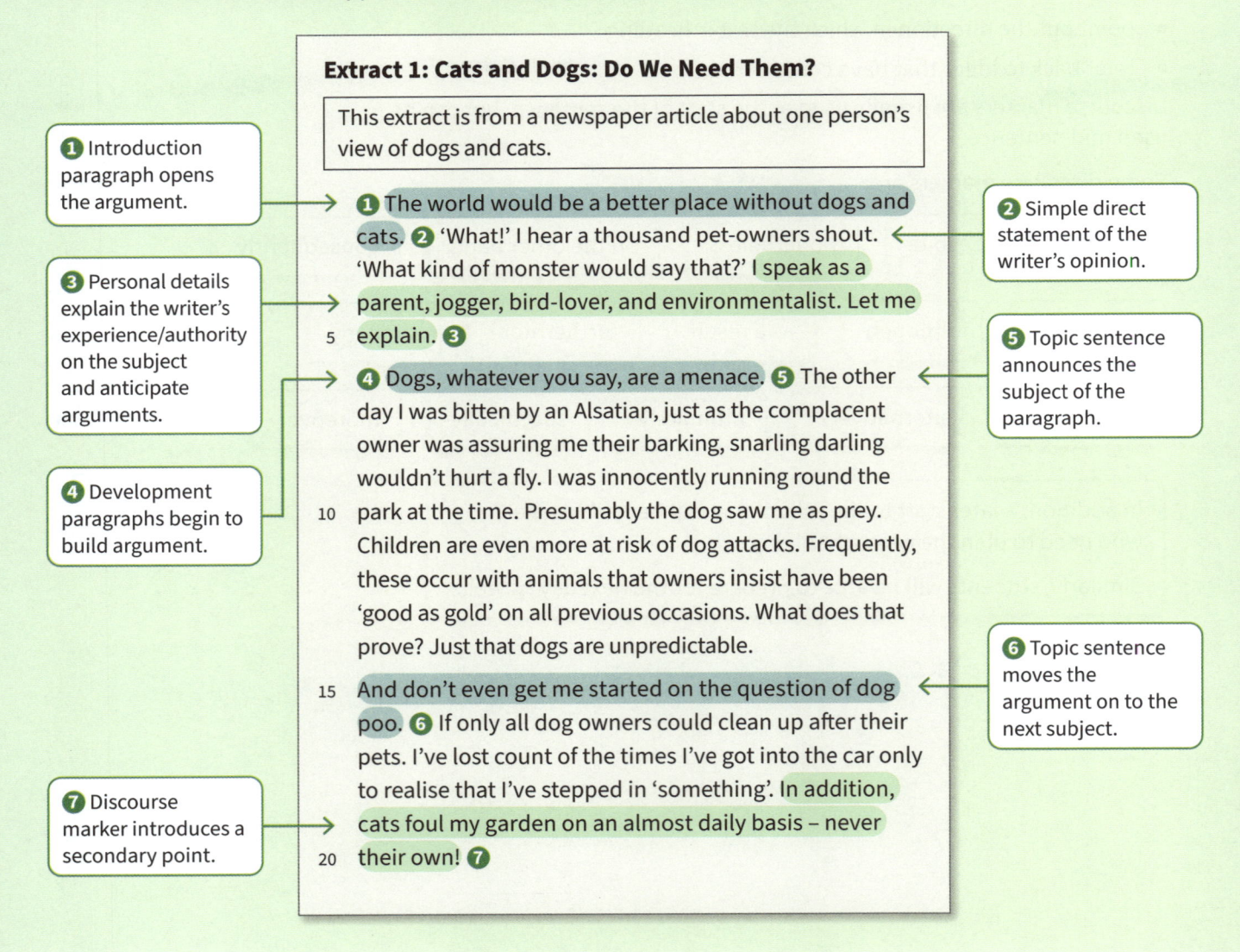

Extract 1: Cats and Dogs: Do We Need Them?

This extract is from a newspaper article about one person's view of dogs and cats.

❶ The world would be a better place without dogs and cats. ❷ 'What!' I hear a thousand pet-owners shout. 'What kind of monster would say that?' I speak as a parent, jogger, bird-lover, and environmentalist. Let me
5 explain. ❸

❹ Dogs, whatever you say, are a menace. ❺ The other day I was bitten by an Alsatian, just as the complacent owner was assuring me their barking, snarling darling wouldn't hurt a fly. I was innocently running round the
10 park at the time. Presumably the dog saw me as prey. Children are even more at risk of dog attacks. Frequently, these occur with animals that owners insist have been 'good as gold' on all previous occasions. What does that prove? Just that dogs are unpredictable.

15 And don't even get me started on the question of dog poo. ❻ If only all dog owners could clean up after their pets. I've lost count of the times I've got into the car only to realise that I've stepped in 'something'. In addition, cats foul my garden on an almost daily basis – never
20 their own! ❼

❶ Introduction paragraph opens the argument.

❸ Personal details explain the writer's experience/authority on the subject and anticipate arguments.

❹ Development paragraphs begin to build argument.

❼ Discourse marker introduces a secondary point.

❷ Simple direct statement of the writer's opinion.

❺ Topic sentence announces the subject of the paragraph.

❻ Topic sentence moves the argument on to the next subject.

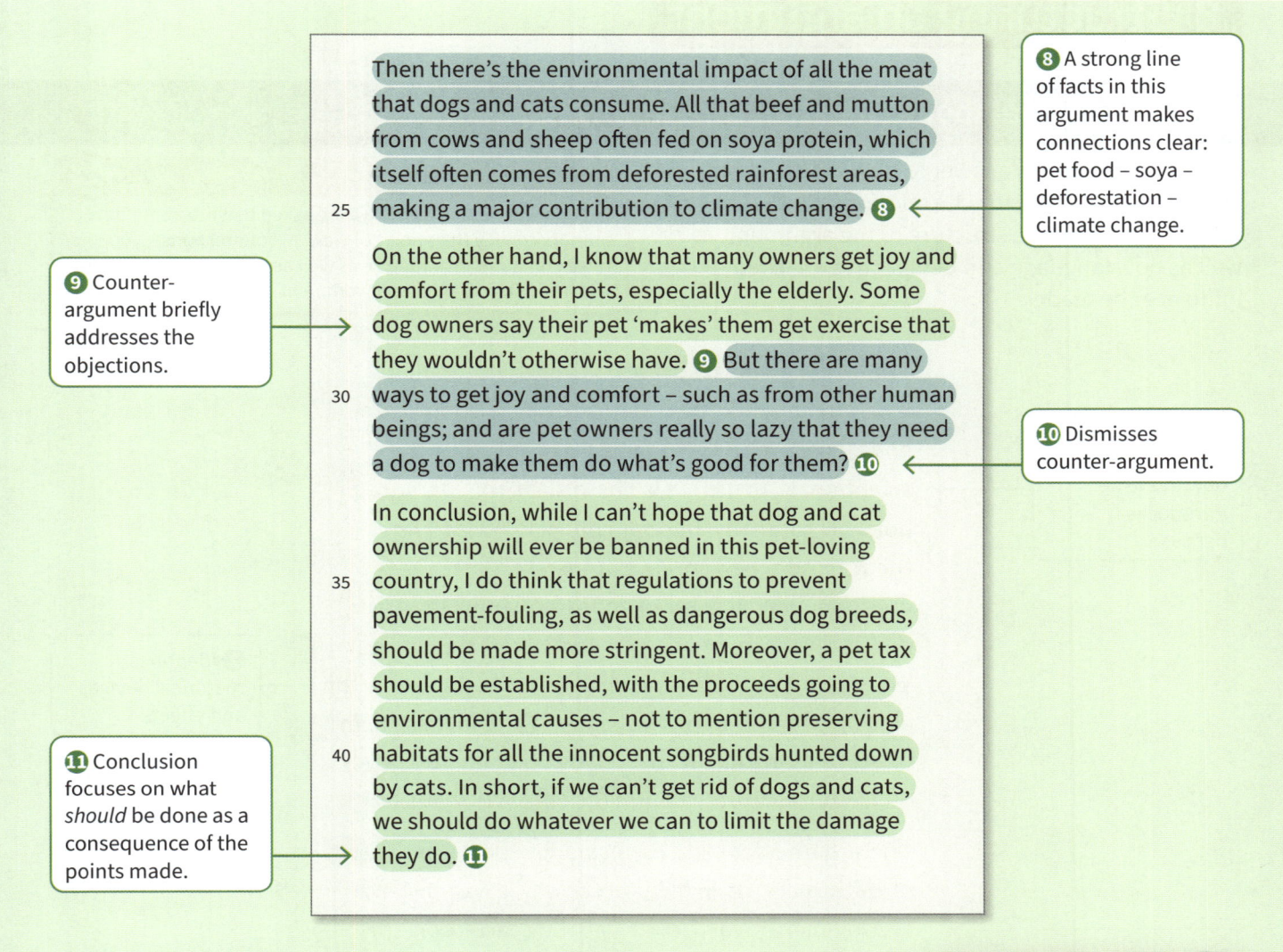

Then there's the environmental impact of all the meat that dogs and cats consume. All that beef and mutton from cows and sheep often fed on soya protein, which itself often comes from deforested rainforest areas,
25 making a major contribution to climate change. ⑧

⑧ A strong line of facts in this argument makes connections clear: pet food – soya – deforestation – climate change.

On the other hand, I know that many owners get joy and comfort from their pets, especially the elderly. Some dog owners say their pet 'makes' them get exercise that they wouldn't otherwise have. ⑨ But there are many
30 ways to get joy and comfort – such as from other human beings; and are pet owners really so lazy that they need a dog to make them do what's good for them? ⑩

⑨ Counter-argument briefly addresses the objections.

⑩ Dismisses counter-argument.

In conclusion, while I can't hope that dog and cat ownership will ever be banned in this pet-loving
35 country, I do think that regulations to prevent pavement-fouling, as well as dangerous dog breeds, should be made more stringent. Moreover, a pet tax should be established, with the proceeds going to environmental causes – not to mention preserving
40 habitats for all the innocent songbirds hunted down by cats. In short, if we can't get rid of dogs and cats, we should do whatever we can to limit the damage they do. ⑪

⑪ Conclusion focuses on what *should* be done as a consequence of the points made.

This argument states its case at the outset. It then works its way paragraph by paragraph through the objections to dogs and cats: danger, faeces, and climate change. Then it considers a counter-argument and dismisses it, before concluding with recommendations for action.

TIP

If you're unsure of a **statistic** in your own writing, you could make a similar impact using a phrase such as 'The vast majority of …' or 'In most cases …'.

8 Knowledge

Knowledge

CONCEPT

8 Structuring an argument

How can I write about the structure of an argument?

Here is one student's answer to how the point of view is conveyed in Extract 1 on pages 58–59. They draw attention to the structure of the argument, as well as how language and perspective are used to influence the reader.

> **QUESTION CONNECTION**
>
> In Paper 2 Question 3, you will be asked to write about how authors convey their point of view. In your response, you must comment on structure as well as language. Your marks will be limited if you do not comment on both.

❶ Identifies how the writer introduces her case.

❷ Identifies rhetorical devices and effects.

❸ Identifies the argument structure.

❹ Identifies the counter-argument and its dismissal.

❺ Identifies how the writer concludes, including her own feelings.

> The writer begins with a bold opening opinion: 'The world would be a better place without cats and dogs', which will succeed in capturing the attention of readers. ❶ The rest of this paragraph goes on to justify the opinion, acknowledging the opposite view in an exaggerated rhetorical question: 'What kind of monster would say that?' and listing four positive credentials of the writer: 'parent, jogger, bird-lover, environmentalist' with the aim of 'winning over' the reader. ❷ It invites them to see the argument in: 'Let me explain' to convey an established understanding between them both.
>
> The argument builds by including three paragraphs of both facts, as in 'The other day I was bitten', and opinions: 'don't even get me started on the question of dog poo'. ❸ A counter-argument is challenged briefly, beginning with a discourse marker: 'On the other hand, I know that many owners get joy' and dismissed. ❹ A summarising conclusion paragraph and statement ('In short, if we can't get rid of dogs and cats') emphasises the writer's personal opinion in a bold way to the reader, creating a cohesive argument, as this was the way the argument began. ❺

Notice how this student finds a variety of ways to sum up how the writer's argument progresses, identifying what each stage does. Look for the following sentence starters:

- The writer begins …
- The rest of this paragraph …
- The argument builds …
- A summarising conclusion …

> **TIP**
>
> When commenting on a writer's argument, remember to explain the effects of how it is presented, its structure, and how it leads the reader through a series of linked ideas in order to persuade them to adopt a viewpoint.

How can I structure an argument in my own writing?

Paper 2 Questions 8 and 9 will ask you to write your own text for a particular purpose. This may require you to express an opinion. It is essential to plan your response.

Explore the argument

First consider the question, and the text form, audience, and purpose of the response it asks you for.

For example, the question could be:

> 'Job satisfaction is much more important than how much you earn.'
>
> Write an article for a magazine in which you argue your point of view on this statement.
>
> You could write about:
> - what *gives* job satisfaction
> - how much do you really need to earn
> - why one is more important than the other
>
> as well as any other ideas you might have.

To plan an answer to this, first think about the question, using the prompts in the bullet points unless you wish to focus on your own ideas.

You could see what ideas you can come up with for two of the bullet points using spider diagrams like the ones below.

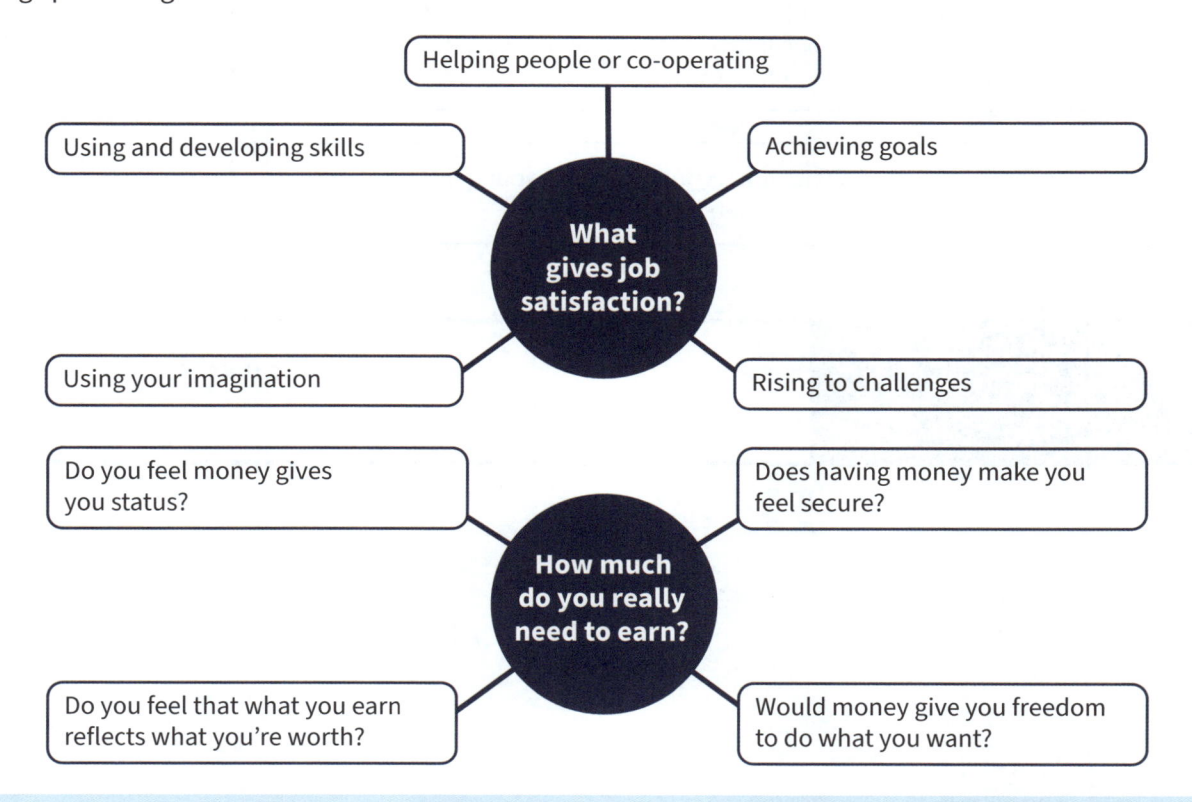

What gives job satisfaction?
- Helping people or co-operating
- Using and developing skills
- Achieving goals
- Using your imagination
- Rising to challenges

How much do you really need to earn?
- Do you feel money gives you status?
- Does having money make you feel secure?
- Do you feel that what you earn reflects what you're worth?
- Would money give you freedom to do what you want?

8 Knowledge

Knowledge — CONCEPT

8 Structuring an argument

Build a cohesive argument

Focus on one main point of view to build a cohesive argument. You will address the opposite view in your one counter-argument paragraph, but the task requires you to argue a particular opinion.

First, make sure you know the purpose of the text and its audience. Think about how to argue your point successfully and have the most impact, such as through rhetorical language and considering which tone and perspective to use. Refer to pages 18–41 for more details about these.

For the question on page 61, you could then structure your argument like this:

1. Introduction: how our society values wealth and celebrity and material possessions. Then asking if there is more to life.

2. Exploring some of the things you have listed that seem most important to you, with some examples from the world of work, e.g. a nurse helping others, or an artist using their imagination.

3. Counter-argument: exploring how people might argue in favour of money being important, e.g. gaining respect or admiration, freedom to travel, money to buy possessions. You could begin with a discourse marker, such as 'On the other hand …'.

4. Your reasons for preferring job satisfaction; for example, that it lasts long after material possessions have become boring, or that money is never satisfying on its own.

5. Conclusion: how you would advise others, for example a young person choosing a career, and why.

> **TIP**
> Check your plan to make sure that it is *cohesive* – that one idea leads on to the next and it makes sense as a whole.

Key terms: Make sure you can write a definition for each of these key terms.

counter-argument   discourse marker   fact
opinion   statistic   topic sentence

Retrieval **CONCEPT** 8

Use the following questions to check your understanding of the knowledge covered in this section. Then cover the answers column with a piece of paper and write down as many as you can. Check and repeat.

Questions | Answers

#	Question	Answer
1	A topic sentence always comes at the end of a paragraph. True or false?	False. It normally comes at the start.
2	Is this a fact or an opinion? *It's always worthwhile to take a holiday abroad.*	An opinion. This is because it cannot be proven or backed up with evidence.
3	Planning a response takes up valuable time that would be better spent on writing that response. True or false?	False. It is important to plan to organise your ideas and build a cohesive argument.
4	What is a *cohesive* argument? Choose from: • One that you stick to. • One that is passionately argued. • One that makes sense as a whole.	One that makes sense as a whole
5	What is a 'counter-argument'? Choose from: • An opposing viewpoint to your own. • An argument that disproves your own. • An especially persuasive argument.	An opposing viewpoint to your own
6	What is the effect of this discourse marker? 'On the other hand …'?	It warns the reader that you are about to explore a view that differs from the one you have just been writing about.
7	Discourse markers can only be used at the start of a sentence. True or false?	False. You could, for example, write: 'Cats, *on the other hand*, don't need to be taken for walks.'
8	What discourse marker could you use to indicate that you are going to introduce another similar point?	Possible answers include: 'In addition'; 'Additionally'; or 'Moreover'.
9	What would the discourse marker 'Consequently' indicate?	That you were about to write about something that was a result of the last thing you mentioned.

Previous questions

Now go back and use these questions to check your knowledge of previous topics.

Questions | Answers

#	Question	Answer
1	What is a circular narrative?	A story that ends in the same or similar place to where it began.
2	If a story starts *in media res*, what does this mean?	The story starts in the middle of the action. It then goes on to reveal what happened before and after this event.

8 Retrieval

Knowledge EXAM

Paper 1: Overview

Questions

In the exam, the questions will be printed in the answer booklet. The source texts will be in a separate document.

The following are examples of the question types. They relate to the source text on pages 214–215, *Far from the Madding Crowd* by Thomas Hardy. The exam will include the same question types in the same order each year. The source texts will be different.

Q1 | Identify information   AO1

This question tests AO1 – identifying explicit and implicit information and ideas.

> **Q1** From lines 1 to 5, identify a word or phrase which shows that there has already been lightning. **[1 mark]**

This question tests your ability to:
- focus on the section of text specified in the question
- select one piece of relevant information.

Q2 | Identify information   AO1

This question tests AO1 – identifying explicit and implicit information and ideas.

> **Q2** Read this extract.
>
> Give **two** things that the reader learns about Bathsheba.
>
> You may use your own words or quotations from the text. **[2 marks]**

This question tests your ability to:
- focus on the section of text printed with the question
- identify and underline the key words in the question
- identify two pieces of information about the character or subject indicated.

Q3 | Analyse how the writer uses language and structure   AO2

This question tests the second part of AO2 – analysing how writers use language and structure to achieve effects and influence readers, using relevant subject terminology to support their views.

> **Q3** Read this extract.
>
> How does the writer use language and structure to describe the effects of the lightning on Gabriel and Bathsheba?
>
> Support your views with reference to the text. **[6 marks]**

This question tests your ability to:
- identify relevant language features
- identify relevant structural features
- describe their effect in the text
- explain their impact on the reader
- use subject terminology and quotations to support your ideas.

Q4 | Evaluate critically

AO4

This question tests AO4 – Evaluating texts critically and using appropriate textual references.

Q4 In this extract, there is an attempt to create a growing sense of tension.

Evaluate how successfully this is achieved.

Support your views with detailed reference to the text.

[15 marks]

This question tests your ability to:
- consider the whole extract
- make references to specific parts of the text that support your judgements
- use evaluative language to show you are making a judgement about the writer's effectiveness
- consider the setting, ideas, themes, and events to make your judgement.

Q5 and Q6 | Imaginative writing

AO5 **AO6**

This question tests AO5 – communicating clearly, effectively, and imaginatively; selecting and adapting tone, style, and register for different forms, purposes, and audiences; and organising information and ideas, using structural and grammatical features to support coherence and cohesion of texts.

It also tests AO6 – using a range of vocabulary and sentence structures for clarity, purpose, and effect, with accurate spelling and punctuation.

Questions 5 and 6 are imaginative writing tasks. You must choose to respond to one of them. One, usually Question 5, will be a text prompt; the other will be based on two images provided. Both tasks will be loosely linked to themes in the text in Section A: Reading.

Q5 Write about a time when you, or someone you know, took a risk. Your response could be real or imagined.

Or

Q6 Look at the images provided. Write about a time when you, or someone you know, experienced a storm.

[40 marks]

Includes 16 marks for the range of vocabulary and sentence structures for clarity, purpose and effect, with accurate use of spelling and punctuation.

This question tests your ability to:
- respond in the appropriate form of either a narrative (story) or a description
- use an appropriate tone and style to suit your chosen content
- organise your writing, choosing vocabulary carefully and varying sentence structures for effect.

Knowledge 65

Knowledge EXAM

Paper 1: Reading the source / Question 1

Reading the source

In Paper 1, Section A: Reading, there will be four questions to answer about a source text. Before answering any questions, you must remember to read the source text in full.

Aim to spend the first five minutes of the exam carefully reading and annotating the text. It will be:

- approximately 650 words
- a fiction text from the 19th-century.

There will be a short introduction to the source. Be sure to read this, as it will give you some important information, such as the setting, characters, or what is happening and where.

Some source texts will include a glossary explaining one or two unusual words. These glossed words will be starred, so double check their meaning when you come across them during your reading.

In the Paper 1 section of this book, Sources 1–4 will be used for learning and practice. These are on pages 214–221.

Question 1: Overview

Focus	Marks	Time	AO
Explicit information	1 mark	2 minutes	AO1

You should have already spent five minutes at the start of the exam reading the whole source for Paper 1. Question 1 is based on a small part of the text. It tests your ability to read specific lines and *identify a word or phrase* which shows something.

Question 1 will always follow the same format:

> **Q1** From lines x to x, identify a word or phrase…
>
> [1 mark]

You must select and copy out one piece of relevant information from the given lines.

LINK
See page 3 for the difference between explicit and implicit information.

TIP
Make sure you read the question carefully. At the start of an exam, it is easy to rush and miss the point of the task.

P1/Q1

Question 1: Strategy

Follow the steps below to respond to a Question 1 task.

> **Step 1**: Re-read the question and make sure you know what the key focus is. It is usually found at the end of the question, detailing exactly what you need to look for.

> **Step 2**: Underline or put brackets round the specified lines, and re-read them. Highlight possible words or phrases which address the key focus.

> **Step 3**: Select the word or phrase that shows what is specified in the question most clearly.

Question 1: Example

Below is a sample Question 1 task. In the exam, the relevant lines will not be printed out in the question, so you will need to find them in the source text. They will normally be near the beginning. You may find it helpful to mark the relevant lines to make sure you keep looking at the correct section of text.

> From **lines x–x**, identify a **word or phrase** which shows **that there has already been lightning.** [1 mark]

This question needs you to quote a word or phrase – it requires no explanation.

You will be given specific lines to use to answer this question (usually from the start of the text). Stick to those lines. Anything you say from elsewhere in the text will gain no marks.

The question will ask you to quote a word or phrase that shows *one* specific thing. You must focus your answer on that thing and nothing else.

Source 1: *Far from the Madding Crowd* **by Thomas Hardy**

Before Oak had laid his hands upon his tools again out leapt the fifth flash, with the spring of a serpent and the shout of a fiend. It was green as an emerald, and the reverberation was stunning.

LINK

This question refers to an extract from Source 1: *Far from the Madding Crowd*. The full text is on pages 214–215.

Knowledge 67

Knowledge EXAM

Paper 1: Reading the source / Question 1

Question 1: Sample answers

Now read the following sample answers to the Question 1 example on page 67, alongside the examiner's comments.

Sample answer 1

This answer scores 0 marks.

> laid his hands upon his tools again ✗

This answer is incorrect. The student may have thought that 'again' suggested something that had already happened before, but there is no mention of the lightning.

Sample answer 2

This answer scores the 1 mark available.

> the fifth flash ✓

This answer is correct because the words 'fifth flash' make it clear that there have been previous flashes (of lightning).

The examiner's mark scheme may allow more than one word or phrase to earn the mark. Here, the word 'fifth' on its own might do so, whereas 'flash' would not. Avoid copying a longer phrase that includes irrelevant words.

> **REMEMBER**
> - Keep your answer short. Do not write a full sentence.
> - Use the exact words from the source text: do not put them into your own words.
> - Do not copy out whole sentences or long chunks of text.
> - Do not explain your answer.

Retrieval — EXAM — P1/Q1

Paper 1: Question 1

Use the following questions to check your understanding of the knowledge covered in this section. Then cover the answers column with a piece of paper and write down as many as you can. Check and repeat.

Questions / Answers

#	Questions	Answers
1	What is the focus of Question 1?	Identifying a word or phrase that shows something.
2	How long should you spend on Question 1?	2 minutes
3	How many marks are available for Question 1?	1 mark
4	You need to explain your answer. True or false?	False
5	The lines in the question are just to help you. You can actually give information from anywhere in the source. True or false?	False. You must stick to the given lines.
6	You will not be expected to infer information (work out what the text hints at). True or false?	True
7	Summarise the three steps of the Question 1 strategy.	**Step 1:** identify the key focus of the question. **Step 2:** re-read the lines and highlight any possible answers. **Step 3:** select and copy your chosen word or phrase.

Previous questions

Now go back and use these questions to check your knowledge of previous topics.

Questions / Answers

#	Questions	Answers
1	What kind of source text will you have to comment on in Paper 1?	19th-century prose fiction.
2	Name at least four different fiction genres.	Possible answers include: science fiction; fantasy; romance; historical fiction; thriller; mystery; horror.
3	What is explicit information?	Information that is clearly stated, not just hinted at.

Retrieval

Practice EXAM

Exam-style questions

Answer the exam-style questions on pages 70–71. In the exam, the relevant lines in the extract for Question 1 will not be reprinted in the question paper so you will need to find them in the source text. They have been included here for easy reference.

REMEMBER

In the exam, you will need to read the *whole* source text first, before you start looking at the questions and any specific extracts.

1.1

Q1 From lines 1–4, identify a word or phrase which shows that Catherine (the mistress) wants to annoy her husband. **[1 mark]**

Source 2: *Wuthering Heights* by Emily Brontë

'Have you been listening at the door, Edgar?' asked the mistress, in a tone particularly calculated to provoke her husband, implying both carelessness and contempt of his irritation. Heathcliff, who had raised his eyes at the former speech, gave a sneering laugh at the latter…

LINK

This question refers to an extract from Source 2: *Wuthering Heights* by Emily Brontë. The full text is on pages 216–217.

EXAM TIP

In your answer, you should:
- check the question focus (here, it is that Catherine wants to *annoy her husband*)
- select your answers from the correct part of the source text
- find a word or phrase which shows the focus of the question.

1.2

Q1 From lines 1–4, identify a word or phrase which shows that Frankenstein's creation does not consider himself to look attractive. **[1 mark]**

LINK

This question refers to an extract from Source 3: *Frankenstein* by Mary Shelley. The full text is on pages 218–219.

Source 3: *Frankenstein* by Mary Shelley

What I ask of you is reasonable and moderate; I demand a creature of another sex, but as hideous as myself; the gratification is small, but it is all that I can receive, and it shall content me. It is true, we shall be monsters, cut off from all the world; but on that account we shall be more attached to one
5 another. Our lives will not be happy, but they will be harmless and free from the misery I now feel.

1.3

Q1 From lines 3–6, identify a word or phrase which shows that Pip does not feel comfortable in Miss Havisham's house. **[1 mark]**

> **LINK**
> This question refers to an extract from Source 4: *Great Expectations* by Charles Dickens. The full text is on pages 220–221.

Source 4: *Great Expectations* by Charles Dickens

'Call Estella,' she repeated, flashing a look at me. 'You can do that. Call Estella. At the door.'

To stand in the dark in a mysterious passage of an unknown house, bawling Estella to a scornful young lady neither visible nor responsive, and feeling it
5 a dreadful liberty so to roar out her name, was almost as bad as playing to order. But she answered at last, and her light came along the dark passage like a star.

Knowledge   EXAM

Paper 1: Question 2

Question 2: Overview

Focus	Marks	Time	AO
Explicit and implicit information	2 marks	4 minutes	AO1

Question 2 tests your ability to find explicit and implicit information. It is slightly more challenging than Question 1 because it just gives you the subject and leaves you to decide what information is revealed about it. Question 2 will always follow the same format:

> **Q2** Give **two** things …
>
> You may use your own words or quotations from the text.   **[2 marks]**

You will only have to refer to a set number of lines for Question 2, not the whole source. The specific part of the source is reprinted in your question paper.

The 'two things' could, for example, be about the setting, the weather, or a character. Don't give information from outside of the short extract you are given.

LINK
The knowledge section on page 3 will remind you of the difference between implicit and explicit information. This will help you answer Question 2.

Question 2: Strategy

Follow the steps below to respond to a Question 2 task.

Step 1: Re-read the short extract. Underline the focus of the question.

Step 2: Search for explicit or implicit information on the focus of the question.

Step 3: Select the two things that most clearly address the question focus. For each one, write it as a statement in your own words or quote a short sentence or phrase from the given lines.

Step 4: Double check your response to make sure that:
- you have listed two *different* points (don't repeat the same thing)
- both your points answer the question (they are focused on the topic you have been asked to talk about)
- all your points are from within the given lines (you will not gain marks for information taken from elsewhere).

TIP
There is no need to explain how you infer the information you identify. The examiner will have a list of valid evidence.

P1/Q2

Question 2: Example

Read the sample Question 2 task and the annotations below. Before you complete Question 2, re-read the printed extract, which has been provided for you below the exam question, and underline any points that address the key focus.

> **Q2** Read this extract.
>
> Give **two** things that show the reader that Bathsheba is prepared to work hard.
>
> You may use your own words or quotations from the text. **[2 marks]**

This question asks you to find two pieces of information.

If the information is stated explicitly, you will be able to convey it simply by quoting a phrase from the text. If it is implicit, you will have to infer the meaning and put it in your own words. If you think you have found more than two relevant pieces of information, choose the two about which you feel most confident.

Focus on the given subject – in this case, Bathsheba's willingness to work hard. Search for explicit or implicit information. This might include: information about her appearance, abilities, or character.

Source 1: *Far from the Madding Crowd* by Thomas Hardy

20 'You can bring up some reed-sheaves to me, one by one, ma'am; if you are not afraid to come up the ladder in the dark,' said Gabriel. 'Every moment is precious now, and that would save a good deal of time. It is not very dark when the lightning has been gone a bit.'

'I'll do anything!' she said, resolutely. She instantly took a sheaf upon her
25 shoulder, clambered up close to his heels, placed it behind the rod, and descended for another.

LINK
This question refers to an extract from Source 1: *Far from the Madding Crowd* by Thomas Hardy. The full text is on pages 214–215.

REMEMBER
In this extract there are several things you could identify, but you need only name **two**.

Knowledge 73

Knowledge — EXAM

Paper 1: Question 2

Question 2: Sample answers

Now read the following sample answers to the Question 2 example on page 73, alongside the examiner's comments.

Sample answer 1
This answer scores no marks.

> ❶ She is afraid to come up the ladder but she does anyway. ✗
>
> ❷ She obeys Gabriel, saying 'I'll do anything!'. ✗

❶ The student has not read the extract carefully enough and has therefore said the opposite of what is actually true.

❷ The student has used a relevant phrase in the text, 'I'll do anything!' but misinterpreted it. The word 'resolutely' shows that she is determined to get the work done, rather than being merely obedient.

Sample answer 2
This answer scores both the marks available.

> ❶ She says, 'I'll do anything.' ✓
>
> ❷ She starts work 'instantly'. ✓

❶ The student has given a short, self-evident quotation.

❷ The student has made a correct statement quoting a relevant word – there is no need to paraphrase it.

Examiner's comments
This answer receives full marks.
Statements can be written in different ways and still earn a mark. For example, from this line: '"I'll do anything!" she said, resolutely,' any of these statements would get a mark:

- She is determined.
- She is prepared to do 'anything' to save the corn.
- She has great resolution.
- She is resolute about saving the corn.

REMEMBER
- Keep your answers short. Answers do not need to be in full sentences.
- You can use quotations from the source text, but make sure you only use the word or phrase you need.
- If you need to explain an inference, you can phrase answers in your own way.

Retrieval — EXAM — P1/Q2

Paper 1: Question 2

Use the following questions to check your understanding of the knowledge covered in this section. Then cover the answers column with a piece of paper and write down as many as you can. Check and repeat.

Questions	Answers
1. What is the focus of Question 2?	Identifying explicit and implicit information.
2. How long should you spend on Question 2?	4 minutes
3. How many marks are available for Question 2?	2 marks
4. You should always quote exact words from the source. True or false?	False. You can use the exact words from the text or your own words.
5. You need to explain your answer. True or false?	False
6. You may have to infer information (work out what the text hints at). True or false?	True
7. You might be asked for information on the weather. True or false?	True
8. Summarise the four steps of the Question 2 strategy.	**Step 1:** read the short extract and underline the question focus. **Step 2:** search for explicit or implicit information on the focus. **Step 3:** select the two clearest things for your answers. **Step 4:** double check your response.

Previous questions

Now go back and use these questions to check your knowledge of previous topics.

Questions	Answers
1. How is a metaphor different from a simile?	It speaks of a thing as if it is something else, without using 'like' or 'as'.
2. Explain how the sentence 'The train rocketed past' is more effective than 'The train rushed past like a rocket'.	The word 'rocketed' already conveys the idea of speed, so 'rushed' is unnecessary.
3. What does inferring mean?	Working out meaning that is only hinted at, rather than explicitly stated.

Practice **EXAM**

Exam-style questions

Answer the exam-style questions on pages 76–77. Remember that in the exam you will need to read the whole source text before you start looking at the questions and any specific extracts.

2.1

Q2 Read this extract.

Give **two** things that the reader learns about the speaker, Edgar.

You may use your own words or quotations from the text. **[2 marks]**

Source 2: *Wuthering Heights* by Emily Brontë

'I've been so far forbearing with you, sir,' he said quietly; 'not that I was ignorant of your miserable, degraded character, but I felt you were only partly responsible for that; and Catherine wishing to keep up your
10   acquaintance, I acquiesced – foolishly. Your presence is a moral poison that would contaminate the most virtuous…'

LINK

This question refers to an extract from Source 2: *Wuthering Heights* by Emily Brontë. Remember to first read the full text on pages 216–217.

EXAM TIP

In your answer, you should:
- check the question focus
- select answers which address this focus
- choose the two which most clearly address the question focus.

2.2

Q2 Read this extract.

Give **two** things that the reader learns about Frankenstein's response to the creature's request.

You may use your own words or quotations from the text. **[2 marks]**

Source 3: *Frankenstein* by Mary Shelley

I was moved. I shuddered when I thought of the possible consequences
10   of my consent, but I felt that there was some justice in his argument. His tale and the feelings he now expressed proved him to be a creature of fine sensations, and did I not as his maker owe him all the portion of happiness that it was in my power to bestow?

LINK

This question refers to an extract from Source 3: *Frankenstein* by Mary Shelley. Remember to first read the full text on pages 218–219.

2.3

Q2 Read this extract.

Give **two** things that the reader learns about the room in Miss Havisham's house.

You may use your own words or quotations from the text. **[2 marks]**

LINK

This question refers to an extract from Source 4: *Great Expectations* by Charles Dickens. Remember to first read the full text on pages 220–221.

Source 4: *Great Expectations* by Charles Dickens

It was then I began to understand that everything in the room had stopped, like the watch and the clock, a long time ago. I noticed that Miss Havisham
20 put down the jewel exactly on the spot from which she had taken it up. As Estella dealt the cards, I glanced at the dressing-table again, and saw that the shoe upon it, once white, now yellow, had never been worn.

Knowledge · EXAM

Paper 1: Question 3

Question 3: Overview

Focus: Language and structure
Marks: 6 marks
Time: 14 minutes
AO: AO2

Question 3 is based on a larger section of the text. It tests your ability to explore how the writer's *language and structure choices* affect the reader in this given section. Question 3 will always follow the same format:

> Read this extract.
>
> How does the writer use language and structure to …
>
> Support your views with reference to the text. **[6 marks]**

> **LINK**
> The Writing Knowledge on pages 18, 19, and 24 contains words and phrases to help you with analytical writing.

You will only have to refer to a set number of lines for Question 3, not the whole source. The specific part of the source you are focusing on is reprinted in your question paper.

It is important to note that you will need to comment on how the writer uses both language and structure, and how they use them to achieve a particular aim.

A precise aim will be identified, as in:

- to show the thoughts and feelings of X when …
- to show the thoughts and feelings of the narrator about X
- to describe what happens when …

You must stick to this aim. You will not achieve a high mark if you just write generally about the writer's use of language and structure in the given section. However, you may find that the section is chosen because its focus is largely on the aim identified.

P1/Q3

Question 3: Strategy

Follow the steps below to respond to a Question 3 task.

Step 1: Re-read the extract. Read the question. Underline its key focus.

Step 2: Search for *language and structure features* in the text which relate to the focus.

You must write about both types of feature, though not necessarily equally. There are 6 marks available. If you only write about language or structure, you will not earn more than 2 marks.

Search for and highlight features as you read. Select the four or five features you feel most confident about and use them to write your response. Try writing about the ones you feel most confident about first.

Step 3: Using your annotations and answers from Steps 1 and 2, decide on key features you could talk about in this text.

Step 4: Write your response, supporting your points with reference to the text.

> **TIP**
> If you can talk about how some features combine to create an effect, that can really impress the examiner.

Language and structural features to look for:

Language	Structure
Vocabulary choices	Beginning, middle, end
Figurative language: simile, metaphor, personification	Focus shifts, zooming in and out
Repetition of words in a sentence	Repetition across the whole extract
Emotive language	Punctuation: ellipses, exclamation marks, question marks, etc.
Word classes	Balance of dialogue and description
Dialogue and its style	Sentence types and lengths
Choice of details	How tension and suspense build
Symbolism	Foreshadowing

Knowledge

Knowledge

EXAM

Paper 1: Question 3

Question 3: Example

Read the sample Question 3 task and annotations below.

> **Q3** Read this extract.
>
> How does the writer use language and structure to describe the effects of the lightning on Gabriel and Bathsheba?
>
> Support your views with reference to the text.
>
> **[6 marks]**

You need to talk about the writer's language and structure choices and give examples of them. Include subject terminology where possible.

This question is about *how* language and structures affect the reader. You will gain marks for exploring what the reader might think or feel when they read the text, and how the language and structure choices the writer has made might create those responses. This is the most important part of your response.

The focus of the question is on the *effects* of the lightning on Gabriel and Bathsheba. This means you would be looking for *language* that describes the lightning flashes as perceived by Gabriel and Bathsheba and how this section is *structured* to convey their experience to the reader. They are on a corn rick in a storm. The lightning flashes are beautiful but charged with electricity that could kill them.

You will need to find words and phrases, language features and techniques, sentence forms, and elements of structural progression that help create meaning in this extract.

> **TIP**
>
> Structure can refer to an effect within one or more sentences, as in the withholding of information in lines 28–31. It can also refer to a whole passage, as in the shift of focus from the lightning to the characters.

80 Paper 1: Question 3

P1/Q3

Source 1: *Far from the Madding Crowd* by Thomas Hardy

At her third ascent the rick suddenly brightened with the brazen glare of shining majolica* – every knot in every straw was visible. On the slope in front of him appeared two human shapes, black as jet. The rick lost its sheen – the shapes vanished. Gabriel turned his head. It had been
30 the sixth flash which had come from the east behind him, and the two dark forms on the slope had been the shadows of himself and Bathsheba. Then came the peal. It hardly was credible that such a heavenly light could be the parent of such a diabolical sound.

'How terrible!' she exclaimed, and clutched him by the sleeve. Gabriel
35 turned, and steadied her on her aerial perch by holding her arm. At the same moment, while he was still reversed in his attitude, there was more light, and he saw, as it were, a copy of the tall poplar tree on the hill drawn in black on the wall of the barn. It was the shadow of that tree, thrown across by a secondary flash in the west.

40 The next flare came. Bathsheba was on the ground now, shouldering another sheaf, and she bore its dazzle without flinching – thunder and all – and again ascended with the load.

majolica: *shiny, brightly coloured pottery*

LINK

This question refers to an extract from Source 1: *Far from the Madding Crowd* by Thomas Hardy. The full text is on pages 214–215.

The source text has been chosen because there are interesting things to say about its language and structure: you just have to work your way through it to find them.

A writer may combine structural features with language. For example, a short, significant phrase might be repeated at key moments to build tension.

Make sure that your answer:

- focuses on both *language* and *structural* features – though not necessarily equally
- refers to the text (this doesn't always have to be a quotation) and is relevant to the question focus
- uses subject terminology where appropriate.

Listing subject terminology alone will not earn marks. You must talk about how those named features create impact.

Knowledge

Knowledge — EXAM

Paper 1: Question 3

Question 3: Sample answers

Now read the following sample answers to the Question 3 example on page 80, alongside the examiner's comments.

Sample answer 1

This answer scores around half the marks available.

❶ The student begins in an unfocused way, but makes a point about the question focus – how the writer presents the lightning's effect on the characters, correctly identifying a device but not analysing it and not relating it to the focus.

❸ Uses evidence to show the effect of the lightning on a character, and makes a structural point; however, this is not accurate or developed.

> It is a dark and stormy night. Gabriel finds all the flashes very confusing. It goes from being really bright, 'brazen glare' to 'black as jet'. This is a simile. Then he realised what the 'two dark forms' were — the 'shadows of himself and Bathsheba'. **❶** It is also quite strange that the light is 'heavenly' and 'diabolical'. This is like it's good and evil at the same time. **❷** Bathsheba seems frightened by all the lightning. That's why she 'clutched him by the sleeve' at the start. But the extract develops because by the end she is not that bothered because 'she bore its dazzle without flinching'. **❸** The structure of the extract has a lot of switching between light and dark, which is confusing. This also means there is a lot of brightness and shadow. Gabriel notices this more than Bathsheba. He sees the 'human shapes' at the start and the brightness of the straw, and the shadow of the 'poplar tree'. He also notices the awful sound of the thunder which must be pretty scary. **❹**

❷ Points out a paradox but without relating it to the question focus of the effect of the lightning on Gabriel and Bathsheba. There is also a slight misunderstanding: it is the *sound* of the lightning that is 'diabolical'.

❹ Makes a structural point, though it is very vague and there is a lack of real analysis.

Examiner's comments

The student comments on both language and structural features, but begins in a narrative style and does not always stick to the question focus of how the writer presents the lightning's effect on the characters. Some points are not quite supported by evidence, such as 'Gabriel finds all the flashes very confusing.' One language device is correctly identified, but this point is not developed. Other points, similarly, are not as well developed as they could be. The comments on structure do identify a feature of the passage, but they are weak and do not analyse the effects in sufficient detail.

P1/Q3

Sample answer 2

This is one section of a longer answer. It scores high marks.

> The writer makes the reader feel the danger that Gabriel and Bathsheba are in by showing the dramatic sight and sound of the lightning from their viewpoint. ❶ He first shows its frightening appearance in the image 'the brazen glare of shining majolica'. This says that it is very bright and personifies it as bold and fierce, as if it does not care about humans, including Gabriel and Bathsheba. ❷ The writer presents the lightning as beautiful, but also dangerous in the personification of the 'heavenly light' as a 'parent' of something 'diabolical'. The adjective 'diabolical' implies that the lightning seems evil to Gabriel. ❸ The writer uses withholding information, at first just showing the reader what the characters see – 'two human shapes, black as jet', and then explaining that these were 'the shadows of himself and Bathsheba'. This creates suspense, as Gabriel first sees the shapes, then understands them. He uses the same technique later with the 'copy of the tall poplar tree'. The 'black as jet' simile makes the characters' experience very dramatic. ❹ The focus moves from how Gabriel experiences the lightning to Bathsheba's exclamation. This reveals her fear, as does the verb 'clutched', which implies her needing Gabriel's reassurance because she is afraid of the lightning. Later, however, we see she has overcome this, as she bears the 'dazzle' without 'flinching' (jumping), and ignores it. ❺

❶ The student makes the point that the description here is from the characters' viewpoint (largely Gabriel's), showing the relevance of later points to the question focus.

❷ The student makes a point about the lightning's impact on Gabriel and Bathsheba, explains the image, using terminology correctly, and explains its effects on the reader.

❸ This focuses closely on figurative language and word choices, still sticking to the question focus.

❹ Names and comments on a structural technique, explaining its effect on the character and the reader.

❺ This combines commentary on structure – how the passage develops – and word choices, explaining how key words reveal Bathsheba's reactions to the lightning.

QUESTION CONNECTION

You will also analyse language features in your answer to Paper 2 Question 3.

Knowledge

Knowledge — EXAM

Paper 1: Question 3

Examiner's comments
The student correctly identifies and sticks to the exact focus of the question: 'the effects of the lightning' on both characters, not just writing about the lighting itself or wandering onto other aspects of the text. The response analyses the effects of both language and structural features, even showing how they work together. It provides textual evidence and uses relevant subject terminology.

TIP
It's good to use technical terms, but if you can't remember them, just describe what a particular word, phrase, or technique does; e.g. juxtaposition 'gives a very different image/tone', while a simile 'creates an image'.

REMEMBER

- Make a precise point linked to the question focus which is supported by evidence.
- Briefly zoom in on a few words and language or structural features and *analyse* their effect on the reader.
- Use phrases such as 'We see…', 'showing the reader…', 'This creates…', or 'this reveals…'. These demonstrate that you understand the effect of a feature, earning you more marks.

Key term — Make sure you can write a definition for this key term.

listing

Retrieval — EXAM — P1/Q3

Paper 1: Question 3

Use the following questions to check your understanding of the knowledge covered in this section. Then cover the answers column with a piece of paper and write down as many as you can. Check and repeat.

Questions | Answers

#	Question	Answer
1	What is the focus of Question 3?	Commenting on the effect of the writer's language and structural choices.
2	How long should you spend on Question 3?	14 minutes
3	How many marks are available for Question 3?	6 marks
4	You will earn the most marks if you just write about language. True or false?	False. You have to write about both language and structure.
5	Name at least three language features.	Choose from: figurative language: simile, metaphor, personification; repetition of words in a sentence; emotive language; word classes; dialogue and its style; choice of details; symbolism.
6	Name at least three structure features.	Choose from: beginning, middle, end; focus shifts, zooming in and out; repetition across the whole extract; punctuation; balance of dialogue and description; sentence types and lengths; how tension and suspense build; foreshadowing.
7	You will earn some marks for just identifying language or structure features. True or false?	False. You must analyse their effect.
8	Summarise the four steps for tackling this question.	**Step 1:** re-read the short extract. Underline the question focus. **Step 2:** search for language and structure features relevant to the question focus. **Step 3:** choose four to five features to write about. **Step 4:** write your response.

Previous questions

Now go back and use these questions to check your knowledge of previous topics.

Questions | Answers

#	Question	Answer
1	What is 'inferring' information?	Working out (deducing) what the text hints at.
2	What is 'explicit' information?	Information that is clearly stated.
3	What is 'narrative structure'?	The way that a writer organises and presents a story to the reader.

Retrieval 85

Practice EXAM

Exam-style questions

Answer the exam-style questions on pages 86–87. Remember that in the exam, you will need to read the whole source text first before you start looking at the question and specific extract.

3.1

Q3 Read this extract.

How does the writer use language and structure to describe the conflict at Wuthering Heights?

Support your views with reference to the text. **[6 marks]**

LINK

This question refers to an extract from Source 2: *Wuthering Heights* by Emily Brontë. The full text is on pages 216–217.

Source 2: *Wuthering Heights* by Emily Brontë

'Oh, heavens! In old days this would win you knighthood!' exclaimed Mrs
40 Linton. 'We are vanquished! we are vanquished! Heathcliff would as soon lift a finger at you as the king would march his army against a colony of mice. Cheer up! you sha'n't be hurt! Your type is not a lamb, it's a sucking leveret*.'

'I wish you joy of the milk-blooded coward, Cathy!' said her friend. 'I compliment you on your taste. And that is the slavering*, shivering thing you
45 preferred to me! I would not strike him with my fist, but I'd kick him with my foot, and experience considerable satisfaction. Is he weeping, or is he going to faint for fear?'

The fellow approached and gave the chair on which Linton rested a push. He'd better have kept his distance: my master quickly sprang erect, and
50 struck him full on the throat a blow that would have levelled a slighter man. It took his breath for a minute; and while he choked, Mr Linton walked out by the back door into the yard, and from thence to the front entrance.

sucking leveret: *a young hare still being fed by its mother*
slavering: *dribbling from the mouth, often in hunger or anticipation*

EXAM TIP

In your answer, you should:
- identify interesting language and structural features
- write about their effect on the reader
- consider how language and structure often work together, as in the repetition of a particular word in several sentences.

3.2

Q3 Read this extract.

How does the writer use language and structure to present the character of Frankenstein's creation?

Support your views with reference to the text. **[6 marks]**

LINK

This question refers to an extract from Source 3: *Frankenstein* by Mary Shelley. The full text is on pages 218–219.

Source 3: *Frankenstein* by Mary Shelley

'If you consent, neither you nor any other human being shall ever see us again; I will go to the vast wilds of South America. My food is not that of man; I do not destroy the lamb and the kid to glut my appetite; acorns and berries afford me sufficient nourishment. My companion will be of the same nature
20 as myself and will be content with the same fare. We shall make our bed of dried leaves; the sun will shine on us as on man and will ripen our food. The picture I present to you is peaceful and human, and you must feel that you could deny it only in the wantonness* of power and cruelty. Pitiless as you have been towards me, I now see compassion in your eyes; let me seize the
25 favourable moment and persuade you to promise what I so ardently desire.'

'You propose,' replied I, 'to fly from the habitations of man, to dwell in those wilds where the beasts of the field will be your only companions. How can you, who long for the love and sympathy of man, persevere in this exile?

wantonness: *wickedness*

3.3

Q3 Read this extract.

How does the writer use language and structure to describe Miss Havisham and her room?

Support your views with reference to the text. **[6 marks]**

LINK

This question refers to an extract from Source 4: *Great Expectations* by Charles Dickens. The full text is on pages 220–221.

Source 4: *Great Expectations* by Charles Dickens

It was then I began to understand that everything in the room had stopped, like the watch and the clock, a long time ago. I noticed that Miss Havisham
20 put down the jewel exactly on the spot from which she had taken it up. As Estella dealt the cards, I glanced at the dressing-table again, and saw that the shoe upon it, once white, now yellow, had never been worn. I glanced down at the foot from which the shoe was absent, and saw that the silk stocking on it, once white, now yellow, had been trodden ragged. Without
25 this arrest of everything, this standing still of all the pale decayed objects, not even the withered bridal dress on the collapsed form could have looked so like grave-clothes, or the long veil so like a shroud.

So she sat, corpse-like, as we played at cards; the frillings and trimmings on her bridal dress, looking like earthy paper. I knew nothing then of the
30 discoveries that are occasionally made of bodies buried in ancient times, which fall to powder in the moment of being distinctly seen; but, I have often thought since, that she must have looked as if the admission of the natural light of day would have struck her to dust.

Practice

Knowledge EXAM

Paper 1: Question 4

Question 4: Overview

Focus: How successfully the writer has achieved an aim
Marks: 15 marks
Time: 35 minutes
AO: AO4

Question 4 is based on the whole source text. It gives you a statement about what the author has tried to do, and asks you to **evaluate** – to **critically** respond to – how successfully this **aim** has been achieved. Question 4 will always follow the same format:

> **Q4** In this extract, there is an attempt to …
> Evaluate how successfully this is achieved.
> Support your views with detailed reference to the text. **[15 marks]**

This is not a question about analysing details of language and structure, but about evaluating the author's use of ideas, events, themes, or settings. The stated author's aim could be anything, but the task will always be to evaluate the author's success, giving a critical **judgement** which is supported by references to the text.

It is important to evaluate the author's aim as identified in the question. This will be quite precise, as in:

- to show the relationship between …
- to create an atmosphere of …
- to create a sense of …

Make sure you stick to this aim. Remember, too, that you can if you wish be critical of the text. However, the text will have been chosen for its literary merit, so don't expect to find a lot to criticise.

Paper 1: Question 4

Question 4: Strategy

Follow the steps below to respond to a Question 4 task.

Step 1: Re-read the statement of author's intention in the question. Highlight the key focus of the statement; for example:

'In this extract, there is an attempt to create a growing sense of tension.'

Think about what these key words mean.

Step 2: Re-read the source text. Highlight sections that especially relate to the focus of the question. Add notes in the margin on how they do this.

If there are parts that you feel are less successful, mark those too. However, you may well only find good points. If you mention a weakness, be sure to give evidence.

Step 3: Plan your answer, considering the following:
- How far do you agree with the statement, and why?
- What elements of the text make it successful in achieving the stated aim?
- Work out the best order in which to deal with your points. This might be in chronological order, working through the text, but it may be better to deal with one element (such as setting) at a time.

Step 4: Write your response, including the elements from your plan which best support the stated aim and making sure that you include evidence.

TIP

Try to work methodically through the source when answering a question; it can help avoid missing important sections of the text.

Knowledge — EXAM

Paper 1: Question 4

Question 4: Example

Read the sample Question 4 and annotations below. Remember that it is based on the whole source text.

> **Q4** In this extract, there is an attempt to **create a growing sense of tension**.
> **Evaluate** how successfully this is achieved.
> Support your views with **detailed reference to the text**.
>
> **[15 marks]**

- You will be given a statement about what the author is trying to do.
- Your response should explain how far you think the author has succeeded. You must 'evaluate' the text, which involves analysing the author's use of ideas, events, themes, or settings and their effects to achieve the stated aim.
- It is vital to provide textual evidence in the form of short quotations or references.
- Students often lose marks on this question because they just write an analysis of the text without making a judgement about the writer's success in achieving the aim.

You will be given a context box at the top of the source that tells you important information about the text. Read this!

Source 1: *Far from the Madding Crowd* by Thomas Hardy

> This extract is taken from the novel *Far from the Madding Crowd* by Thomas Hardy, written in 1874. A farmer, Bathsheba, is working with Gabriel Oak trying to save her harvest from a coming storm, because her husband has got all her workers drunk.

Before Oak had laid his hands upon his tools again out leapt the fifth flash, with the spring of a serpent and the shout of a fiend. It was green as an emerald, and the reverberation was stunning. What was this the light revealed to him? In the open ground before him, as he looked over the ridge
5   of the rick, was a dark and apparently female form. Could it be that of the only venturesome woman in the parish – Bathsheba? The form moved on a step: then he could see no more.

'Is that you, ma'am?' said Gabriel to the darkness.

'Who is there?' said the voice of Bathsheba,

10   'Gabriel. I am on the rick, thatching.'

'O, Gabriel! – and are you? I have come about them. The weather awoke me, and I thought of the corn. I am so distressed about it – can we save it anyhow? I cannot find my husband. Is he with you?'

'He is not here.'

15   'Do you know where he is?'

'Asleep in the barn.'

LINK

This question refers to Source 1: *Far from the Madding Crowd* by Thomas Hardy. The text can also be found on pages 214–215.

'He promised that the stacks should be seen to, and now they are all neglected! Can I do anything to help? Liddy is afraid to come out. Fancy finding you here at such an hour! Surely I can do something?'

20 'You can bring up some reed-sheaves to me, one by one, ma'am; if you are not afraid to come up the ladder in the dark,' said Gabriel. 'Every moment is precious now, and that would save a good deal of time. It is not very dark when the lightning has been gone a bit.'

'I'll do anything!' she said, resolutely. She instantly took a sheaf upon her
25 shoulder, clambered up close to his heels, placed it behind the rod, and descended for another. At her third ascent the rick suddenly brightened with the brazen glare of shining majolica – every knot in every straw was visible. On the slope in front of him appeared two human shapes, black as jet. The rick lost its sheen – the shapes vanished. Gabriel turned his head. It had been
30 the sixth flash which had come from the east behind him, and the two dark forms on the slope had been the shadows of himself and Bathsheba. Then came the peal. It hardly was credible that such a heavenly light could be the parent of such a diabolical sound.

'How terrible!' she exclaimed, and clutched him by the sleeve. Gabriel
35 turned, and steadied her on her aerial perch by holding her arm. At the same moment, while he was still reversed in his attitude, there was more light, and he saw, as it were, a copy of the tall poplar tree on the hill drawn in black on the wall of the barn. It was the shadow of that tree, thrown across by a secondary flash in the west.

40 The next flare came. Bathsheba was on the ground now, shouldering another sheaf, and she bore its dazzle without flinching – thunder and all – and again ascended with the load.

There was then a silence everywhere for four or five minutes, and the crunch of the spars*, as Gabriel hastily drove them in, could again be distinctly
45 heard. He thought the crisis of the storm had passed. But there came a burst of light.

'Hold on!' said Gabriel, taking the sheaf from her shoulder, and grasping her arm again.

Heaven opened then, indeed. The flash was almost too novel for its
50 inexpressibly dangerous nature to be at once realised, and they could only comprehend the magnificence of its beauty. It sprang from east, west, north, south, and was a perfect dance of death. The forms of skeletons appeared in the air, shaped with blue fire for bones – dancing, leaping, striding, racing around, and mingling altogether in unparalleled confusion. With these were
55 intertwined undulating snakes of green, and behind these was a broad mass of lesser light. Simultaneously came from every part of the tumbling sky what may be called a shout; since, though no shout ever came near it, it was more of the nature of a shout than of anything else earthly.

---

majolica: *shiny, brightly coloured pottery*
spar: *a sharpened wooden rod*

Knowledge

EXAM

Paper 1: Question 4

Question 4: Sample answers

Now read the following sample answers to the Question 4 example question on page 90, alongside the examiner comments.

Sample answer 1

This answer scores less than half the marks available.

① The response identifies the essential source of the tension, but without focusing on the 'growing sense of tension' in the question. The opening sentence focuses on excitement rather than tension. There is a misunderstanding about why Bathsheba is 'distressed'.

> This is a very exciting description of a storm. The characters are in great danger being perched up high and in danger of being struck by lightning anytime. Despite this they have to work against the clock without any help. If they don't manage to protect the corn it will get wet in the storm. Bathsheba is also upset about her husband. ①
> The writer makes it very clear that the thunder and lightning are both dangerous and frightening. The thunder has loud 'reverberations' and the lightning is 'diabolical', 'a serpent', and 'a fiend'. Calling it 'a serpent' is a metaphor which means it is a snake. ②
> One way in which the writer creates a lot of tension is through how it is dark one moment and dazzling the next, so the characters are confused about what is going on. In fact at first they don't even know they're both there. ③
> When it goes completely quiet, this is less tense, so not good. The biggest part of the storm like dancing skeletons comes after this. The characters find it beautiful, like a firework display. Probably they can enjoy it as the worry is over. ④

② This paragraph starts well, with a hint of evaluation of the writer's effects, but drifts into attempted analysis of language, which is not the focus of Question 4.

③ This makes a point about the use of light and dark, and its effect on the characters, but without development or textual reference. The last sentence is unclear.

④ The student misinterprets an important structural point (the silence), and fails to link it to the exact focus of the question or back it up with evidence.

P1/Q4

Examiner's comments
This response does identify the key source of tension in the text, but fails to focus closely on the 'growing sense of tension'. It also drifts into language analysis without linking it to setting, ideas, events, or themes – the focus of Question 4. Several points start well but are undeveloped and, essentially, lack the support of textual reference. There is one mention of the writer, but little real evidence of an understanding of the author aiming to create particular effects on the reader, and how well this is achieved. Nor does it move from beginning to end of the extract in its comments, which is a useful way to track how the text develops.

Key terms — Make sure you can write a definition for these key terms.

aim   critical   evaluate   judgement

Knowledge

Knowledge — EXAM

Paper 1: Question 4

Sample response 2

This is part of an answer which scores high marks.

❶ The answer quickly identifies the key source of tension and focuses on setting and the combination of urgency and physical danger, coupled with the lack of other help. The student uses well-chosen short quotations as evidence.

> First the author places this scene in a highly dangerous setting. The characters are alone on a corn rick in an electrical storm at night, so they could easily be struck by lightning. From the start, the author conveys the storm's power by the 'shout' of the lightning and the 'stunning' impact of the thunder. There is immediate tension between this danger and their urgent need to save the corn, indicated by Bathsheba being 'so distressed' about its possible ruin. What's more, they must do this on their own, as her husband is 'asleep'. ❶ A particularly effective way in which tension is created is the contrasting of dark and light, and the characters' resulting uncertainty. The author makes the reader identify with Gabriel by showing the setting from his viewpoint, using questions like 'What was this the light revealed to him?' to convey the idea of uncertainty, at the same time withholding information from the reader. It is effective that Gabriel is not even sure who is coming, and nor is the reader. He can only see an 'apparently female form', and must ask, 'Is that you, ma'am?' to know who it is. Similarly, the author creates tension well by Bathsheba having ask, 'Who is there?' This creates tension through the characters not knowing who they are with. ❷

❷ Evaluates a technique and its effect on the reader – the contrast of light and dark and how it enables the withholding of information, in turn creating tension.

94   Paper 1: Question 4

P1/Q4

> The author adds tension well by Bathsheba saying, 'I'll do anything,' followed by Gabriel saying, 'every moment is precious'. This creates the idea of desperation that adds to the mounting tension. The loud thunder and flashes of lightning make Bathsheba clutch Gabriel's sleeve, her gesture very effectively showing her fear. ❸ After a cleverly placed silence that lulls both Gabriel and the reader into a false sense of security, the tension climaxes in the final paragraph with the lightning's 'dance of death'. The author suggests that the characters might be so struck by its beauty that they forget its 'inexpressibly dangerous nature'. ❹

❸ Introduces dialogue and action as means of creating further tension. Uses evaluative language in 'adds tension well' and 'very effectively showing'.

❹ Evaluates ('cleverly') elements from throughout the text, focusing exactly on the question wording in 'mounting tension' and 'tension climaxes'.

Examiner's comments

This answer scores highly by keeping focused on the precise wording of the question, evaluating the author's creation of a 'growing sense of tension', covering several key ways in which this is done, and using suitably evaluative language, such as 'very effectively'. It covers setting, ideas, themes, and events. Overall, the student has thought carefully about the stated aim and how well the writer has achieved effects, even commenting on how the writer has made the reader identify with one character.

REMEMBER

- You must evaluate the statement in the exam question throughout your answer.
- You must write a critical personal response that gives clear judgements about the aim.
- You must consider how far the ideas, events, themes, or settings in the extract successfully express its aim.
- The quality and clarity of your evaluation is important: every point you make should connect to the question aim and be supported with evidence from the text.

Knowledge

Retrieval

EXAM

Paper 1: Question 4

Use the following questions to check your understanding of the knowledge covered in this section. Then cover the answers column with a piece of paper and write down as many as you can. Check and repeat.

Questions | Answers

#	Question	Answer
1	What is the focus of Question 4?	How successfully the writer has achieved a stated aim.
2	How long should you spend on Question 4?	35 minutes
3	How many marks are available for Question 4?	15 marks
4	What is 'evaluative' language?	Language that expresses your assessment of something, such as: 'A particularly effective feature is …'
5	Name at least three aspects of the text that you could analyse in your Question 4 evaluation.	Choose from: ideas, events, themes, or settings.
6	How much of the source text should you consider in Question 4?	All of it.
7	In this question statement, what key topic should you focus on? 'In this extract, there is an attempt to show the relationship between Gabriel and Bathsheba.'	The relationship between Gabriel and Bathsheba.
8	You should never criticise the source text. True or false?	False. If you do, you must give your reason and support it with evidence relating to setting, ideas, themes, and events.
9	Summarise the four steps for tackling this question.	**Step 1:** re-read the statement of author's intention and underline the key words. **Step 2:** highlight especially relevant parts of the source text. **Step 3:** plan your answer, focusing on your evaluation and the order in which to present it. **Step 4:** write your response, using supporting evidence.

Previous questions

Now go back and use these questions to check your knowledge of previous topics.

Questions | Answers

#	Question	Answer
1	What is 'withholding information' in a text?	The technique of keeping back information from the reader for effect, such as suspense, and revealing it later.
2	What does 'chronological order' mean?	The straightforward order in time, or in a text, paragraph by paragraph.
3	What is a 'climax'?	The point of greatest excitement.

Practice EXAM P1/Q4

Exam-style questions

Answer the exam-style questions on pages 97–101. To answer these questions, you need to refer to the full source texts.

4.1

Q4 In this extract there is an attempt to convey the characters' emotions.

Evaluate how successfully this is achieved.

Support your views with detailed reference to the text. **[15 marks]**

LINK

This question refers to Source 2: *Wuthering Heights* by Emily Brontë. This source can also be found on pages 216–217.

Source 2: *Wuthering Heights* by Emily Brontë

This extract is taken from the 1847 novel *Wuthering Heights*, by Emily Brontë. The 'mistress' of the house, Catherine, has been talking to her childhood friend Heathcliff, with whom she is very close, against the wishes of her husband Edgar Linton. This part of the story is narrated by a servant, Nelly.

'Have you been listening at the door, Edgar?' asked the mistress, in a tone particularly calculated to provoke her husband, implying both carelessness and contempt of his irritation. Heathcliff, who had raised his eyes at the former speech, gave a sneering laugh at the latter; on purpose, it seemed, to
5 draw Mr Linton's attention to him. He succeeded; but Edgar did not mean to entertain him with any high flights of passion.

'I've been so far forbearing with you, sir,' he said quietly; 'not that I was ignorant of your miserable, degraded character, but I felt you were only partly responsible for that; and Catherine wishing to keep up your
10 acquaintance, I acquiesced – foolishly. Your presence is a moral poison that would contaminate the most virtuous: for that cause, and to prevent worse consequences, I shall deny you hereafter admission into this house, and give notice now that I require your instant departure. Three minutes' delay will render it involuntary and ignominious.'

15 Heathcliff measured the height and breadth of the speaker with an eye full of derision.

'Cathy, this lamb of yours threatens like a bull!' he said. 'It is in danger of splitting its skull against my knuckles. By God! Mr Linton, I'm mortally sorry that you are not worth knocking down!'

20 My master glanced towards the passage, and signed me to fetch the men: he had no intention of hazarding a personal encounter. I obeyed the hint; but Mrs Linton, suspecting something, followed; and when I attempted to call them, she pulled me back, slammed the door to, and locked it.

'Fair means!' she said, in answer to her husband's look of angry surprise. 'If
25 you have not courage to attack him, make an apology, or allow yourself to be beaten. It will correct you of feigning more valour than you possess. No, I'll swallow the key before you shall get it! I'm delightfully rewarded for my kindness to each! After constant indulgence of one's weak nature, and the

Practice EXAM

Exam-style questions

> other's bad one, I earn for thanks two samples of blind ingratitude, stupid to
> 30 absurdity! Edgar, I was defending you and yours; and I wish Heathcliff may
> flog you sick, for daring to think an evil thought of me!'
>
> It did not need the medium of a flogging to produce that effect on the
> master. He tried to wrest the key from Catherine's grasp, and for safety she
> flung it into the hottest part of the fire; whereupon Mr Edgar was taken with
> 35 a nervous trembling, and his countenance grew deadly pale. For his life he
> could not avert that excess of emotion: mingled anguish and humiliation
> overcame him completely. He leant on the back of a chair, and covered
> his face.
>
> 'Oh, heavens! In old days this would win you knighthood!' exclaimed Mrs
> 40 Linton. 'We are vanquished! we are vanquished! Heathcliff would as soon lift
> a finger at you as the king would march his army against a colony of mice.
> Cheer up! you sha'n't be hurt! Your type is not a lamb, it's a sucking leveret*.'
>
> 'I wish you joy of the milk-blooded coward, Cathy!' said her friend. 'I
> compliment you on your taste. And that is the slavering*, shivering thing you
> 45 preferred to me! I would not strike him with my fist, but I'd kick him with my
> foot, and experience considerable satisfaction. Is he weeping, or is he going
> to faint for fear?'
>
> The fellow approached and gave the chair on which Linton rested a push.
> He'd better have kept his distance: my master quickly sprang erect, and
> 50 struck him full on the throat a blow that would have levelled a slighter man.
> It took his breath for a minute; and while he choked, Mr Linton walked out by
> the back door into the yard, and from thence to the front entrance.
>
> **sucking leveret:** *a young hare still being fed by its mother*
> **slavering:** *dribbling from the mouth, often in hunger or anticipation*

EXAM TIP

In your answer, you should:
- evaluate how far the author has achieved the aim
- consider the ideas, events, themes, or settings
- use quotations from the source text to illustrate your points.

4.2

> In this extract there is an attempt to convey the characters' conflicting desires.
>
> Evaluate how successfully this is achieved.
>
> Support your views with detailed reference to the text **[15 marks]**

LINK

This question refers to Source 3: *Frankenstein* by Mary Shelley. The text can also be found on pages 218–219.

Source 3: *Frankenstein* by Mary Shelley

> This extract is taken from the 1818 novel *Frankenstein* by Mary Shelley. A monstrous 'creature' tells his creator, Victor Frankenstein, that he wants a mate. The story is narrated by Frankenstein.

> What I ask of you is reasonable and moderate; I demand a creature of another sex, but as hideous as myself; the gratification is small, but it is all that I can receive, and it shall content me. It is true, we shall be monsters, cut

off from all the world; but on that account we shall be more attached to one
another. Our lives will not be happy, but they will be harmless and free from
the misery I now feel. Oh! My creator, make me happy; let me feel gratitude
towards you for one benefit! Let me see that I excite the sympathy of some
existing thing; do not deny me my request!'

I was moved. I shuddered when I thought of the possible consequences
of my consent, but I felt that there was some justice in his argument.
His tale and the feelings he now expressed proved him to be a creature
of fine sensations, and did I not as his maker owe him all the portion of
happiness that it was in my power to bestow? He saw my change of feeling
and continued,

'If you consent, neither you nor any other human being shall ever see us
again; I will go to the vast wilds of South America. My food is not that of man;
I do not destroy the lamb and the kid to glut my appetite; acorns and berries
afford me sufficient nourishment. My companion will be of the same nature
as myself and will be content with the same fare. We shall make our bed of
dried leaves; the sun will shine on us as on man and will ripen our food. The
picture I present to you is peaceful and human, and you must feel that you
could deny it only in the wantonness* of power and cruelty. Pitiless as you
have been towards me, I now see compassion in your eyes; let me seize the
favourable moment and persuade you to promise what I so ardently desire.'

'You propose,' replied I, 'to fly from the habitations of man, to dwell in those
wilds where the beasts of the field will be your only companions. How can
you, who long for the love and sympathy of man, persevere in this exile?
You will return and again seek their kindness, and you will meet with their
detestation; your evil passions will be renewed, and you will then have a
companion to aid you in the task of destruction. This may not be; cease to
argue the point, for I cannot consent.'

'How inconstant are your feelings! But a moment ago you were moved by my
representations, and why do you again harden yourself to my complaints?
I swear to you, by the earth which I inhabit, and by you that made me, that
with the companion you bestow I will quit the neighbourhood of man and
dwell, as it may chance, in the most savage of places. My evil passions will
have fled, for I shall meet with sympathy! My life will flow quietly away, and
in my dying moments I shall not curse my maker.'

His words had a strange effect upon me. I compassionated him* and
sometimes felt a wish to console him, but when I looked upon him, when
I saw the filthy mass that moved and talked, my heart sickened and my
feelings were altered to those of horror and hatred. I tried to stifle these
sensations; I thought that as I could not sympathize with him, I had no right
to withhold from him the small portion of happiness which was yet in my
power to bestow*.

wantonness: *wickedness*
compassionated him: *felt sorry for him*
bestow: *give*

Practice EXAM

Exam-style questions

4.3

In this extract there is an attempt to convey the narrator's feelings about his visit to Miss Havisham.

Evaluate how successfully this is achieved.

Support your views with detailed reference to the text. **[15 marks]**

> **LINK**
> This question refers to Source 4: *Great Expectations* by Charles Dickens. The text can also be found on pages 220–221.

Source 4: *Great Expectations* by Charles Dickens

This extract is taken from the 1861 novel by Charles Dickens, *Great Expectations*. A young boy, Pip, has been told that he has to visit a strange, rich old woman, Miss Havisham, who is the guardian of a girl, Estella. Miss Havisham wants to see Pip play with Estella. The story is narrated by Pip as an adult.

'Call Estella,' she repeated, flashing a look at me. 'You can do that. Call Estella. At the door.'

To stand in the dark in a mysterious passage of an unknown house, bawling Estella to a scornful young lady neither visible nor responsive, and feeling it
5   a dreadful liberty so to roar out her name, was almost as bad as playing to order. But she answered at last, and her light came along the dark passage like a star.

Miss Havisham beckoned her to come close, and took up a jewel from the table, and tried its effect upon her fair young bosom and against her pretty
10 brown hair. 'Your own, one day, my dear, and you will use it well. Let me see you play cards with this boy.'

'With this boy? Why, he is a common labouring boy!'

I thought I overheard Miss Havisham answer – only it seemed so unlikely, 'Well? You can break his heart.'

15 'What do you play, boy?' asked Estella of myself, with the greatest disdain.

'Nothing but beggar my neighbour, miss.'

'Beggar him,' said Miss Havisham to Estella. So we sat down to cards.

It was then I began to understand that everything in the room had stopped, like the watch and the clock, a long time ago. I noticed that Miss Havisham
20 put down the jewel exactly on the spot from which she had taken it up. As Estella dealt the cards, I glanced at the dressing-table again, and saw that the shoe upon it, once white, now yellow, had never been worn. I glanced down at the foot from which the shoe was absent, and saw that the silk stocking on it, once white, now yellow, had been trodden ragged. Without
25 this arrest of everything, this standing still of all the pale decayed objects, not even the withered bridal dress on the collapsed form could have looked so like grave-clothes, or the long veil so like a shroud.

So she sat, corpse-like, as we played at cards; the frillings and trimmings on her bridal dress, looking like earthy paper. I knew nothing then of the discoveries that are occasionally made of bodies buried in ancient times, which fall to powder in the moment of being distinctly seen; but, I have often thought since, that she must have looked as if the admission of the natural light of day would have struck her to dust.

'He calls the knaves Jacks, this boy!' said Estella with disdain, before our first game was out. 'And what coarse hands he has! And what thick boots!'

I had never thought of being ashamed of my hands before; but I began to consider them a very indifferent pair. Her contempt for me was so strong, that it became infectious, and I caught it.

She won the game, and I dealt. I misdealt, as was only natural, when I knew she was lying in wait for me to do wrong; and she denounced me for a stupid, clumsy labouring-boy.

'You say nothing of her,' remarked Miss Havisham to me, as she looked on. 'She says many hard things of you, but you say nothing of her. What do you think of her?'

'I don't like to say,' I stammered.

'Tell me in my ear,' said Miss Havisham, bending down.

'I think she is very proud,' I replied, in a whisper.

'Anything else?'

'I think she is very pretty.'

'Anything else?'

'I think she is very insulting.' (She was looking at me then with a look of supreme aversion.)

'Anything else?'

'I think I should like to go home.'

'And never see her again, though she is so pretty?'

'I am not sure that I shouldn't like to see her again, but I should like to go home now.'

'You shall go soon,' said Miss Havisham, aloud. 'Play the game out.'

Knowledge EXAM

Paper 1: Questions 5 and 6

Questions 5 and 6: Overview

Focus	Marks	Time	AO
Imaginative writing	40 marks	45 minutes	AO5, AO6

Questions 5 and 6 are imaginative writing tasks. You must respond to one of them. Your account could be based on a real experience you have had, or it could be imagined, or a combination of both.

One, usually Question 5, will be a text prompt; the other question will be based on two images provided for you. Both tasks will be loosely linked to themes in the text in Section A: Reading. Here are examples of Questions 5 and 6:

EITHER

Q5 Write about a time when you, or someone you know, took a risk.

Your response could be real or imagined.

*Your response will be marked for the accurate and appropriate use of vocabulary, spelling, punctuation, and grammar.

[40 marks]

OR

Q6 Look at the images provided.

Write about a time when you visited somewhere for the first time.

Your response could be real or imagined. You may wish to base your response on one of the images.

[40 marks]

> **LINK**
>
> The knowledge section on the following pages will help you with your writing task:
> - figurative language: pages 10–16
> - character: pages 26–32
> - sentence forms: pages 42–46
> - narrative structure: pages 48–54.

P1/Q5-6

Questions 5 and 6 are worth 40 marks, compared with only 24 marks for *all* of the questions in Section A, so it's important to make sure you leave enough time to tackle your chosen question. These questions test both your creative writing skills (AO5) and your technical skills (AO6). Up to 24 marks are awarded for AO5 and up to 16 marks are awarded for AO6.

No audience or purpose is specified for either task, and the instruction is quite general: 'Write about a time…', 'Write about when…'. Use your imagination: there could be several ways in which to interpret the prompt. The wording invites a response that is at least partly **narrative**, with a beginning, middle, and end, but it could include a lot of **description**.

The images are just to inspire you. You do not need to limit yourself to what is in them or describe their contents. You could also treat an image as a metaphor. An image of someone running through the woods could suggest finding a new path in life.

Whichever type of question you choose, think about how you could interpret it in an original and imaginative way to show off your writing skills.

> **TIP**
> It's really important that you allow time to proofread for spelling, punctuation, and grammar. Don't miss out on easy marks for getting these basics right.

Knowledge [EXAM]

Paper 1: Questions 5 and 6

Questions 5 and 6: Strategy

Follow the steps below to respond to a Question 5/6 task.

Step 1: Consider which of the two question options you will answer. Choose the one which will best show off your imagination and creative abilities. Also decide whether you will write a story, a description, or a **monologue**.

Step 2: Write a simple plan of how you will structure your imaginative writing, using the box in the answer booklet. Plan what you will write for the beginning, middle, and end of your response.

Step 3: Write your response. Make sure your work engages your reader and uses language accurately.
- Include effective details and figurative language.
- Vary your word use, punctuation, and sentence structure to show off your range of vocabulary and technical skills.

Step 4: Proofread your work and make corrections for spelling, punctuation, and grammar. Check that everything makes sense.

> **TIP**
> Aim to write a detailed answer. Most successful responses are around two to three sides in length. You should stick to the form you choose – story, description, monologue – throughout your answer.

Question 5 and 6: Key skills

Whether you choose to write a descriptive or narrative response, the same key skills are being assessed. They are detailed below.

Skill	What this means you need to do	Assessment objective
Clear communication	Make sure everything you write is clear and makes sense.	AO5
Quality of ideas	Engage your reader with interesting ideas. Spend time planning how you will use setting, character, or events to make your response engaging.	AO5
Quality of expression	Show that you can phrase your response in interesting ways. Take time to craft what you are writing. Use interesting words.	AO5
Structure and sequence	Plan the sequence of your response – what will happen in what order. Show that you can 'shape' a response by giving it an interesting structure.	AO5
Technical accuracy	Make sure that spelling, punctuation, and expression are as accurate as possible.	AO6
Technical variety	Show that you can use a range of punctuation and sentence types.	AO6

P1/Q5-6

Question 5 and 6: Example

Below are sample Question 5 and 6 tasks.

The question wording will usually ask you to focus on a particular time. This could well suggest a story, but it could also inspire a description or monologue – e.g. someone describing their hometown, which they complain never changes.

This is the key focus. The writing needs to reflect this, but it is up to you how you interpret it. For example, here it could be the narrator's life, winter snow, or a set of traffic lights.

Q5 Write about a time when you, or someone you know, longed for something to change.

Your response could be real or imagined.

*Your response will be marked for the accurate and appropriate use of vocabulary, spelling, punctuation, and grammar. **[40 marks]**

You could write about an actual event or time, a made-up one, or a mixture of both.

Remember that 16 marks are available for this. Choose your words well, and allow time to proofread your writing.

The images are meant to inspire you. You should not attempt to describe exactly what is in them or limit yourself to them.

You could write about an actual event or time, a made-up one, or a mixture of both.

Q6 Look at the images provided.

Write about a time when you, or someone you know, took a risk.

Your response could be real or imagined.

*Your response will be marked for the accurate and appropriate use of vocabulary, spelling, punctuation, and grammar. **[40 marks]**

This is the key focus. The writing needs to reflect this, but it is up to you how you interpret it. For example, here the risk could be physical, financial, or emotional.

Even if you use a picture as inspiration, you could still write about a real experience of your own, or an imagined one.

Remember that 16 marks are available for this. Choose your words well, and allow time to proofread your writing.

Knowledge

Knowledge   EXAM

Paper 1: Questions 5 and 6

Questions 5 and 6: Planning a response

Make a plan before writing. There is a section on the question paper provided for this. The plan doesn't need to be long or detailed, but it can be helpful to make a bullet-point list or a rough mind map, for example, which includes:

- a structure for what you want to write
- some key vocabulary you'd like to use
- some key descriptive moments or devices you will use
- for a story, some key narrative moments or devices you will use
- a setting/location
- a brief note on one or two characters (if you are writing a narrative).

> **LINK**
>
> All the language features and structural devices from the Concept Knowledge section on pages 10–62, and the Writing Knowledge you will explore in the rest of this section, can be used in your writing for Questions 5 and 6.

Structuring your response

Look at the following example of a Question 5 imaginative task:

> **Q5** Write about a time when you, or someone you know, longed for something to change.
>
> Your response could be real or imagined.
>
> *Your response will be marked for the accurate and appropriate use of vocabulary, spelling, punctuation, and grammar. **[40 marks]**

There are *many* ways to structure a narrative piece. Here is just one approach you could use or take some ideas and inspiration from, relating to the question above.

P1/Q5-6

Ask yourself these seven questions:

1. **WAITING:** *Could my character be waiting for something?*
   e.g. Think about where the character is or what they can see. Establish the mood by including details such as the weather or people around them.

2. **SHORT AND SIMPLE action:** *Can I follow a descriptive paragraph with a simple statement about something that happens?*
   This can quickly move your story along – you don't need to describe every detail.

3. **SENSORY** description: *How could I use the senses to build atmosphere?*
   For example, think about a smell or a texture. Consider using something the character senses to trigger a memory.

4. **PAST memory:** *How can you use something that the character remembers?*
   It can be effective to make this different from where they are in the present: it creates a sense that things have changed in their life.

5. **MOTION back to the present:** *How can I use motion to return the character to the present?*
   For example, this could be something dropping and making a noise, something knocking into them, or somehow making them move.

6. **SHIFT to a new place:** *What could a new location do to move the story along?*
   For example, later that day, the character could be at work or somewhere with a friend. Have something small but interesting happen, such as the character receiving a message or a call.

7. **WONDER:** *How can I link the task focus to the character's thoughts?*
   This can be a very short section, but could be a key moment where the character realises something, or suddenly has an idea, which links to the focus of the task.

> **TIP**
> You might also consider using a **motif** to tie your piece together. This is an image or idea which is repeated at different points across the narrative. In the second sample answer, the student has used the colour blue as a motif.

Knowledge 107

Knowledge EXAM

Paper 1: Questions 5 and 6

Using the images

Look at the following example of a Question 5 or 6 image-based imaginative task:

> **Q5/6** Look at the images provided.
>
> Write about a time when you, or someone you know, took on a challenge.
>
> Your response could be real or imagined.
>
> *Your response will be marked for the accurate and appropriate use of vocabulary, spelling, punctuation, and grammar.*
>
> **[40 marks]**

There are many ways to use the images as inspiration. You may have been taught an approach by a teacher or you might have your own ideas. Here is one possible approach you could use or take some ideas and inspiration from.

Paper 1: Questions 5 and 6

P1/Q5-6

Consider these seven questions:

1. **GETTING YOUR INSPIRATION:** *What do the images show? How could they be treated as a metaphor?* Make a quick mind map or spider diagram of your ideas. Note that you could withhold information to keep the reader guessing.

2. **BACKSTORY:** *What might have led up to the moment at which your narrative starts?* This could reveal a lot about your main character. Perhaps they feel a need to prove themselves to a parent, or to their friends. What has made them like this?

3. **MONOLOGUE:** *How could I show what is going on in the character's mind?* You could use the first person. For example: 'I've got to do this. I can't bottle out now. But the sea looks so far down, and those rocks – they're like needles…' Or you could use third person but from their viewpoint: 'He knew he had to do this…'

4. **ZOOM:** *What powerful single image could I zoom in on?* Think of a way to describe something specific in lots of detail. It might be a person, an animal, an object, a sound.

5. **SENSE APPEAL:** *How can I use the senses to engage the reader?* Think of how you can bring your writing to life by using the senses; for example, the sound of the waves, the smell of the sea, the touch of the breeze.

6. **LIGHT:** *How can I use light symbolism in my description?* Light is a very powerful symbol to use in your writing. You can describe light (or darkness) really easily, no matter what the exam image is; for example, 'The sun glared on the water below, making his mind go blank.'

7. **RETURN TO THE BIG METAPHOR:** *How can I return to the starting metaphor?* By returning to the same image that you start with, even if you change it a little by the end, you can create an effective structure. For example, you could begin with a cliff dive and end with the character 'diving' into a difficult challenge – like performing a solo in the school concert.

Follow these tips for descriptive and narrative writing:

SHOW, don't tell – reveal details by describing.

Think about VOICE – first person as a character, or third person as an observer?

Focus on the BIG and the SMALL – zoom in on the tiny details and zoom out to talk about the big picture.

Play with TIME – flash back to the past or foreshadow the future.

Prioritise VOCABULARY – word choices will always be more useful than other more complex devices.

Consider STRUCTURE – you only have 45 minutes, so plan your ending first – a story doesn't have to be action-packed; it just has to take us somewhere.

Knowledge 109

Knowledge **EXAM**

Paper 1: Questions 5 and 6

Question 5 and 6: Sample answers

Now read the following sample answers to the Question 5 and 6 example on page 105, alongside the examiner's comments.

Sample answer 1

This is one paragraph from a longer answer. It receives less than half the marks available.

❶ This establishes a setting and uses a metaphor, but it's a cliché. The words 'I was longing…' focus on the question, but without any interesting language.

❹ This attempts to develop the story by introducing a new idea, though without interesting language. It would be better if the student had chosen either red or orange, and included the description immediately after mentioning Mrs Jones. There are spelling and punctuation errors.

> We were on a school camp one year and it just kept bucketing down all the time, day after day. I was longing for the weather to change. ❶ Our tent was leeking a bit and all our cloths was wet and drenched, so I felt quite cold. Our tent was sagging like a washing line. ❷ I was sharing with a friend, and he said, 'If it keeps on like this our tent is going to get washed away.' Gary agreed. ❸ The teacher in charge Mrs Jones was promising to take us to the beach but it was too rainy, she was a middle-aged woman with red or maybe orange hair. ❹ On our second to last day and there was a little hint of blue in the sky like a cheaky little grin, like maybe it would stop at last. ❺

❷ 'Drenched' is a good word choice, but it would be better not to use 'wet' as well: it repeats the idea but in a weaker way. The 'washing line' simile is not developed (a 'tired old washing line' would be better), and it would be better not to repeat 'Our tent was'. Mentioning the 'cold' appeals to the senses, but more interesting synonyms could be used – e.g. 'I was shivering.' There are spelling and grammar errors.

❸ Dialogue is a good technique to use, but it would be better to introduce the friend with a name and one or two characteristics. It is unclear who 'Gary' is.

❺ The timing adds a little interest and the 'grin' simile is quite effective. It would be better to avoid using 'little' twice. It is unclear what 'it' refers to.

Examiner's comments
The student has chosen an appropriate subject, established a situation, and used some figurative language. There is some use of dialogue, though this could be improved. The response lacks a strong sense of direction. Some of the language is quite interesting, but much of it is unimaginative, with some repetition and an insufficient variety of sentence forms.

P1/Q5-6

Sample answer 2

This is part of a longer answer. It receives high marks.

① The narrative starts with the colour blue, in an attention-grabbing minor sentence, then uses it as a repeated motif.

Flash of blue. ① It flutters past her face, soars up and away past the bus stop, over the top of the brick wall, and is gone. She wraps her thin jacket around her waist against the cold morning and waits. An old man inches along the pavement with a Zimmer frame, and a group of teenagers huddle in a doorway. She watches as the smoke rises from their knot: up, up, and away from this place. Surely something must change soon. ②

The bus comes and she steps on. ③ The familiar scent of stale air greets her as she sinks into a seat at the front. She turns to look out of the window, and gazes mindlessly at the blur of early morning high street through the misted glass. Every day is the same. Suddenly, the sharp smell of cheap aftershave snaps her mind into focus. Alert, she looks around, instinctively shrinking her body into the seat and feeling her fingernails dig into her palm. A man sits across the aisle from her and starts scrolling on his phone. It's not him. She tries to slow her breathing, but all she can see is blue. Blue butterflies. ④

There had been butterflies that day. Fifteen years ago. They were big and beautiful, flooding her vision in a majestic swarm... ⑤

③ A short compound sentence progresses the narrative.

② This is showing, not telling us things the character experiences; e.g. we know the woman is cold because she 'wraps her thin jacket' around herself. The final sentence also links the narrative to the key word in the task: change. The student is clearly answering the question.

④ A strong use of sensory detail. The stale air of the bus is 'familiar' and the aftershave triggers a memory.

⑤ An effective use of flashback to develop the story.

Examiner's comments

This opening sets up an intriguing situation using present tense effectively, making the reader want to know why the character longs for change. The student uses sensory impressions, making them a key part of the narrative development. Vocabulary is chosen well, and there is variety in sentence lengths. The flashback promises to lead the story towards a satisfying conclusion.

TIP

Look out for opportunities to use short sentences, or even 'minor' (grammatically incomplete) sentences for impact. Like this!

Knowledge 111

Knowledge

EXAM

Paper 1: Questions 5 and 6

Question 5 and 6: Sample answers

Now read the following sample answers to the Question 5 and 6 example on page 108, alongside the examiner's comments.

Sample answer 3

This is one section from a longer answer. It receives less than half the marks available.

❶ This establishes a context for the story, and gives some sense of the narrator's character. The list of activities, followed by 'But none…' uses withholding of information to make the reader wonder what the risk actually was, but the language is uninteresting. There are errors in spelling, punctuation, and grammar.

❹ This dialogue does the job of revealing that they are lost, but it is very simple and does nothing to create any sense of suspense.

> I'm not really that brave but sometimes you just have to take a chance. When my mum said one day that we was going on an adventure holiday I was shocked this wasn't my sort of thing at all. We did absailing, kayaking, climbing, even pot-holing. But none of these was the big risk I took. ❶
> Me and my brother Darrel went for a walk in the woods one day.
> We'll be back in time for tea! I shouted. She looked unsure but I tried to assure her. ❷
> We wandered along the woodland paths as happy as squirrells looking at woodpeckers and trees. Before long we thought we ought to get back, it was starting to get so dark we couldn't see nothing. ❸
> 'It's that way,' I said.
> 'No it's this way,' Darrel said. ❹

❷ This moves the story on. The line of dialogue gives information concisely, though it needs quotation marks. 'Assure' is an interesting word choice – though 'reassure' would be better.

❸ This is a very hasty description of the wood, with just two random details. The 'happy as…' comparison is partly effective, but it would be better to link it to the setting: 'as the squirrels leaping in the trees above us'. There are errors in spelling, punctuation, and grammar.

Examiner's comments

This response uses some techniques in a promising way, but the language overall is not very interesting, and the student makes little real use of the woodland setting. It would have been good to have more description here. There is some sense of the story progressing, and a limited use of more interesting vocabulary.

REMEMBER

- Allow 45 minutes to complete this writing task. It is worth 40 out of the 64 marks for Paper 1.
- Planning is essential. Work out the structure of your response before you begin writing.
- Aim to engage your reader with original and interesting content based on the text or visual prompt.
- Use a range of interesting words and language techniques.
- Use a range of punctuation and sentence types.
- Always proofread your work – accuracy is important and valuable!

P1/Q5-6

Sample answer 4

Here is the opening of a response to an image-based writing task, which uses the structure outlined above. It receives high marks.

① The student writes in the third person, but from one character's point of view. The rhetorical question immediately gets the reader's attention and puts them into the mind of the main character. It reveals his inner conflict but withholds its source in order to keep the reader guessing.

④ Leads into a flashback that begins to explain how the character reached the point where the narrative starts. Interesting language, such as 'perched on the precipice' and 'churning sea', expresses a sense of challenge and danger.

⑥ Monologue reveals what is going on in the character's mind, using third-person limited perspective. Short sentences, including one minor sentence – 'Almost home and dry' – create a stream of consciousness and build tension. Longer sentences provide variety and suggest his anxieties. 'Devour' personifies the sea as a frightening monster.

> Why had he agreed to do this? ① He'd been put at the front, so he could easily get up, and climb the steps to the stage when summoned. It looked a long way up. He glanced along the row to where Nadia sat, and she smiled at him encouragingly. Or was she smirking? He couldn't tell anymore. His stomach felt like it was full of rocks — jagged ones. Sweat pricked in his armpits but his hands felt cold and awkward in his lap. Now the head teacher was starting on the daily notices. Somebody had done a thing: it just washed over him like the waves over someone drowning. ②
>
> He began to drift. ③
>
> Now he was there again, on the cliff top at Perravissey, beginning to shiver in his trunks as he perched on the precipice looking down at the churning sea. Billy was already below, swimming strongly towards the beach, having taken the plunge moments earlier. ④
>
> Dan was standing a few feet behind him. 'Come on mate. I'm getting cold here. You're not chicken, are you?' He accompanied this with a clucking sound. ⑤
>
> He knew he had to do this. He couldn't bottle out now. But the sea looked so far down, and those rocks — they were like needles. He told himself: just one jump and a few fleeting seconds of falling, and he'd be swimming for the shore. Almost home and dry. But what if he misjudged it and crashed onto the rocks, a mangled mess of broken limbs for the waves to pick up and devour? ⑥

② *Shows* how the character is feeling rather than just *telling* the reader – which would be less interesting.

③ One-line paragraph emphasises time shift and foreshadows the narrative development.

⑤ Dialogue, with a use of sound, brings the story to life and hints at the character's motivation.

Knowledge

Knowledge

EXAM

Paper 1: Question 5 and 6

> **Examiner's comments**
> This response hooks the reader by drawing them into the main character's inner conflict, making them want to know, from the start, what the outcome will be. There is a strong sense of the character's inner life, but there is also dramatic action and vivid description in the flashback. The response *shows* how the character is feeling, rather than just telling the reader.

You can write your Question 5 or 6 narrative from any perspective you like – it could be in the third person or in the first person. Compare this opening written in the first person with the one above:

> I don't really know why I agreed to do it. I was sitting at the front, where I'd been told to go so that I'd be able to get up easily and get to the steps when I was summoned.

A further way to write it is in the third person, but with an **omniscient** narrator:

> Darren Novak sat in the front row of the St George's School assembly wishing he was somewhere else. He was a slim, dark-haired boy with nervous hands that kept folding and unfolding in his lap.

This gives a different tone to the story. This approach is less direct, but it means you can describe things that would be difficult from another perspective – such as the character's appearance.

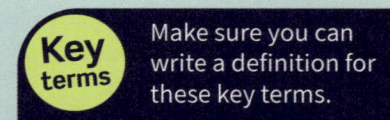

Key terms — Make sure you can write a definition for these key terms.

description   monologue   motif
narrative   omniscient   sensory

Retrieval — EXAM — P1/Q5-6

Paper 1: Question 5 and 6

Use the following questions to check your understanding of the knowledge covered in this section. Then cover the answers column with a piece of paper and write down as many as you can. Check and repeat.

Questions / Answers

#	Question	Answer
1	How long should you spend on Question 5/6?	45 minutes
2	What is the focus of Question 5/6?	Imaginative writing
3	You only have to answer one of the two questions. True or false?	True. You won't get extra marks for answering a second question.
4	How many marks are available for Question 5/6?	40 marks
5	There is usually a loose connection between the fiction text in Section A and the theme of Questions 5 and 6. True or false?	True
6	If you choose the image-based task, you should describe the contents of both images in close detail. True or false?	False. The images are just meant to give you some inspiration for imaginative writing. You should not just describe what is in either of them.
7	You can write in either the first or third person. True or false?	True
8	Summarise the four steps for tackling this question.	**Step 1:** choose one of the two question options. **Step 2:** plan how you will structure your writing, using the box in the answer booklet. **Step 3:** write your response. **Step 4:** proofread and make corrections for spelling, punctuation, and grammar.

Previous questions

Now go back and use these questions to check your knowledge of previous topics.

Questions / Answers

#	Question	Answer
1	What is a narrative 'flashback'?	Going back in time from the 'present' of the narrative to a moment in a character's past.
2	What is foreshadowing?	Hinting at what is to come in the story, so that the reader starts to guess, and so that the ending, when it comes, will seem more inevitable.
3	What is a 'monologue'?	The technique of showing what is going on in the mind of one character, as if they were speaking aloud.

Retrieval

Practice EXAM

Exam-style questions

In the exam, you must answer Question 5 or Question 6. One will be based on a choice of two pictures, and one will use a text prompt. The prompts usually suggest a narrative, though your writing could be largely descriptive rather than involving a complex plot.

Answer the exam-style questions on pages 116–117.

5.1/6.1

Section B: Imaginative Writing

Answer ONE question. You should spend about 45 minutes on this section. Write your answer in the space provided.

EITHER

Q5 Write about a time when you, or someone you know, was lost.

Your response could be real or imagined.

*Your response will be marked for the accurate and appropriate use of vocabulary, spelling, punctuation, and grammar.

[40 marks]

OR

Q6 Look at the images provided.

Write about a time when you visited a busy place.

Your response could be real or imagined. You may wish to base your response on one of the images.

*Your response will be marked for the accurate and appropriate use of vocabulary, spelling, punctuation, and grammar.

[40 marks]

EXAM TIP

As part of your answer, you should:

- read Questions 5 and 6 again, even if you read them when you started the exam
- consider the images before you choose your task
- spend about five minutes planning your answer. It is time well spent as it will help you focus on what to include and help structure your story or description
- proofread your work, carefully checking your spelling, grammar, and punctuation.

P1/Q5-6

5.2/6.2

Q5 Write about a time when you, or someone you know, did something completely unexpected.

Your response could be real or imagined. **[40 marks]**

OR

Q6 Look at the images provided.

Write about a time when you went on a journey.

Your response could be real or imagined. You may wish to base your response on one of the images.

[40 marks]

5.3/6.3

EITHER

Q5 Describe a time when you finally did something you'd always wanted to do.

Your response could be real or imagined.

Your response will be marked for the accurate and appropriate use of vocabulary, spelling, punctuation, and grammar.

[40 marks]

OR

Q6 Look at the images provided. Write about a time when you were unexpectedly free to do whatever you wanted.

Your response could be real or imagined. You may wish to base your response on one of the images.

Your response will be marked for the accurate and appropriate use of vocabulary, spelling, punctuation, and grammar.

[40 marks]

Practice

Knowledge EXAM

Paper 1: Overview

Questions

In the exam, the questions will be printed in the answer booklet. The source texts will be in a separate document.

The following are examples of the question types. They relate to the sources on pages 222–232. The exam will include the same or very similar question types in the same order each year. The source texts will be different.

Q1 | Identify information AO1

This question tests AO1 – identifying explicit and implicit information and ideas.

Q1 From lines 1–5, identify **two** things that Mitchell likes to do at Christmas.

[2 marks]

This question tests your ability to:
- focus on the specified section of Text 1
- identify and copy out relevant explicit or implicit information from the section.

Q2 | Identify information AO1

This question tests AO1 – identifying explicit and implicit information and ideas.

Q2 Read this extract. Give **two** criticisms of Christmas that Mitchell mentions.

You may use your own words or quotations from the text.

[2 marks]

This question tests your ability to:
- focus on the specific topic in the question
- find details in the short extract from Text 1 which link to the topic
- paraphrase or write down relevant short quotations.

118 Paper 2: Overview

P2

Q3 — Analyse how the writer uses language and structure [AO2]

This question tests AO2 – explaining and analysing how writers use language and structure to achieve effects and influence readers, using relevant subject terminology.

Q3 Analyse how the writer uses language and structure to interest and engage the reader.

In your answer you should write about:
- language features and techniques
- structural techniques
- the effect on the reader.

Support your views with detailed reference to the text.

[15 marks]

This question tests your ability to:
- focus on the whole of Text 1
- identify words and phrases, language features and techniques, and sentence forms that help create meaning
- explore what the reader might think or feel when they read the text, and how the specific language choices the writer has made create those feelings
- use subject terminology and quotations to support your ideas.

Q4 — Identify information [AO1]

This question tests AO1 – identifying explicit and implicit information and ideas.

Q4 From lines 1–5, identify **one** feature of the author's train journey.

[1 mark]

This question tests your ability to:
- focus on given lines from Text 2
- look for details which link to the topic
- identify one piece of explicit or implicit information about the topic in the section.

Q5 — Identify information [AO1]

This question tests AO1 – identifying explicit and implicit information and ideas.

Q5 From lines 5–11, identify **one** piece of information about the family.

[1 mark]

This question tests your ability to:
- focus on given lines from Text 2
- look for details which link to the topic
- identify one piece of explicit or implicit information about the topic in the section.

Knowledge 119

Knowledge *EXAM*

Paper 2: Overview

Q6 — Evaluate the text critically   [AO2]

This question tests AO4 – evaluating texts critically, supporting this with appropriate textual references.

Q6 In this extract, the writer attempts to persuade readers to consider simplifying their Christmas.
- Evaluate how successfully this is achieved.
- Support your views with detailed reference to the text.

[15 marks]

This question tests your ability to:
- consider the setting, ideas, themes, and events to make your judgement on how far an effect is achieved
- use evaluative language to show you are making a judgement about the writer's effectiveness
- explain how well the elements of the text you have chosen contribute to the focus given in the question.

Q7(a) — Synthesise information and evidence   [AO1]

This question tests AO1 – selecting and synthesising evidence from different texts.

Q7(a) The two texts are about changes people make in their lives.

What similarities do the people who take up growing vegetables share in these extracts?

Use evidence from **both** texts to support your answer.

[6 marks]

This question tests your ability to:
- focus on the specific topic mentioned in the question
- identify similarities in the whole of both source texts which link to the topic in the second sentence of the question.
- use quotations from both source texts to support your ideas.

P2

Q7(b) | Compare writers' ideas and perspectives [AO3]

This tests AO3 – comparing writers' ideas and perspectives, as well as how these are conveyed, across two or more texts.

Q7(b) Compare how the writers of Text 1 and Text 2 present ideas and perspectives about travel.

You should write about:
- the ideas and perspectives
- how they are presented
- how they are similar/different.

Support your answer with detailed references to the texts.

[14 marks]

This question tests your ability to:
- talk about how the writers of both source texts have ideas and opinions which are different or similar to each other
- identify and explain the effects of techniques the writers use
- identify and compare what the writers think and feel about the topic
- use quotations and references to both texts to support your ideas.

Q8/9 | Write an article, letter, review, text for a speech, section of a guide/textbook/leaflet/booklet [AO5] [AO6]

This question tests AO5 – communicating clearly, effectively, and imaginatively; selecting and adapting tone, style, and register for different forms, purposes, and audiences; and organising information and ideas, using structural and grammatical features to support coherence and cohesion of texts.

It also tests AO6 – using a range of vocabulary and sentence structures for clarity, purpose, and effect, with accurate spelling and punctuation.

You only need to answer one of these questions, either Question 8 or Question 9.

Q8–9 'Developments in science and technology will transform the world for the better in years to come.'

Write a magazine article in which you explore this statement.

In your article, you could include:
- what developments are taking place now
- what you expect the world's future to be like
- how far you think the statement will prove true

as well as any other ideas you might have.

[40 marks]

Includes 16 marks for the range of vocabulary and sentence structures for clarity, purpose, and effect, with accurate use of spelling and punctuation

This question tests your ability to:
- respond in the appropriate form, such as an article, letter, or review, as directed in the question
- organise your writing and use appropriate features of the given form
- write to argue, explain, or persuade as directed in the question
- clearly communicate your point of view on the given statement
- use an appropriate tone, level of formality, and style to suit the given form, purpose, and topic.

Knowledge 121

Knowledge — EXAM

Paper 2: Reading the source / Question 1

Reading the source

In Paper 2, Section A: Reading, there will be eight questions (including the two parts of Question 7) to answer about two linked source texts. You must remember to read both source texts in full before answering any questions.

As for Paper 1, there will be brief introductions to the sources. Be sure to read them, as they will give you important information about the contexts of the texts.

Spend the first 10 minutes of the exam reading the texts carefully. Each source text will be:

- about 650 words
- a non-fiction 20th- or 21st-century text.

Question 1: Overview

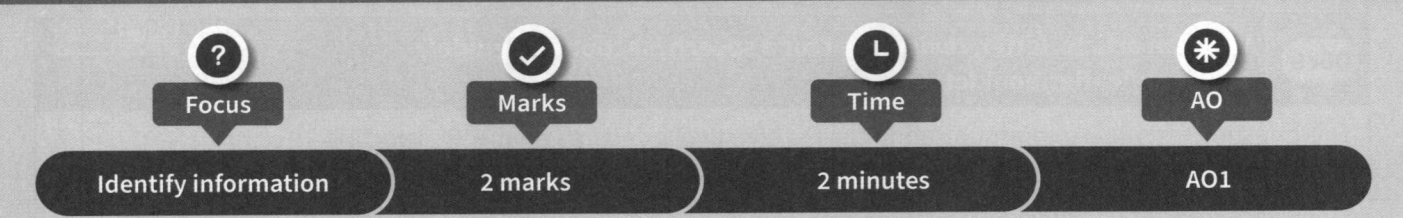

Focus	Marks	Time	AO
Identify information	2 marks	2 minutes	AO1

Question 1 is based on a small section taken from the start of Source 1. It asks you to look at specific lines and then select two things. It tests your ability to find explicit information and write it down using short self-explanatory quotations. It will look like this:

> **Q1** In lines x–x, identify **two** things that…
>
> [2 marks]

LINK

The knowledge section on pages 2–8 will remind you of the difference between explicit and implicit information that will help you to answer this type of question.

P2/Q1

Question 1: Strategy

Follow the steps below to respond to a Question 1 task.

Step 1: Re-read the relevant lines of the source.

Step 2: Underline the relevant information in the extract. Don't attempt to use your own words for this question.

Step 3: Write out your quotations or short **paraphrase**.

> **TIP**
> You will already have read the source texts at the start of the exam; try to recall if you read something relevant then to help you work quickly through this question.

Question 1: Example

Read the sample Question 1 task and annotations below.

Q1 From lines 1–3, identify **two** things that David Mitchell likes to do at Christmas.

[2 marks]

The question could ask you to identify information about a person, thing, action, setting, or event.

There will be a focus – probably the main subject of the few lines selected.

> **LINK**
> This question refers to an extract from Source 5A: 'Bah humbug to all of you who just hate Christmas' by David Mitchell. The full text is on pages 222–223.

Source 5A: 'Bah humbug to all of you who just hate Christmas' by David Mitchell

My official policy on Christmas is that I like it. That says a lot more about me than that I'm partial to a day spent watching TV and stuffing my face. More fundamentally, it shows that I can't stand the thought of our most public and celebratory festival being a lie.

> **TIP**
> You should only spend two minutes on this question: it only carries 2 marks.

Knowledge 123

Knowledge EXAM

Paper 2: Question 1

Question 1: Sample answers

Now read the following sample answers to the Question 1 example on page 123, alongside the examiner's comments.

Sample answer 1

This answer scores 1 mark out of the 2 marks available.

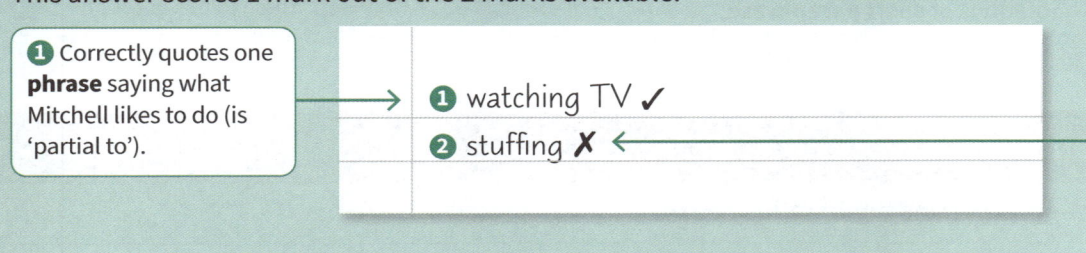

① Correctly quotes one phrase saying what Mitchell likes to do (is 'partial to').

① watching TV ✓
② stuffing ✗

② Quotes only one word, which in this case is not enough. It is not clear that the student has understood the meaning: they may think 'stuffing' is a noun referring to food.

Sample answer 2

This answer scores both the marks available.

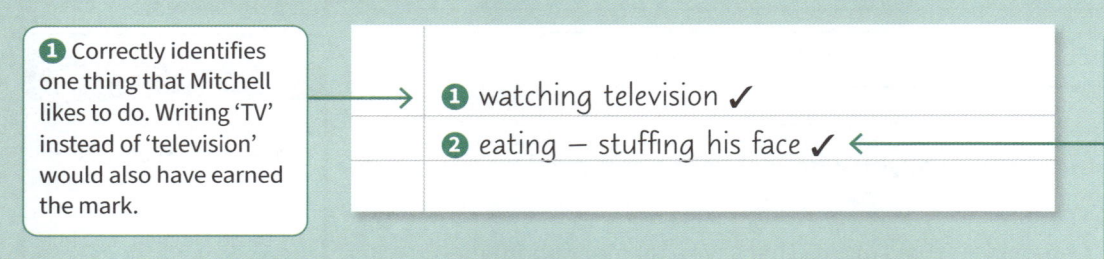

① Correctly identifies one thing that Mitchell likes to do. Writing 'TV' instead of 'television' would also have earned the mark.

① watching television ✓
② eating – stuffing his face ✓

② The student could have earned the mark with 'stuffing my face' or with 'eating', which is an accurate interpretation. However, it is better to quote a word or phrase if possible.

> **REMEMBER**
> - You will be given line numbers. Make sure you select information only from these lines.
> - Keep your answers short.
> - You can use the exact words from the source text, but make sure you use only the part you need.
> - Do not copy out long chunks of text.

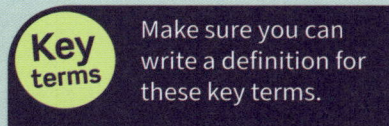

Key terms — Make sure you can write a definition for these key terms.

interpretation   paraphrase   phrase

Paper 2: Reading the source / Question 1

Retrieval — EXAM — P2/Q1

Paper 2: Question 1

Use the following questions to check your understanding of the knowledge covered in this section. Then cover the answers column with a piece of paper and write down as many as you can. Check and repeat.

	Questions	Answers
1	What is the focus of Question 1?	Identifying information
2	How long should you spend on Question 1?	2 minutes
3	How many marks are available for Question 1?	2 marks
4	You can quote exact words from the source. True or false?	True
5	You need to explain your answer. True or false?	False
6	You will not be expected to infer information (work out what the text hints at). True or false?	True
7	You should write a full sentence for each piece of information. True or false?	False: write the minimum – a word or phrase.
8	Summarise the steps for tackling this question.	**Step 1:** Re-read the lines. **Step 2:** Underline any possible answers. **Step 3:** Select and copy your chosen word or phrase.

Previous questions

Now go back and use these questions to check your knowledge of previous topics.

	Questions	Answers
1	What kind of text will you have to comment on in Paper 2?	Modern non-fiction
2	Name at least three different non-fiction genres.	For example: travelogue; biography; autobiography; article; letter.
3	What is 'explicit information'?	Information that is clearly stated, not just hinted at.

Practice EXAM

Exam-style questions

Answer the exam-style questions on pages 126–127. In the exam, the relevant lines in the extract for Question 1 will *not* be reprinted in the question paper so you will need to find them in the source text. They have been included here for easy reference.

> **REMEMBER**
> In the exam, you will need to read the *whole* source text first, before you start looking at the questions and any specific extracts.

1.1

From lines 1–5, identify **two** jobs Claire Ratinon does.

1

2

[2 marks]

LINK

This question refers to an extract from Source 6A: 'I left my job in London to grow food' by Claire Ratinon. The full text is on pages 225–226.

Source 6A: 'I left my job in London to grow food' by Claire Ratinon

In July 2016, I was sitting on the rooftop of a building in central London, listening to the gentle rumble of a nearby beehive, when I realised that my life had changed entirely. I didn't intend to quit – quitting crept up on me. After eight years of working in the media, I was on a path to becoming an
5 organic food grower, with a temporary side hustle of city beekeeping.

EXAM TIP

In your answer, you should:
- check the question focus
- not waste time reading beyond the given lines. The information you need is all within this section of the text
- use short quotations if their sense is clear, or your own words if it's quicker.

1.2

From lines 1–5, identify **two** things about train travel in India.

1

2

[2 marks]

LINK

This question refers to an extract from Source 7A: *Around India in 80 Trains* by Monisha Rajesh. The full text is on pages 227–228.

Source 7A: *Around India in 80 Trains* by Monisha Rajesh

Six-people deep, and growing by the second, the crowd tensed. A single knuckle pressed into my back and betel-nut* breath filled my nostrils as a steady beat rose above the din. Against the peach pink of Mumbai's evening skies, the commuter service curled into view, passengers hanging from
5 the sides like moving livery*.

betel-nut: *nut commonly chewed as a stimulant in India*
livery: *painted symbols indicating ownership*

P2/Q1

1.3

From lines 4–0, identify **two** things the author says about wild swimming.

1

2

[2 marks]

LINK

This question refers to an extract from Source 8A: 'RIP wild swimming! Nature's "cure all" has thrown in the towel' by Eva Wiseman. The full text is on pages 230–231.

Source 8A: 'RIP wild swimming! Nature's "cure all"' has thrown in the towel' by Eva Wiseman

Farewell, wild swimming, it's been fun. Well, not fun. Not 'fun' in the traditional sense of the word. More, it's been baffling, sometimes blood-curdling and, eventually, a banal cliché* flattened by over-use, but this is an obituary of sorts, so we will be kind.

banal cliché: *something that has become boring by repetition*

Knowledge EXAM

Paper 2: Question 2

Question 2: Overview

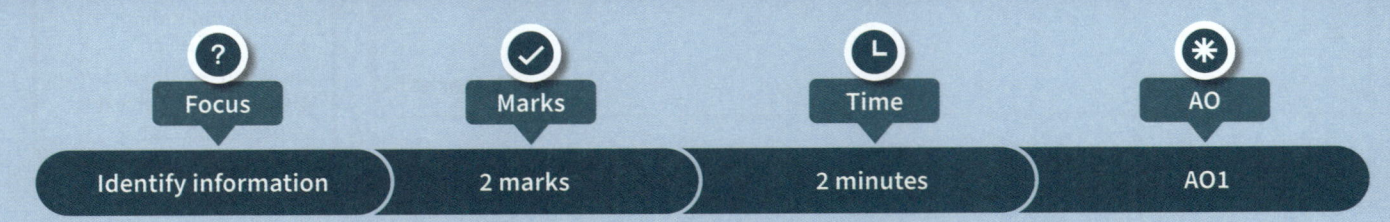

Focus: Identify information
Marks: 2 marks
Time: 2 minutes
AO: AO1

Question 2 is based on a slightly longer section of Source 1 than Question 1. It will ask you to find two pieces of information. This could be explicit or implicit information. It will look like this:

> **Q2** Read this extract.
>
> Give **two** things that…
>
> You may use your own words or quotations from the text.
>
> [2 marks]

Question 2: Strategy

Follow the steps below to respond to a Question 2 task.

Step 1: Identify the focus of the question.

Step 2: Underline the relevant information in the source.

Step 3: Write out your quotations or short paraphrases as shown here:
1 'the sparkle' (or 'Decorations')
2 'the queues' (or 'People queuing in shops')

If you paraphrase, you may need to infer information, as is done here with 'Decorations', but be careful not to change the meaning. You don't need to write sentences.

LINK

The knowledge section on pages 2–8 will remind you of the difference between explicit and implicit information that will help you to answer this type of question.

P2/Q2

Question 2: Example

Read the sample Question 2 task and annotations below. In the exam, the relevant lines will be printed with the question so you do not need to search the source text for them.

> Read this extract.
> Give **two** criticisms of Christmas that David Mitchell mentions.
> You may use your own words or quotations from the text.
>
> [2 marks]

Stick to the *given* extract. Don't take information from the rest of the text.

You need to focus on the *specific* topic mentioned in the question, for example, here it is about criticisms of Christmas. This means that the answer must focus on that and *not* on anything else.

You are looking for details in the source extract which link to the topic (e.g., 'the queues').

Source 5A: 'Bah humbug to all of you who just hate Christmas' by David Mitchell

Other people – my enemies – love to hate Christmas. They rejoice in looking at the sparkle, the bustle, the drinking and the queues and muttering: 'Christmas is a nightmare'; 'We're going to Jane's parents – it's going to be a living hell'; 'The sooner we can forget all the expense and false jollity, this
10 great capitalist hypocrisy dance, the better, I say', as if commerce* were as exclusive to this time of year as mince pies.

commerce: *buying and selling*

LINK
This question refers to an extract from Source 5A: 'Bah humbug to all of you who just hate Christmas' by David Mitchell. The full text is on pages 222–223.

TIP
You should only spend two minutes on this question.

Knowledge 129

Knowledge — EXAM

Paper 2: Question 2

Question 2: Sample answers

Now read the following sample answers to the Question 2 example on page 129, alongside the examiner's comments.

Sample answer 1

This answer scores 1 mark out of the 2 marks available.

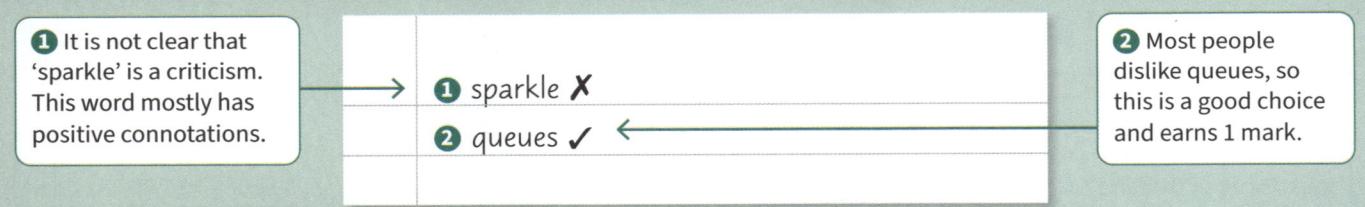

❶ It is not clear that 'sparkle' is a criticism. This word mostly has positive connotations.

❶ sparkle ✗
❷ queues ✓

❷ Most people dislike queues, so this is a good choice and earns 1 mark.

Sample answer 2

This answer scores both the marks available.

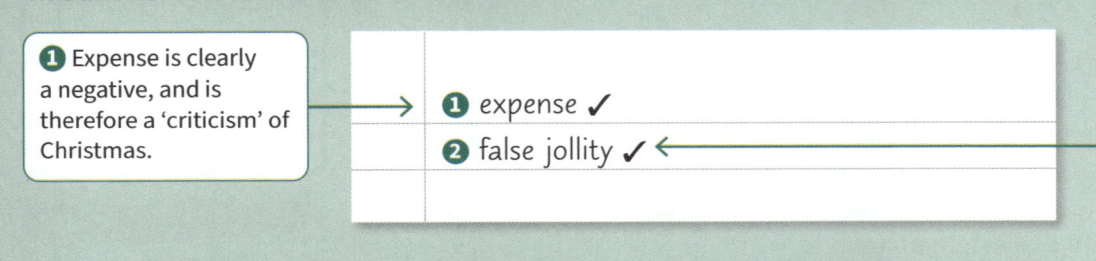

❶ Expense is clearly a negative, and is therefore a 'criticism' of Christmas.

❶ expense ✓
❷ false jollity ✓

❷ Here it is acceptable to quote the phrase, though a **paraphrase** such as 'fake cheerfulness' would also earn the mark.

> **REMEMBER**
> - The lines will be printed for you. Make sure you select information only from these lines.
> - Keep your answers short.
> - You can use the exact words from the source text, but make sure you use only the part you need.
> - Do not copy out long chunks of text.

Retrieval — EXAM — P2/Q2

Paper 2: Question 2

Use the following questions to check your understanding of the knowledge covered in this section. Then cover the answers column with a piece of paper and write down as many as you can. Check and repeat.

Questions / Answers

#	Question	Answer
1	How long should you spend on Question 2?	2 minutes
2	How many marks are available for Question 2?	2 marks
3	What is the focus of Question 2?	Identifying information
4	You can use your own words. True or false?	True
5	There is no need to explain your answer. True or false?	True
6	You might have to infer information. True or false?	True. The information you are asked for could be explicit or implicit.
7	You may be asked for your opinion. True or false?	False
8	You should copy out a full sentence to make sure you include the right information. True or false?	False. Write the minimum – a word or phrase. You could lose the mark by copying out too much.
9	Summarise the steps for tackling this question.	**Step 1:** Identify what you are looking for. **Step 2:** Underline the relevant information. **Step 3:** Write out your quotations or short paraphrases.

Previous questions

Now go back and use these questions to check your knowledge of previous topics.

#	Question	Answer
1	What does 'infer' mean?	Work out an implied meaning.
2	What is an 'opinion'?	A viewpoint, as opposed to a fact.
3	What is 'implicit information'?	Information that is hinted at.

Practice — EXAM

Exam-style questions

Answer the exam-style questions on pages 132–133.

2.1

Read this extract.

Give **two** reasons for the author changing her lifestyle.

You may use your own words or quotations from the text.

[2 marks]

LINK

This question refers to an extract from Source 6A: 'I left my job in London to grow food', by Claire Ratinon. The full text is on pages 225–226.

Source 6A: 'I left my job in London to grow food' by Claire Ratinon

10 I was growing tired of my life in London and I wanted to explore somewhere new, and it was in New York that a seed was (literally and figuratively) sown for my unexpected change of profession. I encountered the alchemy of food growing for the first time at Brooklyn Grange – a rooftop farm that sits above New York's busy streets and overlooks Manhattan. Dusky leaves of Tuscan
15 kale*, peppers and tomatoes in unexpected shapes and colours, striped aubergines wearing spiked sepal* hats – chaos of abundance in the most unlikely of places. I was captivated.

kale: *a leafy vegetable*
sepal: *the outer leaves that protect a flower*

EXAM TIP

In your answer, you should:
- check the question focus
- select your answers from the correct part of the source text
- clearly and precisely list your answers.

2.2

Read this extract.

Give **two** problems experienced by the author.

You may use your own words or quotations from the text.

[2 marks]

LINK

This question refers to an extract from Source 7A: *Around India in 80 Trains* by Monisha Rajesh. The full text is on pages 227–228.

Source 7A: *Around India in 80 Trains* by Monisha Rajesh

10 A slice of papaya in one hand my bag gripped with the other, I battled through elbows, meaty shoulders and thick plaits slicked with coconut oil. In the crush the papaya was knocked to the ground and my sandal came off, but I made it on board and fell sideways into a seat as the train jerked away from the platform. Wiping someone else's sweat from my arm, I watched
15 fellow travellers scrabble for handholds, adjust saris* and pull out phones before relaxing into the ride with a mix of relief and pride. I'd survived my first experience on the infamous Mumbai 'locals'*.

sari: *traditional outfit worn by Indian women*
'locals': *local trains*

P2/Q2

2.3

Read this extract.

Give **two** things that the author feels about wild swimming and wild swimmers.

You may use your own words or quotations from the text.

[2 marks]

LINK

This question refers to an extract from Source 8A: 'RIP wild swimming! Nature's "cure all" has thrown in the towel' by Eva Wiseman. The full text is on pages 230–231.

Source 8A: 'RIP wild swimming! Nature's "cure all" has thrown in the towel', by Eva Wiseman

[...] I am
10 a person quite tied to dry land, and cosiness, and a lack of eels scraping my shins, but I applaud those who did it. Those brave enough to jump straight into lakes, whether for exercise, their mental health, their headaches or their Instagrams. You always knew who was a wild swimmer, because they would tell you, frequently. And I'd applaud until my palms stung, because this was
15 a feat of endurance and bravery so far beyond my own pathetic limits that they might as well have jumped into an active volcano rather than the local pond.

Knowledge EXAM

Paper 2: Question 3

Question 3: Overview

Focus: Analyse language and structure
Marks: 15 marks
Time: 20 minutes
AO: AO2

Question 3 is based on the whole of the first source text in the exam.

This question is similar to Paper 1 Question 3. It is also a language and structure question and uses the same marking criteria. The differences are that it is based on the *whole* of Source 1, not a section of it, and it carries more marks.

This question asks you to explore how the writer uses *language and structure* to interest and engage the reader. Question 3 will always follow the same format. Here is an example:

> **Q3** Analyse how the writer uses language and structure to interest and engage the reader.
>
> In your answer you should write about:
>
> - language features and techniques
> - structural techniques
> - the effect on the reader.
>
> Support your views with detailed reference to the text.
>
> **[15 marks]**

Question 3: Strategy

Follow the steps below to respond to a Question 3 task.

Step 1: Re-read the text and annotate it with language and structure features you could analyse.

To look at language you have to 'zoom in' on vocabulary and devices such as **imagery, contrast,** emotive language, etc.; for structure, you have to 'zoom out' to see what each paragraph is about, and how ideas develop across the text. In between, you should consider sentence structure – for example, simple or complex sentences.

Step 2: Highlight your best points and number them in the order in which you will use them. You could begin by writing about the effect of the overall structure, then zoom in to sentence level, then comment on individual word choices. However, don't stick rigidly to this. If you feel that a word choice works with a structural feature, analyse them both together.

Step 3: Write your response to the question.

> **TIP**
>
> You could pull multiple features out of the whole extract, but you only need to talk about *four or five* in detail if you choose them well and develop your analysis fully.

P2/Q3

Question 3: Example

Read the sample Question 3 task and annotations below.

> This question is about the way language and structure affect the reader.

Q3 Analyse **how the writer** uses **language and structure** to **interest and engage the reader.**

In your answer you should write about:
- language features and techniques
- structural techniques
- their effects on the reader.

Support your views with detailed reference to the text.

[15 marks]

> You should consider the text type and intended reader, in order to be able to consider how language and structure features, including aspects such as tone, will 'engage the reader'.

> Where possible, include subject terminology to give examples of the writer's language and structure choices.

LINK

This question refers to an extract from Source 5A: 'Bah humbug to all of you who just hate Christmas' by David Mitchell. The full text is on pages 222–223.

> You gain marks for exploring what the writer's choices might make the reader think or feel, and why. This is the most important part of your response. You need to find words and phrases, language features and techniques, and structural features that help create meaning in the extract.

TIP

You will be given a context box at the top of the text that gives you important information about it. Make sure you read this!

Source 5A: 'Bah humbug to all of you who just hate Christmas' by David Mitchell

This text is taken from 'Bah humbug to all of you who just hate Christmas' by David Mitchell, a newspaper article published in 2008. David Mitchell is a comedian who is giving his opinion about people who don't like Christmas.

My official policy on Christmas is that I like it. That says a lot more about me than that I'm partial to a day spent watching TV and stuffing my face. More fundamentally, it shows that I can't stand the thought of our most public and celebratory festival being a lie. It is a happy and magical time, I'm insisting,
5 for deeper and more sinister reasons than a liking for Brazil nuts and *Shrek 3*.

Other people – my enemies – love to hate Christmas. They rejoice in looking at the sparkle, the bustle, the drinking and the queues and muttering: 'Christmas is a nightmare'; 'We're going to Jane's parents – it's going to be a living hell'; 'The sooner we can forget all the expense and false jollity, this
10 great capitalist hypocrisy dance, the better, I say,' as if commerce* were as exclusive to this time of year as mince pies.

Knowledge 135

As they grumble and sneer their way through the season – seek each other out for affirmation that it's all just a sick joke and that participating is as joyous as diarrhoea and as prudent as a pyramid scheme* I stand shocked and afraid. To the boy I once was, heart buoyed* by the air of magic, and expectation of an acquisitive* nature about to be satisfied, this is a colossal slap in the face: it has finally all ended in tears.

So I must sustain my policy. It's vulnerable, I know. I'm not at a good time of life for liking Christmas. The childhood enchantment has long gone, as has the excitement about presents, and I have no children to help me rediscover it vicariously*. Meanwhile, shopping is stressful, tree lights never work, turkey's not the best meat in the world and Christmas pudding is weird. If I'm not careful, I'll realise I'm only in it for the booze.

But I'm still too tribal to accept this conclusion. We of the Christmas-liking tribe will keep the Christmas-cynic tribe in perpetual subjugation – they will be made to join in whether they like it or not and particularly if not. They will never, if we can help it, be permitted to 'get away somewhere hot' but, if they do, we can be confident that our allies overseas will besiege them with spray-on snow and piped-in Slade even as they sweat round the pool.

This is a time when we all come together to disagree about how Christmas is supposed to be done. It's not so much 'love thy neighbour' as 'mock the neon Santa on thy neighbour's roof'. I think these divisions might be what saves my pro-Christmas policy because I love asserting my way of celebrating it over everyone else's. In another life, I could have been a great witchfinder general, paranoid anti-communist or warrior ant. I will root out people who slightly differ from me in their Christmas traditions and blow them away with the twin barrels of my British disdain gun, which are, of course, snobbery and inverse snobbery.

To test your suitability for this fight, consider your reaction to the phrase: 'We actually had goose this year.' It's not the nature of your reaction that's important, but its strength. I'm hoping for a strong one. Either: 'Yes of course, goose is a much tastier meat and an older tradition. I can't believe those turkey-eating scum are suffered to live. They should be locked up in the same hell sheds where the bland objects of their culinary affection are chemically spawned.' Or, and this is the one I favour: '[Get] back to Borough Market with your talk of goose deliciousness. We're supposed to eat turkey – that's now the tradition.'

---

commerce: *buying and selling*
pyramid scheme: *a sales scheme: people pay to join and only make money by recruiting others*
buoyed: *lifted up*
acquisitive: *wanting possessions*
vicariously: *through someone else*

P2/Q3

Question 3: Sample answers

Now read the following sample answers to the Question 3 example on page 135, alongside the examiner's comments.

Sample answer 1

This paragraph is from a longer answer. It scores less than half the marks available.

> I think David Mitchell must like Christmas a lot. 'I like it.' Some of the things he likes are 'TV and stuffing my face'. **①** He says he finds it 'happy and magical' but also somehow 'sinister', so he is mixed about it really. **②** When he calls the people who 'hate Christmas' his 'enemies' it is meant to be funny because Christmas is a time of peace and goodwill and if he actually likes it he should not be saying this. **③** Even so David does give some reasons why these people might dislike Christmas, like 'the bustle, the drinking and the queues'. This list helps to convince readers of Christmas being bad or difficult because they are all bad things. **④** The 'grumble and sneer' also makes it seem like the Christmas haters are quite nasty. The words 'joyous as diarrhoea' is a very comical simile that is relatable for many. **⑤** It could appeal to some who worry about eating too much Christmas food making them ill. **⑥**

① This makes obvious statements with simple evidence that is not analysed.

② Presents evidence in the form of embedded quotations, but misunderstands the writer's use of the word 'sinister' and therefore draws the wrong conclusion.

③ This makes a good point about the basis of the writer's humorous approach and offers some analysis, though it is undeveloped. There could be more comment on the choice of the word 'enemies' and its effect.

④ This gives some simple analysis of language, but presents it as if the writer's aim was to put people off Christmas.

⑤ This offers some simple analysis of language, though the effect is not made clear, and it is not made part of the coherent analysis of the writer's methods that is expected.

⑥ This at least acknowledges that there are readers, and what might appeal to them, but it is speculation rather than analysis which again misses the point that the writer is trying to make.

Examiner's comments

This answer identifies, and begins to comment on, some language features, but without developing the analysis of their effect on the reader. There is some misunderstanding and some irrelevance. The answer's strongest feature is its identification of the humour that is the basis of Mitchell's approach. In this section of the answer there is no mention of structure – which has to be addressed to gain the highest levels of marks for this question; though the student might tackle this later on.

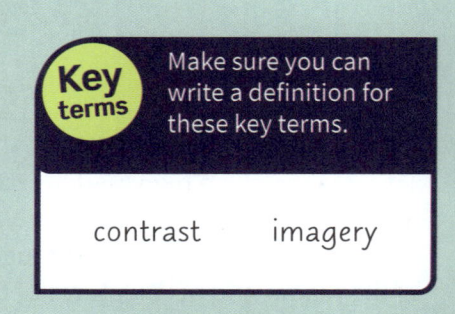

Key terms — Make sure you can write a definition for these key terms.

contrast   imagery

Knowledge

Knowledge — Paper 2: Question 3 (EXAM)

Sample answer 2

This is part of a longer answer. It scores high marks.

---

① The opening statement addresses the question directly, sums up the effect of the extract, and links it to the reaction of the reader.

The writer uses structure and language to interest and engage the reader by humorously showing he is a passionate Christmas lover who strongly disapproves of people who think differently. **①** The opening topic sentence immediately sets the humorous tone for the reader by using a clear, simple sentence coupled with the words 'official policy'. This makes it sound like a political announcement, as if attitudes to Christmas were controlled by government. **②** The writer continues to pull the reader into the joke by beginning the next paragraph with another simple statement juxtaposed to the first. This develops the idea of Christmas-lovers and Christmas-haters being opposed. **③** He calls the 'other people' his 'enemies', humorously exaggerating his feelings towards them. This is developed in his use of the verbs 'grumble' and 'sneer', which imply unpleasantness. **④** This idea of opposition is built up by his characterising the haters as seeing Christmas as being 'as joyous as diarrhoea and as prudent as a pyramid scheme'. These exaggerated comparisons highlight the unacceptable disgust of the Christmas haters. **⑤** Overall, the writer is trying to get the reader on his side. This is clear when he tries to engage the reader in his call to action: 'To test your suitability for this fight...'. His use of the noun 'fight' makes it sound like a battle. **⑥**

QUESTION CONNECTION
You will also analyse language and structure features in your answers to Paper 1 Question 3.

② Analyses the effect of the opening sentence both structurally and in terms of its language.

③ Makes another point that combines elements of language and structure and explores how these features are developed throughout the source text.

④ Zooms in on word choices and analyses their effects, using correct terminology.

⑤ Analysis of structural development ('built up') and the effect of language choices.

⑥ Comments on overall effect of passage, writer's aims, and a particular word choice.

Examiner's comments

This qualifies for a high mark by commenting on both language and structure more or less equally, and weaving together comments on both aspects throughout. It shows an awareness of the reader and how features of the text would be likely to affect them. It makes clear points about the text, backing them up with evidence and explaining effects. It also makes correct and relevant use of terminology, such as 'juxtaposed'.

REMEMBER

- Follow the paragraph structure of point, evidence, zoom, analysis in your response.
- Think about the effect created in the text for the reader and remember to include evidence from the text to support your points.

Retrieval — EXAM — P2/Q3

Paper 2: Question 3

Use the following questions to check your understanding of the knowledge covered in this section. Then cover the answers column with a piece of paper and write down as many as you can. Check and repeat.

Questions	Answers
1. How long should you spend on Question 3?	20 minutes
2. How many marks are there for Question 3?	15 marks
3. What is the focus of Question 3?	How the writer uses language and structure to interest and engage the reader.
4. It is important to identify as many language features as possible. True or false?	False. It is better to explore the effects of a few features (both language and structure) in depth.
5. Why is the intended audience of the extract important?	Writers aim at a particular audience of readers, and this will affect how they attempt to 'engage' readers.
6. Is it acceptable to write only about either language or structure?	No – you must write about both.
7. Summarise the steps for tackling this question.	**Step 1:** re-read the text and annotate it with language and structure features. **Step 2:** highlight your best points and number them in order. **Step 3:** write your response.

Previous questions

Now go back and use these questions to check your knowledge of previous topics.

Questions	Answers
1. What is a 'topic sentence'?	A sentence, usually at the start of a paragraph, that tells readers what subject is coming next – probably for the whole of the paragraph.
2. What is a 'simile'?	An image that makes an idea come to life by comparing one thing with another, using 'like' or 'as'.
3. What is 'exaggeration'?	Making something seem more extreme than it really is, especially for comic effect.

Retrieval

Practice EXAM

Exam-style questions

Answer the exam-style questions on pages 140–145.

3.1

> **Q3** Analyse how the writer uses language and structure to interest and engage the reader.
>
> In your answer you should write about:
> - language features and techniques
> - structural techniques
> - the effect on the reader.
>
> Support your views with detailed reference to the text.
>
> **[15 marks]**

LINK

This question refers to an extract from Source 6A: 'I left my job in London to grow food' by Claire Ratinon. The full text is on pages 225–226.

Source 6A: 'I left my job in London to grow food', by Claire Ratinon

This extract is taken from a *Guardian* newspaper article by Claire Ratinon, published in 2022. She explains how she left her life in London to move to the countryside and grow organic food.

In July 2016, I was sitting on the rooftop of a building in central London, listening to the gentle rumble of a nearby beehive, when I realised that my life had changed entirely. I didn't intend to quit – quitting crept up on me. After eight years of working in the media, I was on a path to becoming an
5   organic food grower, with a temporary side hustle of city beekeeping.

Not long before that point, I was just like the people in the office building below me. My work days were spent behind a desk or lugging around camera equipment, but now I am devoted to a life of nurturing the soil and growing the plants that end up on our plates. [...]

10   I was growing tired of my life in London and I wanted to explore somewhere new, and it was in New York that a seed was (literally and figuratively) sown for my unexpected change of profession. I encountered the alchemy of food growing for the first time at Brooklyn Grange – a rooftop farm that sits above New York's busy streets and overlooks Manhattan. Dusky leaves of Tuscan
15   kale*, peppers and tomatoes in unexpected shapes and colours, striped aubergines wearing spiked sepal* hats – chaos of abundance in the most unlikely of places. I was captivated.

From that day, all I could think about was getting through each week of working in documentary production so that, come the weekend, I could join
20   the other farm workers at Brooklyn Grange while they harvested, planted out and raked the earth to a fine tilth, ready for the next sowing of seeds. After two seasons of volunteering there, I was determined to make growing food a bigger part of my life. So, as the city I'd come to love was celebrating Halloween, I boarded a plane headed for London.

25 By the time I'd moved back to Hackney, I had a job working in the evenings – and occasionally nights – which left my days free to seek out the unlikely spaces where edible plants could be found growing in the city. After a year, I quit that role and tried to take on any job – each day a different one – that meant I could spend my days outside, my hands in the soil. I stepped into all
30 kinds of roles and every one taught me something precious.

Working as a school gardener showed me how little room there is in the school day and national curriculum for children to learn about how food arrives on their plate; training as a beekeeper taught me that growing nectar-rich flowers is a far better way of supporting pollinators than keeping hives;
35 and growing organic salad leaves to supply a veg box that filled the plates of people in Hackney made me realise there is nothing quite so ordinary and yet somehow remarkable than the act of feeding people.

Leaving London in 2019 to move to a more rural location changed the shape of my life. Now, in a garden of my own, I grow vegetables and fruit of my own
40 choosing [...]

I'm probably too romantic in the way I speak about working the land. The fact that it is a difficult and arduous way to make a living is worth stating – if only not to seem delusional. It is work that is backbreaking, exhausting and painfully underpaid. I have sacrificed my bodily wellbeing at its altar many
45 times, yet it remains the most important thing I've ever done.

kale: *a leafy vegetable*
sepal: *the outer leaves that protect a flower*

Practice EXAM

Exam-style questions

3.2

Q3 Analyse how the writer uses language and structure to interest and engage the reader.

In your answer you should write about:
- language features and techniques
- structural techniques
- the effect on the reader.

Support your views with detailed reference to the text.

[15 marks]

LINK

This question refers to an extract from Source 7A: *Around India in 80 Trains* by Monisha Rajesh. The full text is on pages 227–228.

EXAM TIP

In your answer, you should:
- identify language features and structural techniques that you can comment on
- comment in detail on the writer's choices of each example, analysing the effect on the reader
- use quotations, subject terminology, and references to the writer and to the reader.

Source 7A: *Around India in 80 Trains* by Monisha Rajesh

This extract is from a book of travel writing called *Around India in 80 Trains* by Monisha Rajesh. This extract describes her experience of train travel in India.

Six-people deep, and growing by the second, the crowd tensed. A single knuckle pressed into my back and betel-nut* breath filled my nostrils as a steady beat rose above the din. Against the peach pink of Mumbai's evening skies, the commuter service curled into view, passengers hanging from
5 the sides like moving livery*. Braking with a wail and grind of metal, the train slowed into the station and I braced against the surge of bodies from behind. Like relay runners, they began to move before the train had stopped, reaching over my head at the same time as a torrent of polyester shirts and satchels thundered down from the open doorways.

10 A slice of papaya in one hand my bag gripped with the other, I battled through elbows, meaty shoulders and thick plaits slicked with coconut oil. In the crush the papaya was knocked to the ground and my sandal came off, but I made it on board and fell sideways into a seat as the train jerked away from the platform. Wiping someone else's sweat from my arm, I watched
15 fellow travellers scrabble for handholds, adjust saris* and pull out phones before relaxing into the ride with a mix of relief and pride. I'd survived my first experience on the infamous Mumbai 'locals'*.

Inside the carriages, a microcosm* of Indian society spanned the train from one end to the other. With my earphones plugged in and my music turned
20 off, I'd pretend to read while eavesdropping on conversations about end-of-year exams, mean bosses, new girlfriends, old boyfriends and mother-in-law disputes.

In the middle of the night, I'd ease down from my berth for a trip to the loo, invariably putting a socked foot on a stranger's blanket-covered back,

25 mumble my apologies and hope they'd be gone by morning. On other days, I'd board at the opposite end, squeezing on to wooden slats with farmers and fruit sellers who would place guavas in my palm, while joking with their friends through paan*-stained teeth. They'd count their money, touching it to their foreheads with thanks, before sloping off the train and crossing the
30 tracks to find the next customer.

On arrival in Londa, I paced the platform munching on hot, fresh vadas and enquired when the return train would arrive, and was dismayed to discover it wasn't due until 2 a.m. It was barely 6 p.m. Gradually the crowds thinned, the skies turned indigo and there was nothing but the chirp of crickets
35 for company. A lone passenger watched me from a doorway. And he wouldn't leave.

At the other end of the platform I spotted a sweeper and beelined for the elderly man, who led me to a nearby guesthouse where I could stay for a few hours before the train arrived – it was always the kindness of strangers.

40 Just before 2 a.m. I crossed the road to the station as the train was rolling in. With no reservation, I boarded the women's compartment, a dimly lit dormitory of bundled bodies and bare feet. Finding me an unoccupied berth, the ticket inspector gestured for me to climb up. The train sailed out of the station and I wriggled down under the blanket before turning over to see my
45 neighbour watching me. She winked and her diamond nose stud shone in the milky light from the moving platform. I was back in my safe place, back at home.

---

betel-nut: *nut commonly chewed as a stimulant in India*
livery: *painted symbols indicating ownership*
sari: *traditional outfit worn by Indian women*
'locals': *local trains*
microcosm: *a little world*
paan: *betel nut rolled in a betel leaf*

> **TIP**
> This question asks *how* language and structure shape meaning. You need to identify the writer's choices and talk about their effect on the reader.

Practice 143

Practice EXAM

Exam-style questions

3.3

Q3 Analyse how the writer uses language and structure to interest and engage the reader.

In your answer you should write about:
- language features and techniques
- structural techniques
- the effect on the reader.

Support your views with detailed reference to the text.

[15 marks]

LINK

This question refers to an extract from Source 8A: 'RIP wild swimming! Nature's "cure all" has thrown in the towel' by Eva Wiseman. The full text is on pages 230–231.

Source 8A: 'RIP wild swimming! Nature's "cure all" has thrown in the towel' by Eva Wiseman

This is an opinion piece from *The Guardian* newspaper by a regular columnist.

Farewell, wild swimming, it's been fun. Well, not fun. Not 'fun' in the traditional sense of the word. More, it's been baffling, sometimes blood-curdling and, eventually, a banal cliché* flattened by over-use, but this is an obituary of sorts, so we will be kind.

5   Much in the same way Lucozade rebranded itself from medicine to energy drink, in the past decade this hobby pivoted to wellness, adding the 'wild' having spent many years known simply as 'swimming'. Led in no small part by this newspaper, it became a trend, elevated by its health-giving properties and photos of nice ladies grinning in swimwear. It was not for me. No, I am
10 a person quite tied to dry land, and cosiness, and a lack of eels scraping my shins, but I applaud those who did it. Those brave enough to jump straight into lakes, whether for exercise, their mental health, their headaches or their Instagrams. You always knew who was a wild swimmer, because they would tell you, frequently. And I'd applaud until my palms stung, because this was
15 a feat of endurance and bravery so far beyond my own pathetic limits that they might as well have jumped into an active volcano rather than the local pond. But.

But but but. When something becomes a trend, its clock starts ticking. Wild swimming is no different. The first nail in its coffin came with the blunt force
20 of marketing: it was presented as a cure for everything. Feeling sad, feeling a low ache in your temples, feeling burned out, grim from too long online, feeling an unravelling guilt about contributing to the climate crisis, feeling disconnected from your body, disconnected from your community, feeling too many feelings or too few – take your clothes off and jump in the lake.
25 There, nature will cleanse you quickly of all your human agonies and sins. Cured.

It has long bothered me, this idea that nature exists as a wellness product, like a scented candle or very green tea, rather than a system that persists in spite of our many-pronged attempts to control it or, of course, profit from
30 it. The popularity of wild swimming led to an increased interest in similar nature therapies, like 'forest bathing', said to counter illnesses including 'cancer, strokes, gastric ulcers, depression, anxiety and stress'. This morning I received an email advertising a restorative forest bathing retreat with overnight prices starting at £599 – a light lunch is included. Without wanting
35 to sound too much like a red-faced management consultant shouting in a beer garden, that is a lot of money to spend on going for a walk. Isn't it?

I have no doubt these moments of slowness and fresh air do help, but their ability to cure a person of all their pains surely also relies on serious structural support and a little bit of medicine, too. But the nail had been
40 banged: these spiritual experiences had been packaged and given price tags, and the magical sheen was dulled.

The second nail was, well, the sewage. Last year, the images of blissy swimmers we'd become accustomed to were replaced by pictures of floating faeces and stories about people falling horribly ill after ingesting raw sewage.
45 According to the Labour Party's analysis of Environment Agency data, since 2016 water companies have pumped raw sewage into our seas and rivers for more than 9m hours. And last week it was reported that hundreds of landfill dumps containing 'plastics, chemicals and other waste are a ticking timebomb threatening to leach pollution' on to beaches and into the sea.

banal cliché: *something that has become boring by repetition*

TIP

It can be effective to analyse how some features work to create an overall effect. For example, 'surge' and 'torrent' in the first paragraph both have similar meanings.

Knowledge   EXAM

Paper 2: Questions 4 and 5

Questions 4 and 5: Overview

Focus: Identify information | **Marks**: 2 marks (1 mark each) | **Time**: 2 minutes | **AO**: AO1

You should already have spent five minutes at the start of the exam reading the whole of Source 1. Questions 4 and 5 are very similar, both testing your ability to find explicit and implicit information in short, specific sections of the text. They are fairly simple information retrieval questions, resembling Paper 1 Questions 1 and 2.

They will look like this:

> **Q4** From lines x–x, identify **one** feature…
>
> **[1 mark]**

> **Q5** Read this extract…
>
> Identify **one** piece of information…
>
> **[1 mark]**

Questions 4 and 5: Strategy

Follow the steps below to respond to Question 4 and 5 tasks.

Step 1: For Question 4, put brackets around the specified lines in the source text.

Step 1: For Question 5, the lines will be printed for you in the exam paper.

Step 2: Decide which piece of information to use, then underline it.

Step 3: Write out your answer as a quotation or short paraphrase.

P2/Q4-5

Questions 4 and 5: Examples

Read the sample Questions 4 and 5 task and annotations below.

> **Q4** From this extract identify **one** thing the writer says about Christmas.
>
> [1 mark]

The question wording can vary. For example, it could refer to 'one feature' or 'one reason'.

There will be a focus – probably whatever is the main subject of the few lines selected. Both questions will ask you to identify a single piece of information

LINK

These questions refer to an extract from Source 5B: 'Why I skipped Christmas – and why you might like to try it too' by Sandy Summons. The full text is on pages 223–224.

> **Source 5B: 'Why I skipped Christmas – and why you might like to try it too' by Sandy Summons**
>
> Christmas is the most magical time of the year. But is it really? Now I'm no grinch. In fact, I absolutely love Christmas. Yet there was a stage when I needed to have a holiday from this popular holiday. So one year we decided to 'skip Christmas' to simplify our Christmas Day.

> **Q5** Read this extract (from the same text).
>
> Identify **one** reason the author gives for why some people find Christmas stressful.
>
> [1 mark]

> **Source 5B: 'Why I skipped Christmas – and why you might like to try it too' by Sandy Summons**
>
> 5   The festive season is overwhelming for many, especially with increased financial pressures and family obligations. A recent report revealed one in six people believe Christmas is the most stressful time of the year. Family conflict is often rife, with some sort of bickering over presents or food.

If there are several possible pieces of information, don't waste time weighing up which one to include: it's just 1 mark for each question. You will earn no extra marks by giving more than one piece of information, and you will earn no marks at all if you copy out the whole extract.

You may find it is easier to quote a few words than to paraphrase them.

Knowledge   147

Knowledge

EXAM

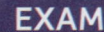

Paper 2: Questions 4 and 5

Questions 4 and 5: Sample answers

Now read the following sample answers to the Questions 4 and 5 example questions on page 147, alongside the examiner's comments.

Sample answers 1

These answers do not score any marks.

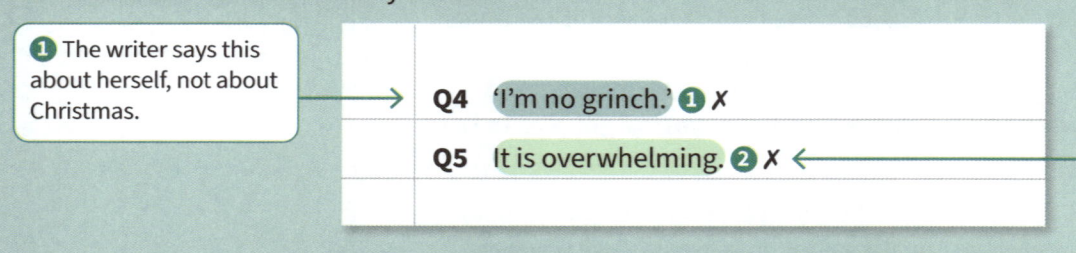

❶ The writer says this about herself, not about Christmas.

Q4 'I'm no grinch.' ❶ ✗

Q5 It is overwhelming. ❷ ✗

❷ This quotes from the text, but 'overwhelming' is really just another word for 'stressful'. It is not a *reason* for people finding Christmas stressful.

Sample answer 2

These answers both score 1 mark each.

❶ The student has quoted a relevant sentence, which is completely acceptable. The answer 'It is magical' would also have earned the 1 mark available.

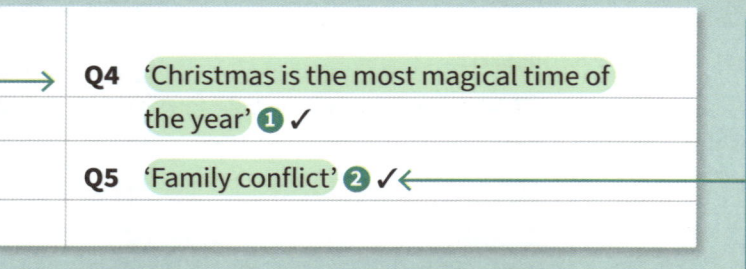

Q4 'Christmas is the most magical time of the year' ❶ ✓

Q5 'Family conflict' ❷ ✓

❷ The student has chosen one correct reason. Other acceptable answers would be: 'financial pressures', 'family obligations', or 'bickering'.

> **REMEMBER**
> - Keep your answers short.
> - You can quote from the source text, but make sure you use only the words you need.
> - Alternatively, you can paraphrase the relevant words.
> - Do not copy out long chunks of text.

Retrieval — EXAM — P2/Q4-5

Paper 2: Questions 4 and 5

Use the following questions to check your understanding of the knowledge covered in this section. Then cover the answers column with a piece of paper and write down as many as you can. Check and repeat.

	Questions	Answers
1	How long should you spend on Questions 4 and 5?	2 minutes (1 minute each)
2	How many marks are available for Questions 4 and 5?	2 marks (1 mark each)
3	What is the focus of Questions 4 and 5?	Retrieving information
4	You need to explain your answers. True or false?	False. Just quote an appropriate phrase or sentence, or put it in your own words.
5	You must write a full sentence. True or false?	False
6	You may be asked to analyse language. True or false?	False
7	Summarise the steps for tackling this question.	**Step 1:** for Question 4, bracket the specified lines. For Question 5, re-read the printed lines. **Step 2:** decide on a piece of information and underline it. **Step 3:** write out your quotation or paraphrase.

Previous questions

Now go back and use these questions to check your knowledge of previous topics.

	Questions	Answers
1	Name two text genres that could be included in Paper 2.	E.g., travelogue; biography; autobiography; article; letter.
2	What is a 'minor' sentence?	One that is grammatically incomplete because it does not have both a subject and a verb.
3	What is a 'relative clause'?	A phrase that only makes sense in relation to the main clause in a sentence, as in 'Darrel, <u>who was tired</u>, slept all the way.'

Practice EXAM

Exam-style questions

Answer the exam-style questions on pages 150–151.

4.1

> **Q4** From lines 1–4, identify **one** thing in the author's garden.
>
> [1 mark]

> **Source 6B:** *Deep Country* **by Neil Ansell**
>
> Without the sheep coming in to trim it, the grass grew in rank tussocks that I had to hack back with a sickle. Besides the fruit tree, the jackdaw ash and the cotoneaster next to the porch, there was one small rhododendron and a clump of blackthorn by the gate.

LINK

These questions refer to an extract from Source 6B: *Deep Country* by Neil Ansell. The full text is on pages 226–227.

5.1

> **Q5** Read this extract (from the same text).
>
> Identify **one** thing that the author did.
>
> [1 mark]

> **Source 6B:** *Deep Country* **by Neil Ansell**
>
> I planted out a larch to stand in for the lonesome pine, and in the southwest corner of the garden a beech, which will one day afford the cottage a little shelter from the prevailing wind. Then a couple of rowans, for berries for the birds, and a buddleia for the butterflies. Apart from a row
> 10 of poppies and wild flowers along the fence, I didn't trouble with flowers. I needed the land for food.

EXAM TIP

In your answer, you should:
- focus only on the specified lines. The information you need is all within this short extract
- focus on the *specific topic* mentioned in the question. This means that the answer must focus on that and *not* on anything else
- clearly and precisely list your answers.

4.2

> **Q4** From lines 1–5, identify **one** feature of the author's train journey.
>
> [1 mark]

> **Source 7B: 'Baghdad to Basra, On the Wrong Side of the Tracks' by Cesar G. Soriano**
>
> Jabar, Sabah and most of the male passengers passed the time on the long train ride by chain-smoking. It wasn't long before the carriages were thick with smoke. For non-smokers like me, relief could only be found by sticking our heads out of the cracked windows or putting our noses to one
> 5 of the many bullet holes.

LINK

These questions refer to an extract from Source 7B: 'Baghdad to Basra, On the Wrong Side of the Tracks' by Cesar G. Soriano. The full text is on pages 229–230.

P2/Q4-5

5.2

Q5 Read this extract.

Identify **one** piece of information about the family.

[1 mark]

Source 7B: 'Baghdad to Basra, On the Wrong Side of the Tracks' by Cesar G. Soriano

Despite all this, across the aisle from me, Abdul Yaseen, his wife and their four children were ecstatic about their first-ever train adventure. They were returning home to Basra after attending a wedding near Baghdad.

4.3

Q4 From lines 1–6, identify **one** thing that Sophie Skellern did.

[1 mark]

LINK

These questions refer to an extract from Source 8B: 'When wild swimming is deeply dangerous' by Helen Carroll. The full text is on pages 231–232.

Source 8B: 'When wild swimming is deeply dangerous' by Helen Carroll

When Sophie Skellern lost her grandma, whom she had nursed through her dying days during the first lockdown, the one thing that helped ease her grief was open-water swimming. Whatever the weather, three times a week, Sophie would pull on her swimming costume and head to the lake at Sale
5 Water Park, near her home in Manchester, where, front crawling through the chilly waters, she would briefly forget her sadness.

5.3

Q5 Read this extract.

Identify **one** thing that helped to save Sophie Skellern.

[1 mark]

Source 8B: 'When wild swimming is deeply dangerous' by Helen Carroll

But last month — if she hadn't had a float and her boyfriend on hand — she could have died while swimming in a lake near Mount Snowdon during a holiday.

Practice 151

Knowledge · EXAM

Paper 2: Question 6

Question 6: Overview

- **Focus:** How successfully the writer has achieved an aim
- **Marks:** 15 marks
- **Time:** 20 minutes
- **AO:** AO4

Question 6 does not ask you to analyse details of language and structure, but to **evaluate** the author's use of ideas, events, themes, or settings. The stated author's aim will vary, but the task will always be to evaluate the author's success in achieving this aim.

Question 6 is based on the whole text. It gives you a statement about what the author has aimed to do in the text, and asks you to *evaluate how successfully* this aim has been achieved. The question wording is largely fixed; the difference is in what *aim* is identified. This question is similar to Paper 1 Question 4.

Here is an example:

> **Q6** In this extract, the writer attempts to…
>
> Evaluate how successfully this is achieved.
>
> Support your views with detailed reference to the text.
>
> [15 marks]

TIP: Students often lose marks on this question because they just write an analysis of the text without critically evaluating its success in achieving the particular aim stated in the question.

The first sentence of the question may state which type of text the source is, e.g., persuasive, entertaining, etc. It will also be where you find the focus of the question. The other parts of the question will always be the same.

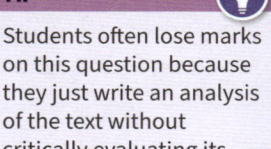

P2/Q6

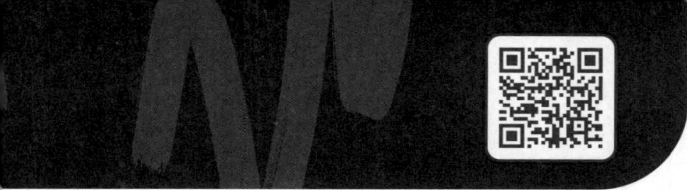

Question 6: Strategy

Follow the steps below to respond to a Question 6 task.

Step 1: Re-read the statement of author's intention in the question. Highlight the statement's key words.

Step 2: Re-read the whole text. Highlight key sections that seem to be trying to persuade the reader. Identify the main thrust of each paragraph – its idea, theme, setting, and any event described, and how it contributes to the big idea in the question.

Step 3: Plan your response, always remembering to focus on *how successful in achieving the aim* a particular feature is.

Mark anything you think is especially successful in persuading the reader. This might include:

- anecdotal evidence
- humour
- **reasoning**
- key ideas.

If there are parts that you feel are less successful, mark those too. Evaluation should weigh up the degree of success. However, you may only find good points. If you find and mention a weakness, be sure to give evidence and an explanation of your view.

Step 4: Decide on the order in which to arrange your points. It may work well just to make your way through each section of the text. With some texts it might be better to deal with each aspect in turn.

Step 5: Write your response.

This question requires you to write an opening statement that starts with a clear indication of how far you think the aim is achieved. You will then analyse the relevant ideas, themes, settings, and events in around 4–6 paragraphs which each:

- respond to the statement
- give evidence to back up your ideas
- evaluate the writer's use of ideas, setting, themes, and events
- use **evaluative language**, such as 'is very effective in…' or 'creates a powerful sense of…'
- explain the effect on the reader
- link to the original statement.

Knowledge

Knowledge — EXAM

Paper 2: Question 6

Question 6: Example

Read the sample Question 6 and annotations below. Remember that it is based on the whole source text.

> **Q6** In this extract, the writer attempts to **persuade the reader to consider simplifying their Christmas.**
>
> **Evaluate how successfully this is achieved.**
>
> **Support your views with detailed reference to the text.**
>
> **[15 marks]**

You will be given a statement about what the author is trying to achieve.

It is vital to provide supportive textual evidence in the form of short quotations or references.

Your response should explain how far you think the author has succeeded. You must 'evaluate' the text – this will involve analysing the use of ideas, events, themes, or settings, and their effects.

TIP

You will be given a context box at the top of the source that provides important information about the text. Be sure to read this!

LINK

This question refers to an extract from Source 5B: 'Why I skipped Christmas – and why you might like to try it too' by Sandy Summons. The full text is on pages 223–224.

Source 5B: 'Why I skipped Christmas – and why you might like to try it too' by Sandy Summons

This extract is from an article, 'Why I skipped Christmas – and why you might like to try it too', by Sandy Summons, in the *Guardian* (December 2022).

Christmas is the most magical time of the year. But is it really? Now I'm no grinch*. In fact, I absolutely love Christmas. Yet there was a stage when I needed to have a holiday from this popular holiday. So one year we decided to 'skip Christmas' to simplify our Christmas Day.

5 The festive season is overwhelming for many, especially with increased financial pressures and family obligations. A recent report revealed one in six people believe Christmas is the most stressful time of the year. Family conflict is often rife, with some sort of bickering over presents or food. And then there's the family member who has too much to drink and thinks it
10 is their duty to sing a 'special' rendition of Mariah Carey's 'All I Want for Christmas'. Unlike friends, we can't choose our relatives!

When I was younger, Christmas Day seemed so much simpler. With only my parents and siblings, it was fun and uncomplicated. We spent time playing with our new toys and wearing the clothing items we received. I
15 still remember getting green knickerbockers one Christmas (for those that don't know, a style of shorts that were very hip back then), and I was utterly delighted. We didn't need anything more.

These days are quite different. My husband and I usually celebrate with our extended families. However, over the years it has become more demanding.
20 It's not that we didn't want to spend time with family. But traipsing all over

the countryside to catch up with relatives and visiting, on average, four to five homes in one day became too much. Yes, at one stage we did that exhausting amount.

One year after being inspired by the movie *Christmas with the Kranks*, we thought we'd change it up. In the movie Tim Allen and Jamie Lee Curtis, who play Luther and Nora Krank, boycott their traditional family Christmas. They choose not to partake in anything Christmas-related including presents, family gatherings, parties, or decorations.

Similarly, we chose to skip the 30C heat, not put up a Christmas tree or to attend our family Christmas festivities. And even though this may seem drastic, to escape the obligations of Christmas we jetted off on an overseas holiday to New York.

While most of our Christmases have been jam-packed, we were able to spend the day how we wanted to. After a lazy breakfast at the hotel, we watched a basketball game at Madison Square Garden, then finished the day walking through a snow-laden Central Park. Spending the time together with our little core family was memorable. It was relaxed and enjoyable.

Funnily enough, skipping our traditional Christmas that year gave us clarity on how we wanted to spend future Christmases. It made us look forward to a simpler Christmas with our extended family. Previously, we had bought presents for our parents, siblings and their partners, plus all their children. It was exhausting, not to mention all the presents destined for either the regifting pile or for landfill. These days only the nieces and nephews aged under 21 receive gifts. In the past, the host would have a meltdown from cooking up a storm, but now we all bring food to share. We realised we enjoyed being with the family but we also wanted to do what makes us happy. To slow down and enjoy stress free, quality time with each other.

grinch: *someone who spoils the enjoyment of others*

Knowledge EXAM

Paper 2: Question 6

Question 6: Sample answers

Now read the following sample answers to the Question 6 example question on page 154, alongside the examiner's comments.

Sample answer 1

This answer scores less than half the marks available.

① This shows misunderstanding of the author's technique, which uses a rhetorical question to interest the reader and raise doubts about the conventional view of Christmas.

> The author begins confusingly because she says Christmas is magical, asks if it is, so it seems like she doesn't think this, then says she 'loves' it, then she 'skipped' it. It's like she can't decide. ①
> The author is successful though in saying that the 'festive season is overwhelming for many, especially with increased financial pressures and family obligations.' This is very true, Christmas has become all about money. She gives reasons why Christmas is hard, like conflict and drunks. It is not successful when she refers to things no one knows, like Mariah Carey and the film later on, 'The Kranks'. ②
> The author compares her olden-day Christmas with her adult one. It used to be 'fun and uncomplicated' which is what people want. Having to visit 'four to five homes' sounds really 'exhausting'. She makes it clear that her Christmas used to be simple when she didn't have many presents, but she still enjoyed it. Now the traipsing is too much. ③
> The last paragraph is the most successful because she found out what really mattered, not having a 'meltdown' but just simple 'quality time'. Most presents end up in 'landfill'. ④

② This gives too long a quotation and fails to explain *why* the author is successful here. It also wanders into a personal opinion on Christmas. The sentence 'She gives reasons…' is too vague and there is no explanation of its effect or success. The evaluation of what is 'not successful' is fairly valid.

③ This is the most successful paragraph because it identifies a structural feature and explains why it works well, although the final sentence could be clearer. Quotation marks should be used for the quoted evidence.

④ A valid opinion is given, though this could be developed more clearly. The point about 'landfill' is not quite accurate, and needs to be developed to make a comment on the wastefulness of Christmas.

Examiner's comments

This response begins with evaluation, but is based on a misunderstanding. Quotation is occasionally used effectively, but not always. The student tends to make promising points that are insufficiently developed, or to refer to the text without explaining sufficiently why it is, or is not, effective. Some statements are vague or inaccurate. The evaluation is not always backed up with evidence.

P2/Q6

Sample answer 2

This is a full answer which scores high marks.

❶ The opening statement refers to the question, indicates the student's assessment, and shows how structural progression helps to make the article persuasive.

The writer argues persuasively for simplifying Christmas by moving from typical Christmas stresses, to memories, to personal anecdote. She hooks the reader by calling Christmas 'magical', but immediately undermines this with a rhetorical question, 'But is it really?' This is effective because it makes readers curious to know more. ❶

The writer first makes it clear that she isn't anti-Christmas — 'I'm no grinch' — and in fact loves it, but she gives the idea that Christmas is hard work by saying she once 'needed to have a holiday' from it. This avoids putting off readers who love Christmas, but makes them interested in why she needed a break. ❷

Her **argument** for avoiding Christmas is sympathetic: 'The festive season is overwhelming for many.' This makes it seem as if she cares about people who find it hard. She follows this with an effective list of reasons, including 'financial pressures', 'family obligations' and 'family conflict' — all things that most readers might relate to. Her statistic that 'one in six' people find Christmas the 'most stressful time of the year' is effective because it makes readers compare this with their own experience. She also avoids being too negative by introducing humour about drunken relatives. ❸

The middle two paragraphs make an accessible contrast between the past ('When I was younger...') and the present ('These days...'). This comparison could help to persuade readers because the old-time Christmas was 'fun and uncomplicated', whereas her modern one is hard work, 'traipsing all over the countryside' to see relatives, which is 'exhausting'. However, her memories may seem sentimental. ❹

She makes 'skipping' Christmas sound like a more enjoyable alternative to 'obligations of Christmas', and her 'jetting off' to New York sounds glamorous. However, this would be less persuasive for readers on lower incomes. The most persuasive idea comes at the end, because 'stress free, quality time' is what most readers want. ❺

❷ Identifies how the writer introduces her ideas and how these ideas would appeal to readers and make them want to read on.

❸ This provides textual evidence using short, well-chosen quotations, interprets it (as sympathetic), and explains the effect on readers. It identifies the use of a statistic and of humour, explaining their persuasive effect. It also successfully refers to the humour without unnecessarily quoting the text.

❹ The student picks out a structural feature which is an important part of the persuasive technique. It also makes a valid criticism based on the readers' possible response.

❺ Here the student weighs up the article, referring to the story and its possible mixed effect on readers, and gives an opinion on what is most effective in the article and why.

Knowledge

Knowledge — EXAM

Paper 2: Question 6

Examiner's comments
This response is clearly focused on the question statement from the start, and remains so. It shows an awareness of the writer's deliberate techniques and their effect on the reader, as well as an awareness of how the text might be more effective for some readers than for others. It evaluates the text using evaluative language, and is not afraid to say in what ways the text is less effective. It is particularly effective in talking about the juxtaposition between the author's childhood and adult Christmases, and how this helps to persuade the reader.

REMEMBER

- You must respond to the statement of author's intention in the question during your answer.
- You must evaluate the ideas, themes, settings, and events presented by the author.
- Consider both successful and unsuccessful attempts to influence the reader.
- You need to support your analysis with relevant evidence from the text.

Key terms — Make sure you can write a definition for these key terms.

argument   evaluate   evaluative language   reasoning

Retrieval — EXAM — P2/Q6

Paper 2: Question 6

Use the following questions to check your understanding of the knowledge covered in this section. Then cover the answers column with a piece of paper and write down as many as you can. Check and repeat.

Questions / Answers

#	Question	Answer
1	How long should you spend on Question 6?	20 minutes
2	How many marks are available for Question 6?	15 marks
3	What is the focus of Question 6?	How successfully the writer has achieved a stated aim.
4	What kind of language is used here? 'This paragraph is especially effective…' 'The author writes very persuasively…' 'A particularly convincing point is…'	Evaluative language
5	You should use your response to explore your own ideas and opinions on topics in a text. True or false?	False
6	How much of the source text should you consider in Question 6?	All of it
7	You can criticise the text. True or false?	True. Note that if you do, you must give your reason and support it with evidence.
8	Summarise the five steps for tackling this question.	**Step 1:** re-read the statement of author's intention and highlight the key words. **Step 2:** highlight especially relevant parts of the source text. **Step 3:** plan your answer, focusing on your evaluation. **Step 4:** decide on the order in which to present your answer. **Step 5:** write your response.

Previous questions

Now go back and use these questions to check your knowledge of previous topics.

#	Question	Answer
1	What is a 'topic sentence' in a text?	One that is given usually at the start of a paragraph to tell the reader what the rest of the paragraph will be about.
2	What is meant by 'juxtaposition'?	Placing two ideas or images next to each other to highlight differences or similarities.
3	What pronouns are typically used in a 'first-person' viewpoint?	'I', 'we'

Retrieval 159

Practice EXAM

Exam-style questions

Answer the exam-style questions on pages 160–163.

6.1

Q6 In this extract there is an attempt to convey what it is like to live alone in the countryside.

Evaluate how successfully this is achieved.

Support your views with detailed reference to the text.

[12 marks]

LINK

This question refers to an extract from Source 6B: *Deep Country* by Neil Ansell. The full text is on pages 226–227.

Source 6B: *Deep Country* by Neil Ansell

This extract is taken from *Deep Country*, by Neil Ansell, who left a life in London, living communally and working with teenagers in care, to live alone in a remote cottage in Wales, where he managed to grow his own food on previously uncultivated land.

Without the sheep coming in to trim it, the grass grew in rank tussocks that I had to hack back with a sickle. Besides the fruit tree, the jackdaw ash and the cotoneaster next to the porch, there was one small rhododendron and a clump of blackthorn by the gate. Once, before my time, a solitary pine had
5 stood guard over the house from above the quarry wall, but it had been unlucky.... I planted out a larch to stand in for the lonesome pine, and in the southwest corner of the garden a beech, which will one day afford the cottage a little shelter from the prevailing wind. Then a couple of rowans, for berries for the birds, and a buddleia for the butterflies. Apart from a row
10 of poppies and wild flowers along the fence, I didn't trouble with flowers. I needed the land for food.

Although I planted a patch of herbs – coriander, dill and parsley, which were unavailable locally – my priority was the heavy vegetables. I didn't want to be hauling sackfuls of potatoes up the mountainside when I could be
15 growing them myself. Preparing the land was hard work; the roots of the grass grew deep and tangled. Then I had to pick out all the rocks, carefully lift any daffodil bulbs for transplantation elsewhere, and lime the soil. Each year I would dig an extra patch, and prepare another for the next year by pegging down a sheet of tarpaulin with bricks to kill off the grass. I didn't
20 want to use any pesticides, and besides the lime I bought no fertilizer. Each winter, when the bats were long gone to their hibernation roost, I would clamber up into the loft and shovel up bagfuls of guano*. It was dry and powdery and odourless, and it seemed somehow appropriate that the bats who shared my home with me should help me grow my food.

25 I had never grown anything before, I had never stayed in one place long enough to even think about it, and had no idea what would grow well at this altitude, and in a location so exposed to the elements, so it was a process of trial and error. Each year I would try a few new things; if they grew well they would become a fixture; if they failed I would abandon them and try
30 something else. I had a small patch of early potatoes, and a larger patch of

main crops. I got a metal dustbin which I kept in the pantry and would fill it to the top with these, enough to last the whole year. Onions and garlic I hung on strings on the woodshed wall, as the mice didn't ever bother them. Garlic was the only thing I planted in autumn; growing garlic seems magical in its
35 simplicity. Take a head of garlic, break it into cloves and plant them in a row. By the next year each clove will have turned into a new head.

Carrots and parsnips I stored in the ground and lifted when I needed them. The carrots in particular were a revelation; they are hard to grow in most places because of the depredations of the carrot fly, but the altitude here
40 kept my crop pest-free. They grew to over a pound in weight without becoming woody, were such a deep orange they were almost red, and tasted better than any others I have had before or since.

guano: *droppings from bats or seabirds*

EXAM TIP

In your answer, you should:

- consider the whole of the source text
- respond to the statement of author's intention in your answer
- evaluate the ideas, themes, settings, and events presented by the author
- support your analysis with evidence form the source text.

6.2

Q6 In this extract there is an attempt to interest the reader in train travel.

Evaluate how successfully this is achieved.

Support your views with detailed reference to the text.

[12 marks]

LINK

This question refers to an extract from Source 7B: 'Baghdad to Basra, On the Wrong Side of the Tracks' by Cesar G. Soriano. The full text is on pages 229–230.

Source 7B: 'Baghdad to Basra, On the Wrong Side of the Tracks' by Cesar G. Soriano

This extract is taken from Cesar G. Soriano's essay 'Baghdad to Basra, On the Wrong Side of the Tracks' from *Best of Lonely Planet Travel Writing*. The writer describes a long train journey in Iraq.

Jabar, Sabah and most of the male passengers passed the time on the long train ride by chain-smoking. It wasn't long before the carriages were thick with smoke. For non-smokers like me, relief could only be found by sticking our heads out of the cracked windows or putting our noses to one
5 of the many bullet holes. Despite all this, across the aisle from me, Abdul Yaseen, his wife and their four children were ecstatic about their first-ever train adventure. They were returning home to Basra after attending a wedding near Baghdad. 'I like the train because it's more comfortable, slow and lets the kids have a chance to see the countryside,' he said. His wide-
10 eyed children were peering from the windows, wearing their best clothes, reminiscent of a time when travelling was actually an occasion for dressing up. Abdul's nine-year-old daughter, Haba, surprised to see an American on board, latched onto us and peppered me with questions in broken English: 'Mister, where you from? You married? You have children? You like Arabian
15 music? You like Jennifer Lopez? Mister, buy me Pepsi!'

Around 4pm the train pulled into the station in Nasiriyah, one of the largest cities in southern Iraq. But, unlike our stops at other cities, the train did

Practice EXAM

Exam-style questions

> not immediately pull out but sat at the platform. And sat. And sat. There was no announcement or explanation for our delay. The thermometer
> 20 on the platform read 100°F. Inside, the train was becoming a steel oven, baking us alive. Within minutes, we were drenched in sweat. The stench of body odour, dirty baby diapers and the raw sewage on the tracks became unbearable. An old woman fainted and was carried outside into the shade and doused with water, and many more of us followed her out into the air.
> 25 Angry passengers took out their rage on the conductor, who explained that the station manager had refused to give clearance for the train to proceed. Apparently there was only one working track between Nasiriyah and Basra, and a northbound cargo train already had dibs*. An hour later, without a whistle or warning, the train began pulling out of the station. Of course, most
> 30 of us were still out on the platform and had to run and jump back onto the moving train.
>
> South of Nasiriyah, we reached the most scenic point of the journey. The endless monochrome images of brown, dusty villages were replaced by lush, green landscape, fields of corn, alfalfa and date palms. This was the Arab
> 35 Marshland, a fertile region between the Tigris and Euphrates Rivers that is the legendary location of the Garden of Eden. The setting sun blazed into the windows of the right side of the train. There were no curtains or shades to pull down, so passengers took chewing gum from their mouths and used it to stick newspapers onto the windows to shield their heads from the sun. Ah,
> 40 so that was why there was gum stuck all over the windows.
>
> **dibs:** *priority*

6.3

Q6 In this extract there is an attempt to convey the risks of wild swimming. Evaluate how successfully this is achieved.

Support your views with detailed reference to the text.

[12 marks]

> **LINK**
>
> This question refers to an extract from Source 8B: 'When wild swimming is deeply dangerous' by Helen Carroll. The full text is on pages 231–232.

Source 8B: 'When wild swimming is deeply dangerous' by Helen Carroll

This extract is from an article published in the *Daily Mail*: 'When wild swimming is deeply dangerous' by Helen Carroll (July 2021).

> When Sophie Skellern lost her grandma, whom she had nursed through her dying days during the first lockdown, the one thing that helped ease her grief was open-water swimming. Whatever the weather, three times a week, Sophie would pull on her swimming costume and head to the lake at Sale
> 5 Water Park, near her home in Manchester, where, front crawling through the

chilly waters, she would briefly forget her sadness. In fact, wild swimming left Sophie, 29, feeling so exhilarated that it had never occurred to her what a risky form of exercise it can be. But last month — if she hadn't had a float and her boyfriend on hand — she could have died while swimming in a lake near Mount Snowdon during a holiday.

'I was half a mile from the water's edge when both my calves cramped up and I couldn't move or kick them, the pain was so intense,' recalls Sophie, shuddering at the memory of what happened in Llyn Gwynant. 'I felt almost paralysed from the waist down as I lay on my back trying to float. Luckily I knew to immediately lie on my back and put the tow float I was pulling across my chest. Someone new to this may not have had a float with them and I dread to think what would have happened if I'd panicked. That's when people drown. However, the 30 minutes it took for the cramping to pass were among the scariest of my life. Fortunately, my partner, Jack, was also in the lake, in a kayak about 100 metres away. He noticed I'd stopped swimming and was on my back and I was able to raise my arm and beckon him over.

'It was a tiny one-person kayak, so there was no way he could have pulled me in, or even towed me back to shore, but he stayed beside me, giving me sips of water, while I tried to point my toes to stretch out the muscles, until the cramping finally eased enough for normal sensations to return to my legs. It would have been so easy to start hyperventilating. However, thankfully, I forced myself to keep taking deep breaths and stay calm, because getting stressed and anxious in water is the very worst thing you can do. After half an hour, my legs felt strong enough for Jack to escort me back to the shore.'

Sophie, who organises art exhibitions and is studying for a PhD, believes her legs cramped because she had not drunk enough water and had become dehydrated in the heat, nor had she left enough of a gap between eating lunch and getting into the water — mistakes she will not repeat.

She's one of many women who enjoy so-called 'wild swimming', which has caught on like wildfire in recent years. Barely a day goes by without someone in the public eye — supermodel Helena Christensen, TV presenters Fearne Cotton and Susannah Constantine and even former Prime Minister David Cameron are all fans — espousing its virtues. From improving sleep, boosting immunity and metabolism, to 'significantly reducing' symptoms of anxiety and depression, outdoor swimming is seen by many as a cure-all.

Yet despite its benefits, there is no denying that swimming in open water is far riskier than a trip to your local pool. Since the heatwave began on July 14, at least 40 people have lost their lives in open water — rivers, lakes, natural pools and the sea — treble the usual rate of water deaths, which average 19 a year.

But wild swimming poses risks whatever the weather, with dangers including near freezing temperatures, water-born contaminants and hidden obstructions.

Knowledge — EXAM

Paper 2: Question 7(a)

Question 7(a): Overview

- **Focus:** Similarities between two texts
- **Marks:** 6 marks
- **Time:** 8 minutes
- **AO:** AO1

Question 7(a) is based on the whole of Source texts 1 and 2. It tests the second part of AO1: 'Select and **synthesise** evidence from different texts.'

Synthesising is bringing together shared elements from two sources, finding links between them, and summarising this information in the sources.

The question will ask you to find **similarities** between texts, focusing on a particular thing, such as people or their experiences. You will be looking for information that the texts have in common. The question will look like this:

> **Q7(a)** The two texts are about…
>
> What similarities do…
>
> Use evidence from **both** texts to support your answer.   **[6 marks]**

You should try to find *three* similarities with quotations from *each* text. Whenever you comment on one text, make sure you tie it in to a similarity with the other text.

> **TIP**
> Look for factual information. In Question 7(a) you will not be asked to compare the writers' views and perspectives, or to write about differences.

P2/Q7(a)

Question 7(a): Strategy

Follow the steps below to respond to a Question 7(a) task.

Step 1: Read the question – what is the focus? Identify the specific thing you are being asked to look for.

Step 2: Read both source texts again and highlight anything you find which is linked to the question focus. Make brief notes on the similarities. These could be in two columns.

Step 3: Look back through the sections you have highlighted and find *three* clear similarities between the information in the two texts. You should use quotations from *each* text.

Step 4: Write your response.

You might find some of the **comparative** words and phrases below helpful.

> whereas...   on the other hand...   however...   similarly...
> in the same way that...   likewise...

You might also find it useful to model some of your sentences on the sentence starters below.

> The two writers are similar in that ...
> One thing the two events have in common is ...
> Both explorers show ...
> Another similarity is that ...
> The writers are also alike in their ...

Knowledge

Knowledge EXAM

Paper 2: Question 7(a)

Question 7(a): Example

Read the sample Question 7(a) and annotations below. Remember that this question will relate to the whole of both sources. In the exam, you will have to refer back to the sources provided separately. They will not be reprinted with the exam question.

> **Q7(a)** The two texts are about Christmas.
> What similarities do the writers share in these extracts?
> Use evidence from both texts to support your answer.
> [40 marks]

Focus on the specific topic mentioned in the question; for example, here it is about Christmas. This means that the answer must focus on this and not on anything else.

You must use details from the whole of both texts for this question.

You are looking for similarities which link to the topic (e.g., their awareness of other people's attitudes in the above question). You are not looking for differences, or comparing writing techniques.

You may need to infer information (work it out from the textual clues) to find similarities. The information may not be stated explicitly. Any similarities you make need to be supported by evidence from both sources.

Source 5A: 'Bah humbug to all of you who just hate Christmas' by David Mitchell

This text is taken from 'Bah humbug to all of you who just hate Christmas' by David Mitchell, a newspaper article published in 2008. David Mitchell is a comedian who is giving his opinion about people who don't like Christmas.

My official policy on Christmas is that I like it. That says a lot more about me than that I'm partial to a day spent watching TV and stuffing my face. More fundamentally, it shows that I can't stand the thought of our most public and celebratory festival being a lie. It is a happy and magical time, I'm insisting,
5 for deeper and more sinister reasons than a liking for Brazil nuts and *Shrek 3*.

Other people – my enemies – love to hate Christmas. They rejoice in looking at the sparkle, the bustle, the drinking and the queues and muttering: 'Christmas is a nightmare'; 'We're going to Jane's parents – it's going to be a living hell'; 'The sooner we can forget all the expense and false jollity, this
10 great capitalist hypocrisy dance, the better, I say,' as if commerce* were as exclusive to this time of year as mince pies.

As they grumble and sneer their way through the season – seek each other out for affirmation that it's all just a sick joke and that participating is as joyous as diarrhoea and as prudent as a pyramid scheme* I stand shocked
15 and afraid. To the boy I once was, heart buoyed* by the air of magic, and expectation of an acquisitive* nature about to be satisfied, this is a colossal slap in the face: it has finally all ended in tears.

So I must sustain my policy. It's vulnerable, I know. I'm not at a good time of life for liking Christmas. The childhood enchantment has long gone, as has

LINK

This question refers to the whole text of Source 5A: 'Bah humbug to all of you who just hate Christmas', by David Mitchell, and the whole text of Source 5B: 'Why I skipped Christmas – and why you might like to try it too', by Sandy Summons. These sources can also be found on pages 222–224.

TIP

Remember to compare the specific thing the question says you should look for. Don't lose marks by comparing the texts as a whole!

the excitement about presents, and I have no children to help me rediscover it vicariously*. Meanwhile, shopping is stressful, tree lights never work, turkey's not the best meat in the world and Christmas pudding is weird. If I'm not careful, I'll realise I'm only in it for the booze.

But I'm still too tribal to accept this conclusion. We of the Christmas-liking tribe will keep the Christmas-cynic tribe in perpetual subjugation – they will be made to join in whether they like it or not and particularly if not. They will never, if we can help it, be permitted to 'get away somewhere hot' but, if they do, we can be confident that our allies overseas will besiege them with spray-on snow and piped-in Slade even as they sweat round the pool.

This is a time when we all come together to disagree about how Christmas is supposed to be done. It's not so much 'love thy neighbour' as 'mock the neon Santa on thy neighbour's roof'. I think these divisions might be what saves my pro-Christmas policy because I love asserting my way of celebrating it over everyone else's. In another life, I could have been a great witchfinder general, paranoid anti-communist or warrior ant. I will root out people who slightly differ from me in their Christmas traditions and blow them away with the twin barrels of my British disdain gun, which are, of course, snobbery and inverse snobbery.

To test your suitability for this fight, consider your reaction to the phrase: 'We actually had goose this year.' It's not the nature of your reaction that's important, but its strength. I'm hoping for a strong one. Either: 'Yes of course, goose is a much tastier meat and an older tradition. I can't believe those turkey-eating scum are suffered to live. They should be locked up in the same hell sheds where the bland objects of their culinary affection are chemically spawned.' Or, and this is the one I favour: '[Get] back to Borough Market with your talk of goose deliciousness. We're supposed to eat turkey – that's now the tradition.'

---

commerce: *buying and selling*
pyramid scheme: *a sales scheme: people pay to join and only make money by recruiting others*
buoyed: *lifted up*
acquisitive: *wanting possessions*
vicariously: *through someone else*

Knowledge

Paper 2: Question 7(a)

Source 5B: 'Why I skipped Christmas – and why you might like to try it too' by Sandy Summons

> This extract is from an article, 'Why I skipped Christmas – and why you might like to try it too', by Sandy Summons, in the *Guardian* (December 2022).

Christmas is the most magical time of the year. But is it really? Now I'm no grinch*. In fact, I absolutely love Christmas. Yet there was a stage when I needed to have a holiday from this popular holiday. So one year we decided to 'skip Christmas' to simplify our Christmas Day.

5 The festive season is overwhelming for many, especially with increased financial pressures and family obligations. A recent report revealed one in six people believe Christmas is the most stressful time of the year. Family conflict is often rife, with some sort of bickering over presents or food. And then there's the family member who has too much to drink and thinks it
10 is their duty to sing a 'special' rendition of Mariah Carey's 'All I Want for Christmas'. Unlike friends, we can't choose our relatives!

When I was younger, Christmas Day seemed so much simpler. With only my parents and siblings, it was fun and uncomplicated. We spent time playing with our new toys and wearing the clothing items we received. I
15 still remember getting green knickerbockers one Christmas (for those that don't know, a style of shorts that were very hip back then), and I was utterly delighted. We didn't need anything more.

These days are quite different. My husband and I usually celebrate with our extended families. However, over the years it has become more demanding.
20 It's not that we didn't want to spend time with family. But traipsing all over the countryside to catch up with relatives and visiting, on average, four to five homes in one day became too much. Yes, at one stage we did that exhausting amount.

One year after being inspired by the movie *Christmas with the Kranks*, we
25 thought we'd change it up. In the movie Tim Allen and Jamie Lee Curtis, who play Luther and Nora Krank, boycott their traditional family Christmas. They choose not to partake in anything Christmas-related including presents, family gatherings, parties, or decorations.

Similarly, we chose to skip the 30C heat, not put up a Christmas tree or to attend our family Christmas festivities. And even though this may seem drastic, to escape the obligations of Christmas we jetted off on an overseas holiday to New York.

While most of our Christmases have been jam-packed, we were able to spend the day how we wanted to. After a lazy breakfast at the hotel, we watched a basketball game at Madison Square Garden, then finished the day walking through a snow-laden Central Park. Spending the time together with our little core family was memorable. It was relaxed and enjoyable.

Funnily enough, skipping our traditional Christmas that year gave us clarity on how we wanted to spend future Christmases. It made us look forward to a simpler Christmas with our extended family. Previously, we had bought presents for our parents, siblings and their partners, plus all their children. It was exhausting, not to mention all the presents destined for either the regifting pile or for landfill. These days only the nieces and nephews aged under 21 receive gifts. In the past, the host would have a meltdown from cooking up a storm, but now we all bring food to share. We realised we enjoyed being with the family but we also wanted to do what makes us happy. To slow down and enjoy stress free, quality time with each other.

---

grinch: *someone who spoils the enjoyment of others*

Knowledge — EXAM

Paper 2: Question 7(a)

Question 7(a): Sample answers

Now read the following sample answers to the question on page 166, alongside the examiner's comments.

Sample answer 1

This answer receives less than half the marks available.

❶ The opening sentence is unhelpful in answering the question. The student chooses evidence poorly, missing the irony of Source A's exaggeration, quoting Source B out of context, and attempting to identify a difference, when the question asks for similarities.

> Both writers both say a lot of different and the same things about Christmas. Writer 1 really loves it, 'I like it', and thinks people who hate it should be 'locked up in the same hell sheds', Writer 2 likes to go on holiday at Christmas 'I needed to have a holiday' and so is different to Writer 1 this way. ❶ Both writers had lovely childhood Christmases. David has 'an air of magic' and for Writer 2 it was 'fun and uncomplicated'. ❷ David says he finds 'shopping is stressful, tree lights never work'. The other one is also stressed by it — 'Christmas is the most stressful time of the year'. ❸

❷ The evidence here is more helpful, though it is not well presented. Christmas had 'an air of magic' for the young David Mitchell, rather than it being he who had the air of magic.

❸ The student has spotted the use of 'stressful' in both texts, and therefore identified a superficial similarity without taking into account that the Source A writer loves Christmas, and the Source B writer is quoting a report on how people view it.

Examiner's comments
The answer makes some valid points, with a little evidence, but includes an inaccurate conclusion and shows misunderstandings of the text. The response needs more detailed exploration and examples of similarities to achieve a higher mark.

REMEMBER

- You must identify the specific focus of the question rather than just comparing the texts.
- You must refer to the whole of both source texts.
- Look for clear similarities and select evidence to support your points.
- Using comparative terms in your answer will allow you to keep the focus on similarities.

P2/Q7(a)

Sample answer 2

This full answer receives high marks.

> Both writers have expectations about Christmas based on nostalgic childhood memories. Mitchell recalls his heart being 'buoyed by the air of magic', while Summons remembers her Christmases as 'fun and uncomplicated'. Both talk about what presents they were given. Summons remembers her 'green knickerbockers' and Mitchell remembers his 'expectation' of presents. ❶ The writers are also alike in showing an awareness of the attitudes of others. Mitchell talks about people hating 'the bustle, the drinking and the queues', while Summons acknowledges that Christmas is 'overwhelming for many', and the problem of people having 'too much to drink'. ❷ Both also like to watch TV and films. Mitchell admits he is 'partial to a day spent watching TV' and has a 'liking for… Shrek 3', while Summons says she and her family were 'inspired by the movie Christmas with the Kranks'. ❸ In addition they both have strong views on Christmas. Mitchell says he loves to assert his 'way of celebrating it', while Summons is so convinced that her family's avoidance of Christmas was a success that she recommends it to her readers. ❹

❶ States the main similarity that links the two source texts, and develops this with examples and well-chosen evidence.

❷ Finds a further similarity, with supportive evidence.

❸ Comments on a small but valid similarity.

❹ Makes a strong statement of similarity inferred from the evidence.

Examiner's comments

This is a detailed response that shows full understanding and synthesis of relevant similarities. There is detailed exploration of both texts and examples are well chosen. The response manages to stay focused on the topic – the writers themselves, rather than their arguments about Christmas.

Key terms — Make sure you can write a definition for these key terms.

comparative   similarity   synthesise

Knowledge 171

Retrieval — EXAM

Paper 2: Question 7(a)

Use the following questions to check your understanding of the knowledge covered in this section. Then cover the answers column with a piece of paper and write down as many as you can. Check and repeat.

Questions / Answers

#	Question	Answer
1	How long should you spend on Question 7(a)?	8 minutes
2	How many marks are available for Question 7(a)?	6 marks
3	What is the focus of Question 7(a)?	Identifying similarities between two texts
4	What kind of language is used here? 'Similarly…' 'Likewise…' 'Whereas…' 'however…'	Comparative language
5	You must compare the relative success of each text. True or false?	False
6	You need to provide evidence for the similarities you point out. True or false?	True
7	You will be given two texts to compare that are similar in subject matter. True or false?	True
8	You may need to infer. True or false?	True – some information in the source texts may be implied.
9	Summarise the four steps for tackling this question.	**Step 1**: identify the specific thing you are being asked to look for. **Step 2**: re-read both sources again and highlight anything linked to the question focus. Make notes on the similarities. **Step 3**: find *three* clear similarities between the information in the two texts. **Step 4**: write your response.

Previous questions

Now go back and use these questions to check your knowledge of previous topics.

#	Question	Answer
1	What are the key aspects of a text that determine their content and style?	Text type, audience, purpose
2	What is meant by 'evaluation' of a text?	Judging its success
3	What pronouns are typically used in a 'third-person' viewpoint?	'She', 'he'

Practice

EXAM — **P2/Q7(a)**

Exam-style questions

Answer the exam-style questions on pages 173–181. Before you answer each of these questions, you should have already read the full source text.

7(a).1

Q7(a) The two texts are about changes people make in their lives.

What similarities do the people who take up growing vegetables share in these extracts?

Use evidence from **both** texts to support your answer. [6 marks]

LINK

This question refers to the whole text of Source 6A: 'I left my job in London to grow food' by Claire Ratinon, and the whole text of Source 6B: *Deep Country* by Neil Ansell. These sources can also be found on pages 225–227.

Source 6A: 'I left my job in London to grow food' by Claire Ratinon

This extract is taken from a *Guardian* newspaper article by Claire Ratinon, published in 2022. She explains how she left her life in London to move to the countryside and grow organic food.

In July 2016, I was sitting on the rooftop of a building in central London, listening to the gentle rumble of a nearby beehive, when I realised that my life had changed entirely. I didn't intend to quit – quitting crept up on me. After eight years of working in the media, I was on a path to becoming an
5   organic food grower, with a temporary side hustle of city beekeeping.

Not long before that point, I was just like the people in the office building below me. My work days were spent behind a desk or lugging around camera equipment, but now I am devoted to a life of nurturing the soil and growing the plants that end up on our plates. [...]

10 I was growing tired of my life in London and I wanted to explore somewhere new, and it was in New York that a seed was (literally and figuratively) sown for my unexpected change of profession. I encountered the alchemy of food growing for the first time at Brooklyn Grange – a rooftop farm that sits above New York's busy streets and overlooks Manhattan. Dusky leaves of Tuscan
15 kale*, peppers and tomatoes in unexpected shapes and colours, striped aubergines wearing spiked sepal* hats – chaos of abundance in the most unlikely of places. I was captivated.

From that day, all I could think about was getting through each week of working in documentary production so that, come the weekend, I could join
20 the other farm workers at Brooklyn Grange while they harvested, planted out and raked the earth to a fine tilth, ready for the next sowing of seeds. After two seasons of volunteering there, I was determined to make growing food a bigger part of my life. So, as the city I'd come to love was celebrating Halloween, I boarded a plane headed for London.

25 By the time I'd moved back to Hackney, I had a job working in the evenings – and occasionally nights – which left my days free to seek out the unlikely spaces where edible plants could be found growing in the city. After a year, I quit that role and tried to take on any job – each day a different one – that meant I could spend my days outside, my hands in the soil. I stepped into all
30 kinds of roles and every one taught me something precious.

Practice

Practice EXAM

Exam-style questions

Working as a school gardener showed me how little room there is in the school day and national curriculum for children to learn about how food arrives on their plate; training as a beekeeper taught me that growing nectar-rich flowers is a far better way of supporting pollinators than keeping hives;
35 and growing organic salad leaves to supply a veg box that filled the plates of people in Hackney made me realise there is nothing quite so ordinary and yet somehow remarkable than the act of feeding people.

Leaving London in 2019 to move to a more rural location changed the shape of my life. Now, in a garden of my own, I grow vegetables and fruit of my own
40 choosing [...]

I'm probably too romantic in the way I speak about working the land. The fact that it is a difficult and arduous way to make a living is worth stating – if only not to seem delusional. It is work that is backbreaking, exhausting and painfully underpaid. I have sacrificed my bodily wellbeing at its altar many
45 times, yet it remains the most important thing I've ever done.

kale: *a leafy vegetable*
sepal: *the outer leaves that protect a flower*

Source 6B: *Deep Country* by Neil Ansell

This extract is taken from *Deep Country* by Neil Ansell, who left a life in London, living communally and working with teenagers in care, to live alone in a remote cottage in Wales, where he managed to grow his own food on previously uncultivated land.

Without the sheep coming in to trim it, the grass grew in rank tussocks that I had to hack back with a sickle. Besides the fruit tree, the jackdaw ash and the cotoneaster next to the porch, there was one small rhododendron and a clump of blackthorn by the gate. Once, before my time, a solitary pine had
5 stood guard over the house from above the quarry wall, but it had been unlucky.... I planted out a larch to stand in for the lonesome pine, and in the southwest corner of the garden a beech, which will one day afford the cottage a little shelter from the prevailing wind. Then a couple of rowans, for berries for the birds, and a buddleia for the butterflies. Apart from a row
10 of poppies and wild flowers along the fence, I didn't trouble with flowers. I needed the land for food.

Although I planted a patch of herbs – coriander, dill and parsley, which were unavailable locally – my priority was the heavy vegetables. I didn't want to be hauling sackfuls of potatoes up the mountainside when I could be
15 growing them myself. Preparing the land was hard work; the roots of the grass grew deep and tangled. Then I had to pick out all the rocks, carefully lift any daffodil bulbs for transplantation elsewhere, and lime the soil. Each year I would dig an extra patch, and prepare another for the next year by pegging down a sheet of tarpaulin with bricks to kill off the grass. I didn't

20 want to use any pesticides, and besides the lime I bought no fertilizer. Each winter, when the bats were long gone to their hibernation roost, I would clamber up into the loft and shovel up bagfuls of guano*. It was dry and powdery and odourless, and it seemed somehow appropriate that the bats who shared my home with me should help me grow my food.

25 I had never grown anything before, I had never stayed in one place long enough to even think about it, and had no idea what would grow well at this altitude, and in a location so exposed to the elements, so it was a process of trial and error. Each year I would try a few new things; if they grew well they would become a fixture; if they failed I would abandon them and try
30 something else. I had a small patch of early potatoes, and a larger patch of main crops. I got a metal dustbin which I kept in the pantry and would fill it to the top with these, enough to last the whole year. Onions and garlic I hung on strings on the woodshed wall, as the mice didn't ever bother them. Garlic was the only thing I planted in autumn; growing garlic seems magical in its
35 simplicity. Take a head of garlic, break it into cloves and plant them in a row. By the next year each clove will have turned into a new head.

Carrots and parsnips I stored in the ground and lifted when I needed them. The carrots in particular were a revelation; they are hard to grow in most places because of the depredations of the carrot fly, but the altitude here
40 kept my crop pest-free. They grew to over a pound in weight without becoming woody, were such a deep orange they were almost red, and tasted better than any others I have had before or since.

guano: *droppings from bats or seabirds*

> **EXAM TIP**
>
> In your answer, you should:
> - refer to the whole of both source texts
> - look for similarities, not differences
> - identify the specific focus of the question
> - look for at least three clear similarities between the texts
> - select evidence to support your points.

Practice EXAM

Exam-style questions

7(a).2

> **Q7(a)** The two texts are about travellers in foreign countries.
>
> What similarities do the travellers' experiences share in these extracts?
>
> Use evidence from **both** texts to support your answer. **[6 marks]**

LINK

This question refers to the whole text of Source 7A: *Around India in 80 Trains* by Monisha Rajesh, and the whole text of Source 7B: 'Baghdad to Basra, On the Wrong Side of the Tracks' by Cesar G. Soriano. These sources can also be found on pages 227–230.

Source 7A: *Around India in 80 Trains* by Monisha Rajesh

This extract is from a book of travel writing called *Around India in 80 Trains* by Monisha Rajesh. This extract describes her experience of train travel in India.

Six-people deep, and growing by the second, the crowd tensed. A single knuckle pressed into my back and betel-nut* breath filled my nostrils as a steady beat rose above the din. Against the peach pink of Mumbai's evening skies, the commuter service curled into view, passengers hanging from
5 the sides like moving livery*. Braking with a wail and grind of metal, the train slowed into the station and I braced against the surge of bodies from behind. Like relay runners, they began to move before the train had stopped, reaching over my head at the same time as a torrent of polyester shirts and satchels thundered down from the open doorways.

10 A slice of papaya in one hand my bag gripped with the other, I battled through elbows, meaty shoulders and thick plaits slicked with coconut oil. In the crush the papaya was knocked to the ground and my sandal came off, but I made it on board and fell sideways into a seat as the train jerked away from the platform. Wiping someone else's sweat from my arm, I watched
15 fellow travellers scrabble for handholds, adjust saris* and pull out phones before relaxing into the ride with a mix of relief and pride. I'd survived my first experience on the infamous Mumbai 'locals'*.

Inside the carriages, a microcosm* of Indian society spanned the train from one end to the other. With my earphones plugged in and my music turned
20 off, I'd pretend to read while eavesdropping on conversations about end-of-year exams, mean bosses, new girlfriends, old boyfriends and mother-in-law disputes.

In the middle of the night, I'd ease down from my berth for a trip to the loo, invariably putting a socked foot on a stranger's blanket-covered back,
25 mumble my apologies and hope they'd be gone by morning. On other days, I'd board at the opposite end, squeezing on to wooden slats with farmers and fruit sellers who would place guavas in my palm, while joking with their friends through paan*-stained teeth. They'd count their money, touching it to their foreheads with thanks, before sloping off the train and crossing the
30 tracks to find the next customer.

On arrival in Londa, I paced the platform munching on hot, fresh vadas and enquired when the return train would arrive, and was dismayed to discover it wasn't due until 2 a.m. It was barely 6 p.m. Gradually the crowds thinned, the skies turned indigo and there was nothing but the chirp of crickets for company. A lone passenger watched me from a doorway. And he wouldn't leave.

At the other end of the platform I spotted a sweeper and beelined for the elderly man, who led me to a nearby guesthouse where I could stay for a few hours before the train arrived – it was always the kindness of strangers.

Just before 2 a.m. I crossed the road to the station as the train was rolling in. With no reservation, I boarded the women's compartment, a dimly lit dormitory of bundled bodies and bare feet. Finding me an unoccupied berth, the ticket inspector gestured for me to climb up. The train sailed out of the station and I wriggled down under the blanket before turning over to see my neighbour watching me. She winked and her diamond nose stud shone in the milky light from the moving platform. I was back in my safe place, back at home.

betel-nut: *nut commonly chewed as a stimulant in India*
livery: *painted symbols indicating ownership*
sari: *traditional outfit worn by Indian women*
'locals': *local trains*
microcosm: *a little world*
paan: *betel nut rolled in a betel leaf*

Source 7B: 'Baghdad to Basra, On the Wrong Side of the Tracks' by Cesar G. Soriano

This extract is taken from Cesar G. Soriano's essay 'Baghdad to Basra, On the Wrong Side of the Tracks' from *Best of Lonely Planet Travel Writing*. The writer describes a long train journey in Iraq.

Jabar, Sabah and most of the male passengers passed the time on the long train ride by chain-smoking. It wasn't long before the carriages were thick with smoke. For non-smokers like me, relief could only be found by sticking our heads out of the cracked windows or putting our noses to one of the many bullet holes. Despite all this, across the aisle from me, Abdul Yaseen, his wife and their four children were ecstatic about their first-ever train adventure. They were returning home to Basra after attending a wedding near Baghdad. 'I like the train because it's more comfortable, slow and lets the kids have a chance to see the countryside,' he said. His wide-eyed children were peering from the windows, wearing their best clothes, reminiscent of a time when travelling was actually an occasion for dressing up. Abdul's nine-year-old daughter, Haba, surprised to see an American on board, latched onto us and peppered me with questions in broken English: 'Mister, where you from? You married? You have children? You like Arabian music? You like Jennifer Lopez? Mister, buy me Pepsi!'

Around 4pm the train pulled into the station in Nasiriyah, one of the largest cities in southern Iraq. But, unlike our stops at other cities, the train did not immediately pull out but sat at the platform. And sat. And sat. There

Practice

EXAM

Exam-style questions

was no announcement or explanation for our delay. The thermometer
20 on the platform read 100°F. Inside, the train was becoming a steel oven, baking us alive. Within minutes, we were drenched in sweat. The stench of body odour, dirty baby diapers and the raw sewage on the tracks became unbearable. An old woman fainted and was carried outside into the shade and doused with water, and many more of us followed her out into the air.
25 Angry passengers took out their rage on the conductor, who explained that the station manager had refused to give clearance for the train to proceed. Apparently there was only one working track between Nasiriyah and Basra, and a northbound cargo train already had dibs*. An hour later, without a whistle or warning, the train began pulling out of the station. Of course, most
30 of us were still out on the platform and had to run and jump back onto the moving train.

South of Nasiriyah, we reached the most scenic point of the journey. The endless monochrome images of brown, dusty villages were replaced by lush, green landscape, fields of corn, alfalfa and date palms. This was the Arab
35 Marshland, a fertile region between the Tigris and Euphrates Rivers that is the legendary location of the Garden of Eden. The setting sun blazed into the windows of the right side of the train. There were no curtains or shades to pull down, so passengers took chewing gum from their mouths and used it to stick newspapers onto the windows to shield their heads from the sun. Ah,
40 so that was why there was gum stuck all over the windows.

dibs: *priority*

7(a).3

Q7(a) The two texts are about swimming.

What similarities do the experiences described share in these extracts?

Use evidence from **both** texts to support your answer. **[6 marks]**

> **LINK**
>
> This question refers to the whole text of Source 8A: 'RIP wild swimming! Nature's "cure all" has thrown in the towel' by Eva Wiseman, and the whole text of Source 8B: 'When wild swimming is deeply dangerous' by Helen Carroll. These sources can also be found on pages 230–232.

Source 8A: 'RIP wild swimming! Nature's "cure all" has thrown in the towel' by Eva Wiseman

This is an opinion piece from the *Guardian* newspaper by a regular columnist.

Farewell, wild swimming, it's been fun. Well, not fun. Not 'fun' in the traditional sense of the word. More, it's been baffling, sometimes blood-curdling and, eventually, a banal cliché* flattened by over-use, but this is an obituary of sorts, so we will be kind.

5 Much in the same way Lucozade rebranded itself from medicine to energy drink, in the past decade this hobby pivoted to wellness, adding the 'wild' having spent many years known simply as 'swimming'. Led in no small part by this newspaper, it became a trend, elevated by its health-giving properties and photos of nice ladies grinning in swimwear. It was not for me. No, I am
10 a person quite tied to dry land, and cosiness, and a lack of eels scraping my shins, but I applaud those who did it. Those brave enough to jump straight into lakes, whether for exercise, their mental health, their headaches or their Instagrams. You always knew who was a wild swimmer, because they would tell you, frequently. And I'd applaud until my palms stung, because this was
15 a feat of endurance and bravery so far beyond my own pathetic limits that they might as well have jumped into an active volcano rather than the local pond. But.

But but but. When something becomes a trend, its clock starts ticking. Wild swimming is no different. The first nail in its coffin came with the blunt force
20 of marketing: it was presented as a cure for everything. Feeling sad, feeling a low ache in your temples, feeling burned out, grim from too long online, feeling an unravelling guilt about contributing to the climate crisis, feeling disconnected from your body, disconnected from your community, feeling too many feelings or too few – take your clothes off and jump in the lake.
25 There, nature will cleanse you quickly of all your human agonies and sins. Cured.

It has long bothered me, this idea that nature exists as a wellness product, like a scented candle or very green tea, rather than a system that persists in spite of our many-pronged attempts to control it or, of course, profit from
30 it. The popularity of wild swimming led to an increased interest in similar nature therapies, like 'forest bathing', said to counter illnesses including 'cancer, strokes, gastric ulcers, depression, anxiety and stress'. This morning I received an email advertising a restorative forest bathing retreat with overnight prices starting at £599 – a light lunch is included. Without wanting

Practice

Practice EXAM

Exam-style questions

35 to sound too much like a red-faced management consultant shouting in a beer garden, that is a lot of money to spend on going for a walk. Isn't it?

I have no doubt these moments of slowness and fresh air do help, but their ability to cure a person of all their pains surely also relies on serious structural support and a little bit of medicine, too. But the nail had been
40 banged: these spiritual experiences had been packaged and given price tags, and the magical sheen was dulled.

The second nail was, well, the sewage. Last year, the images of blissy swimmers we'd become accustomed to were replaced by pictures of floating faeces and stories about people falling horribly ill after ingesting raw sewage.
45 According to the Labour Party's analysis of Environment Agency data, since 2016 water companies have pumped raw sewage into our seas and rivers for more than 9m hours. And last week it was reported that hundreds of landfill dumps containing 'plastics, chemicals and other waste are a ticking timebomb threatening to leach pollution' on to beaches and into the sea.

banal cliché: *something that has become boring by repetition*

Source 8B: 'When wild swimming is deeply dangerous' by Helen Carroll

This extract is from an article published in the *Daily Mail*: 'When wild swimming is deeply dangerous' by Helen Carroll (July 2021).

When Sophie Skellern lost her grandma, whom she had nursed through her dying days during the first lockdown, the one thing that helped ease her grief was open-water swimming. Whatever the weather, three times a week, Sophie would pull on her swimming costume and head to the lake at Sale
5 Water Park, near her home in Manchester, where, front crawling through the chilly waters, she would briefly forget her sadness. In fact, wild swimming left Sophie, 29, feeling so exhilarated that it had never occurred to her what a risky form of exercise it can be. But last month — if she hadn't had a float and her boyfriend on hand — she could have died while swimming in a lake near
10 Mount Snowdon during a holiday.

'I was half a mile from the water's edge when both my calves cramped up and I couldn't move or kick them, the pain was so intense,' recalls Sophie, shuddering at the memory of what happened in Llyn Gwynant. 'I felt almost paralysed from the waist down as I lay on my back trying to float. Luckily
15 I knew to immediately lie on my back and put the tow float I was pulling across my chest. Someone new to this may not have had a float with them and I dread to think what would have happened if I'd panicked. That's when people drown. However, the 30 minutes it took for the cramping to pass were among the scariest of my life. Fortunately, my partner, Jack, was also in the
20 lake, in a kayak about 100 metres away. He noticed I'd stopped swimming and was on my back and I was able to raise my arm and beckon him over.

'It was a tiny one-person kayak, so there was no way he could have pulled me in, or even towed me back to shore, but he stayed beside me, giving me sips of water, while I tried to point my toes to stretch out the muscles, until the cramping finally eased enough for normal sensations to return to my legs. It would have been so easy to start hyperventilating. However, thankfully, I forced myself to keep taking deep breaths and stay calm, because getting stressed and anxious in water is the very worst thing you can do. After half an hour, my legs felt strong enough for Jack to escort me back to the shore.'

Sophie, who organises art exhibitions and is studying for a PhD, believes her legs cramped because she had not drunk enough water and had become dehydrated in the heat, nor had she left enough of a gap between eating lunch and getting into the water — mistakes she will not repeat.

She's one of many women who enjoy so-called 'wild swimming', which has caught on like wildfire in recent years. Barely a day goes by without someone in the public eye — supermodel Helena Christensen, TV presenters Fearne Cotton and Susannah Constantine and even former Prime Minister David Cameron are all fans — espousing its virtues. From improving sleep, boosting immunity and metabolism, to 'significantly reducing' symptoms of anxiety and depression, outdoor swimming is seen by many as a cure-all.

Yet despite its benefits, there is no denying that swimming in open water is far riskier than a trip to your local pool. Since the heatwave began on July 14, at least 40 people have lost their lives in open water — rivers, lakes, natural pools and the sea — treble the usual rate of water deaths, which average 19 a year.

But wild swimming poses risks whatever the weather, with dangers including near freezing temperatures, water-born contaminants and hidden obstructions.

Knowledge — EXAM

Paper 2: Question 7(b)

Question 7(b): Overview

- **Focus:** Comparing writers' ideas and perspectives
- **Marks:** 14 marks
- **Time:** 20 minutes
- **AO:** AO3

Question 7(b) is based on the whole of both source texts. This question asks you to:

- identify the ideas in the texts
- compare what attitudes or perspectives are expressed
- compare how they are conveyed.

'Ideas' refers to the main topics or subject matter. 'Perspectives' refers to the authors' different attitudes to these ideas.

Question 7(b) will look like this:

> **Q7(b)** Compare how the writers of Text 1 and Text 2 present ideas and perspectives about…
>
> You should write about:
> - the ideas and perspectives
> - how they are presented
> - how they are similar/different.
>
> Support your answer with detailed references to the texts. **[14 marks]**

TIP
Try to find at least three points of comparison, with quotations, from each text.

Remember to offer a balanced consideration of the texts. Keep your focus roughly equal on each text.

In Question 7(a) you explored points of similarity between both source texts. You need to use your skills of identifying and **interpreting** information and ideas more widely for Question 7(b). You must look for differences as well, and focus both on writer's perspectives and on their **methods** of presenting them, such as themes, language, and/or structure.

P2/Q7(b)

Question 7(b): Strategy

Follow the steps below to respond to a Question 7(b) task.

Step 1: Read the question. Highlight the question focus.

Step 2: Read both texts. Identify the ideas about the key topic across both texts and then identify where the perspectives are the same or different. Next, consider how the methods used by the writer, such as themes, language, and/or structure, are used to convey this.

Step 3: Go back through both texts and narrow down your selection to choose a list of key quotations which show what the writers think and feel about the topic.

Step 4: Go back through the quotations you have identified from both texts and find at least three linked pairs of quotations which show that the writer's ideas are different or similar (as instructed in the question).

Step 5: Write your response.

> **LINK**
>
> The language features you could talk about for this question are covered in the Concept Knowledge sections on pages 10–24. Look for word classes, imagery, figurative language features and techniques, listing, repetition, contrast, and emotive language.

Try to find at least three points of comparison, with quotations, from each text. You must compare throughout your answer: if you make a point about one source, immediately consider how the second source is similar or different. Back up your ideas with evidence.

A writer has many methods at their disposal, so think about not only *what* they say, but *how* they say it when you select points to write about. Make sure you also understand the technique so you can write about it well.

Knowledge

Knowledge EXAM

Paper 2: Question 7(b)

Question 7(b): Example

Read the sample Question 7(b) and annotations below.

> **Q7(b)** **Compare** how the writers of Text 1 and Text 2 **present ideas** and **perspectives** about Christmas.
>
> You should write about:
> - the ideas and perspectives
> - how they are presented
> - **how they are similar/different**.
>
> Support your answer with detailed references to the texts.
>
> [14 marks]

You will need to talk about what ideas connect the texts, how the writers have different or similar perspectives on them, and how they are conveyed.

You also need to identify what the writers think and feel about the topic – whether they are positive or negative about it, how they react to things, and how they describe them.

You need to talk about how writers express their ideas – this is about how they use methods such as word choices, imagery, and emotive language.

Focus on similarities and differences about the given topic.

LINK

This question refers to the whole text of Source 5A: 'Bah humbug to all of you who just hate Christmas' by David Mitchell, and the whole text of Source 5B: 'Why I skipped Christmas – and why you might like to try it too' by Sandy Summons. These sources can also be found on pages 222–224.

TIP

There will be a context box at the top of the source giving you important information about the text. Make sure you read it!

Source 5A: 'Bah humbug to all of you who just hate Christmas' by David Mitchell

> This text is taken from 'Bah humbug to all of you who just hate Christmas' by David Mitchell, a newspaper article published in 2008. David Mitchell is a comedian who is giving his opinion about people who don't like Christmas.

My official policy on Christmas is that I like it. That says a lot more about me than that I'm partial to a day spent watching TV and stuffing my face. More fundamentally, it shows that I can't stand the thought of our most public and celebratory festival being a lie. It is a happy and magical time, I'm insisting,
5 for deeper and more sinister reasons than a liking for Brazil nuts and *Shrek 3*.

Other people – my enemies – love to hate Christmas. They rejoice in looking at the sparkle, the bustle, the drinking and the queues and muttering: 'Christmas is a nightmare'; 'We're going to Jane's parents – it's going to be a living hell'; 'The sooner we can forget all the expense and false jollity, this
10 great capitalist hypocrisy dance, the better, I say,' as if commerce* were as exclusive to this time of year as mince pies.

As they grumble and sneer their way through the season – seek each other out for affirmation that it's all just a sick joke and that participating is as joyous as diarrhoea and as prudent as a pyramid scheme* I stand shocked
15 and afraid. To the boy I once was, heart buoyed* by the air of magic, and expectation of an acquisitive* nature about to be satisfied, this is a colossal slap in the face: it has finally all ended in tears.

184 Paper 2: Question 7(b)

So I must sustain my policy. It's vulnerable, I know. I'm not at a good time of life for liking Christmas. The childhood enchantment has long gone, as has
20 the excitement about presents, and I have no children to help me rediscover it vicariously*. Meanwhile, shopping is stressful, tree lights never work, turkey's not the best meat in the world and Christmas pudding is weird. If I'm not careful, I'll realise I'm only in it for the booze.

But I'm still too tribal to accept this conclusion. We of the Christmas-liking
25 tribe will keep the Christmas-cynic tribe in perpetual subjugation – they will be made to join in whether they like it or not and particularly if not. They will never, if we can help it, be permitted to 'get away somewhere hot' but, if they do, we can be confident that our allies overseas will besiege them with spray-on snow and piped-in Slade even as they sweat round the pool.

30 This is a time when we all come together to disagree about how Christmas is supposed to be done. It's not so much 'love thy neighbour' as 'mock the neon Santa on thy neighbour's roof'. I think these divisions might be what saves my pro-Christmas policy because I love asserting my way of celebrating it over everyone else's. In another life, I could have been a great
35 witchfinder general, paranoid anti-communist or warrior ant. I will root out people who slightly differ from me in their Christmas traditions and blow them away with the twin barrels of my British disdain gun, which are, of course, snobbery and inverse snobbery.

To test your suitability for this fight, consider your reaction to the phrase:
40 'We actually had goose this year.' It's not the nature of your reaction that's important, but its strength. I'm hoping for a strong one. Either: 'Yes of course, goose is a much tastier meat and an older tradition. I can't believe those turkey-eating scum are suffered to live. They should be locked up in the same hell sheds where the bland objects of their culinary affection are
45 chemically spawned.' Or, and this is the one I favour: '[Get] back to Borough Market with your talk of goose deliciousness. We're supposed to eat turkey – that's now the tradition.'

---

commerce: *buying and selling*
pyramid scheme: *a sales scheme: people pay to join and only make money by recruiting others*
buoyed: *lifted up*
acquisitive: *wanting possessions*
vicariously: *through someone else*

Knowledge — EXAM

Paper 2: Question 7(b)

Source 5B: 'Why I skipped Christmas – and why you might like to try it too' by Sandy Summons

> This extract is from an article, 'Why I skipped Christmas – and why you might like to try it too', by Sandy Summons, in the *Guardian* (December 2022).

Christmas is the most magical time of the year. But is it really? Now I'm no grinch*. In fact, I absolutely love Christmas. Yet there was a stage when I needed to have a holiday from this popular holiday. So one year we decided to 'skip Christmas' to simplify our Christmas Day.

5 The festive season is overwhelming for many, especially with increased financial pressures and family obligations. A recent report revealed one in six people believe Christmas is the most stressful time of the year. Family conflict is often rife, with some sort of bickering over presents or food. And then there's the family member who has too much to drink and thinks it
10 is their duty to sing a 'special' rendition of Mariah Carey's 'All I Want for Christmas'. Unlike friends, we can't choose our relatives!

When I was younger, Christmas Day seemed so much simpler. With only my parents and siblings, it was fun and uncomplicated. We spent time playing with our new toys and wearing the clothing items we received. I
15 still remember getting green knickerbockers one Christmas (for those that don't know, a style of shorts that were very hip back then), and I was utterly delighted. We didn't need anything more.

These days are quite different. My husband and I usually celebrate with our extended families. However, over the years it has become more demanding.
20 It's not that we didn't want to spend time with family. But traipsing all over the countryside to catch up with relatives and visiting, on average, four to five homes in one day became too much. Yes, at one stage we did that exhausting amount.

One year after being inspired by the movie *Christmas with the Kranks*, we
25 thought we'd change it up. In the movie Tim Allen and Jamie Lee Curtis, who play Luther and Nora Krank, boycott their traditional family Christmas. They choose not to partake in anything Christmas-related including presents, family gatherings, parties, or decorations.

Similarly, we chose to skip the 30C heat, not put up a Christmas tree or to
attend our family Christmas festivities. And even though this may seem drastic, to escape the obligations of Christmas we jetted off on an overseas holiday to New York.

While most of our Christmases have been jam-packed, we were able to spend the day how we wanted to. After a lazy breakfast at the hotel, we watched a basketball game at Madison Square Garden, then finished the day walking through a snow-laden Central Park. Spending the time together with our little core family was memorable. It was relaxed and enjoyable.

Funnily enough, skipping our traditional Christmas that year gave us clarity on how we wanted to spend future Christmases. It made us look forward to a simpler Christmas with our extended family. Previously, we had bought presents for our parents, siblings and their partners, plus all their children. It was exhausting, not to mention all the presents destined for either the regifting pile or for landfill. These days only the nieces and nephews aged under 21 receive gifts. In the past, the host would have a meltdown from cooking up a storm, but now we all bring food to share. We realised we enjoyed being with the family but we also wanted to do what makes us happy. To slow down and enjoy stress free, quality time with each other.

---

grinch: *someone who spoils the enjoyment of others*

Knowledge

EXAM

Paper 2: Question 7(b)

Question 7(b): Sample answers

Now read the following sample answers to the Question 7(b) example question on page 184, alongside the examiner's comments.

Sample answer 1

This is part of a longer answer. It receives less than half the marks available.

① Makes a broadly correct comparison, but with only a partial understanding of the second writer's comments – which are presented with an unnecessarily long quotation.

The big difference is really that the first writer has a good attitude to Christmas, 'I like it', and the second has a negative attitude when she says it is 'overwhelming' and there is 'increased financial pressures and family obligations'. ① With Text 1 the writer even says the people who 'hate Christmas' are his enemies but he admits there are bad things too like 'drinking and the queues and muttering'. In Text 2 she says it is now 'the most stressful time of the year', but she also admits it used to be fun as a child. ② There is also a big difference in how they give their ideas and views. David makes it a joke about his enemies and how he wants to 'blow them away'. On the other hand, writer 2 tells a story about going to New York to skip Christmas and it was 'relaxed and enjoyable'. ③

② Makes a valid observation, picking up on how each writer says positive and negative things about Christmas, but without explaining this well. The word 'muttering' is misunderstood and quoted out of context.

③ This is a potentially useful piece of language to comment on, but the student hasn't clearly labelled it and their comment is very general rather than specific to what's happening in the source.

Examiner's comments

There are some valid comparisons, but the student needs to develop the idea that, while both writers comment on the stresses of Christmas, Mitchell is essentially a lover of Christmas and Summons is arguing the case for 'skipping' it. Some evidence is lacking, not well chosen, or not explained sufficiently to make the comparison clear. There is a very broad comment on methods, but not on language or structure.

REMEMBER

- You must identify the specific focus of the question.
- You must refer to the whole of both source texts.
- Compare the texts by finding similarities and differences.
- Select evidence from both texts to support your points.

P2/Q7(b)

Sample answer 2

This is part of a longer answer that receives high marks.

> Both texts explore attitudes to Christmas but with different aims and approaches. The Text 1 writer entertains readers with exaggerated views, in which he sees those who 'love to hate Christmas' as 'enemies'. He develops this idea, seeing himself as a member of the 'Christmas-liking tribe', and using comic rhetoric to mock how he insists he is right, comparing himself, in an extreme list of three, with a 'witchfinder... paranoid anticommunist or warrior ant'. ❶ The Text 2 writer, on the other hand, uses less humour, and makes a serious case for a simpler, family-based Christmas, with 'quality time with each other'. She uses negative language like 'meltdown from cooking' to convey the demands of Christmas that she wants to avoid. ❷ One thing they have in common is childhood. The Text 1 writer says he 'can't stand' the idea of Christmas 'being a lie'. This goes back to 'the boy I once was'. He cannot bear the 'magic... ending in tears', suggesting his emotional attachment to it. The Text 2 writer also has nostalgia for 'fun and uncomplicated' Christmases, but whereas Text 1 defends a dream of Christmas, Text 2 recommends bringing back what was good about it. ❸ One structural difference in approach is that the Text 1 writer gradually develops the idea of a tribal fight over Christmas, while the Text 2 writer builds up to an anecdote used to make her point: her family went away to avoid the demands of Christmas, and found it 'relaxed and enjoyable'. ❹

❶ The topic sentence summarises similarities and differences to be explored later. The student then comments on the Text 1 writer's main aim and approach, giving evidence and commenting on language with confidence.

❷ Compares ideas and methods in the second text, noting differences and using short, well-chosen quotations.

❸ States a similarity – the idea of childhood, but explains how the writers deal with it differently and reach different conclusions. Comparative language ('but whereas') adds clarity.

❹ Makes a structural difference incorporating the writers' ideas and methods. It can be effective to write about similarities and differences within one sentence, as in this example.

Examiner's comments

This response considers a range of comparisons, exploring similarities and differences between the texts. There is exploration and analysis of ideas and perspectives, and comment on how language is used to convey them. Evidence is taken from both texts in a balanced way and is used to clarify and back up points made.

Key terms — Make sure you can write a definition for these key terms.

interpret   methods

Knowledge 189

Retrieval — EXAM

Paper 2: Question 7(b)

Use the following questions to check your understanding of the knowledge covered in this section. Then cover the answers column with a piece of paper and write down as many as you can. Check and repeat.

Questions	Answers
1. How long should you spend on Question 7(b)?	20 minutes
2. How many marks are available?	14 marks
3. What is the focus of Question 7(b)?	Comparing writers' ideas and perspectives.
4. How much of each text will you need to refer to?	The whole of both texts
5. How many pairs of references or quotations should you aim to consider?	At least three
6. You can write mostly about whichever text you find more interesting. True or false?	False. You must write equally about both texts.
7. You may be given two texts that have no topics or themes in common. True or false?	False. There will always be similarities between the texts.
8. Summarise the five steps for tackling this question.	**Step 1**: highlight the question focus. **Step 2**: identify ideas about the key topic in both texts. Identify similarities / differences in perspective and writers' methods. **Step 3**: choose key quotations showing what the writers think / feel about the topic. **Step 4**: find three linked pairs of quotations which show that the writer's ideas are different or similar. **Step 5**: write your response.

Previous questions

Now go back and use these questions to check your knowledge of previous topics.

Questions	Answers
1. What is meant by 'narrative viewpoint'?	The point of view from which a story is told, such as first-person or third-person.
2. What technique is used here and what is its effect? *Inside, the train was becoming a steel oven.*	Metaphor. It shows how hot and uncomfortable the train was.

Practice

EXAM

P2/Q7(b)

Exam-style questions

Answer the exam-style questions on pages 191–199.

7(b).1

Q7(b) Compare how the writers present ideas and perspectives about growing food.

You should write about:
- the ideas and perspectives
- how they are presented
- how they are similar/different.

Support your answer with detailed references to the texts.

[14 marks]

> **LINK**
> This question refers to the whole text of Source 6A: 'I left my job in London to grow food' by Claire Ratinon, and the whole text of Source 6B: *Deep Country* by Neil Ansell. These sources can also be found on pages 225–227.

Source 6A: 'I left my job in London to grow food' by Claire Ratinon

This extract is taken from a *Guardian* newspaper article by Claire Ratinon, published in 2022. She explains how she left her life in London to move to the countryside and grow organic food.

In July 2016, I was sitting on the rooftop of a building in central London, listening to the gentle rumble of a nearby beehive, when I realised that my life had changed entirely. I didn't intend to quit – quitting crept up on me. After eight years of working in the media, I was on a path to becoming an
5   organic food grower, with a temporary side hustle of city beekeeping.

Not long before that point, I was just like the people in the office building below me. My work days were spent behind a desk or lugging around camera equipment, but now I am devoted to a life of nurturing the soil and growing the plants that end up on our plates. […]

10 I was growing tired of my life in London and I wanted to explore somewhere new, and it was in New York that a seed was (literally and figuratively) sown for my unexpected change of profession. I encountered the alchemy of food growing for the first time at Brooklyn Grange – a rooftop farm that sits above New York's busy streets and overlooks Manhattan. Dusky leaves of Tuscan
15 kale*, peppers and tomatoes in unexpected shapes and colours, striped aubergines wearing spiked sepal* hats – chaos of abundance in the most unlikely of places. I was captivated.

From that day, all I could think about was getting through each week of working in documentary production so that, come the weekend, I could join
20 the other farm workers at Brooklyn Grange while they harvested, planted out and raked the earth to a fine tilth, ready for the next sowing of seeds. After two seasons of volunteering there, I was determined to make growing food a bigger part of my life. So, as the city I'd come to love was celebrating Halloween, I boarded a plane headed for London.

25 By the time I'd moved back to Hackney, I had a job working in the evenings – and occasionally nights – which left my days free to seek out the unlikely

Practice EXAM

Exam-style questions

spaces where edible plants could be found growing in the city. After a year, I quit that role and tried to take on any job – each day a different one – that meant I could spend my days outside, my hands in the soil. I stepped into all
30 kinds of roles and every one taught me something precious.

Working as a school gardener showed me how little room there is in the school day and national curriculum for children to learn about how food arrives on their plate; training as a beekeeper taught me that growing nectar-rich flowers is a far better way of supporting pollinators than keeping hives;
35 and growing organic salad leaves to supply a veg box that filled the plates of people in Hackney made me realise there is nothing quite so ordinary and yet somehow remarkable than the act of feeding people.

Leaving London in 2019 to move to a more rural location changed the shape of my life. Now, in a garden of my own, I grow vegetables and fruit of my own
40 choosing [...]

I'm probably too romantic in the way I speak about working the land. The fact that it is a difficult and arduous way to make a living is worth stating – if only not to seem delusional. It is work that is backbreaking, exhausting and painfully underpaid. I have sacrificed my bodily wellbeing at its altar many
45 times, yet it remains the most important thing I've ever done.

kale: *a leafy vegetable*
sepal: *the outer leaves that protect a flower*

Source 6B: *Deep Country* by Neil Ansell

This extract is taken from *Deep Country* by Neil Ansell, who left a life in London, living communally and working with teenagers in care, to live alone in a remote cottage in Wales, where he managed to grow his own food on previously uncultivated land.

Without the sheep coming in to trim it, the grass grew in rank tussocks that I had to hack back with a sickle. Besides the fruit tree, the jackdaw ash and the cotoneaster next to the porch, there was one small rhododendron and a clump of blackthorn by the gate. Once, before my time, a solitary pine had
5 stood guard over the house from above the quarry wall, but it had been unlucky…. I planted out a larch to stand in for the lonesome pine, and in the southwest corner of the garden a beech, which will one day afford the cottage a little shelter from the prevailing wind. Then a couple of rowans, for berries for the birds, and a buddleia for the butterflies. Apart from a row
10 of poppies and wild flowers along the fence, I didn't trouble with flowers. I needed the land for food.

Although I planted a patch of herbs – coriander, dill and parsley, which were unavailable locally – my priority was the heavy vegetables. I didn't want to be hauling sackfuls of potatoes up the mountainside when I could be growing them myself. Preparing the land was hard work; the roots of the grass grew deep and tangled. Then I had to pick out all the rocks, carefully lift any daffodil bulbs for transplantation elsewhere, and lime the soil. Each year I would dig an extra patch, and prepare another for the next year by pegging down a sheet of tarpaulin with bricks to kill off the grass. I didn't want to use any pesticides, and besides the lime I bought no fertilizer. Each winter, when the bats were long gone to their hibernation roost, I would clamber up into the loft and shovel up bagfuls of guano*. It was dry and powdery and odourless, and it seemed somehow appropriate that the bats who shared my home with me should help me grow my food.

I had never grown anything before, I had never stayed in one place long enough to even think about it, and had no idea what would grow well at this altitude, and in a location so exposed to the elements, so it was a process of trial and error. Each year I would try a few new things; if they grew well they would become a fixture; if they failed I would abandon them and try something else. I had a small patch of early potatoes, and a larger patch of main crops. I got a metal dustbin which I kept in the pantry and would fill it to the top with these, enough to last the whole year. Onions and garlic I hung on strings on the woodshed wall, as the mice didn't ever bother them. Garlic was the only thing I planted in autumn; growing garlic seems magical in its simplicity. Take a head of garlic, break it into cloves and plant them in a row. By the next year each clove will have turned into a new head.

Carrots and parsnips I stored in the ground and lifted when I needed them. The carrots in particular were a revelation; they are hard to grow in most places because of the depredations of the carrot fly, but the altitude here kept my crop pest-free. They grew to over a pound in weight without becoming woody, were such a deep orange they were almost red, and tasted better than any others I have had before or since.

guano: *droppings from bats or seabirds*

Practice — EXAM

Exam-style questions

7(b).2

Q7(b) Compare how the writers of Text 1 and Text 2 present ideas and perspectives about travel.

You should write about:
- the ideas and perspectives
- how they are presented
- how they are similar/different.

Support your answer with detailed references to the texts. **[14 marks]**

> **LINK**
> This question refers to the whole text of Source 7A: *Around India in 80 Trains* by Monisha Rajesh, and Source 7B: 'Baghdad to Basra, On the Wrong Side of the Tracks' by Cesar G. Sorlano. These sources can also be found on pages 227–230.

> **EXAM TIP**
> In your answer, you should:
> - refer to the whole of both source texts
> - compare the texts by exploring both similarities and differences
> - focus on the ideas and perspectives presented by the author, and how they are presented
> - select evidence from both texts to support your points.

Source 7A: *Around India in 80 Trains* by Monisha Rajesh

This extract is from a book of travel writing called *Around India in 80 Trains* by Monisha Rajesh. This extract describes her experience of train travel in India.

Six-people deep, and growing by the second, the crowd tensed. A single knuckle pressed into my back and betel-nut* breath filled my nostrils as a steady beat rose above the din. Against the peach pink of Mumbai's evening skies, the commuter service curled into view, passengers hanging from
5 the sides like moving livery*. Braking with a wail and grind of metal, the train slowed into the station and I braced against the surge of bodies from behind. Like relay runners, they began to move before the train had stopped, reaching over my head at the same time as a torrent of polyester shirts and satchels thundered down from the open doorways.

10 A slice of papaya in one hand my bag gripped with the other, I battled through elbows, meaty shoulders and thick plaits slicked with coconut oil. In the crush the papaya was knocked to the ground and my sandal came off, but I made it on board and fell sideways into a seat as the train jerked away from the platform. Wiping someone else's sweat from my arm, I watched
15 fellow travellers scrabble for handholds, adjust saris* and pull out phones before relaxing into the ride with a mix of relief and pride. I'd survived my first experience on the infamous Mumbai 'locals'*.

Inside the carriages, a microcosm* of Indian society spanned the train from one end to the other. With my earphones plugged in and my music turned
20 off, I'd pretend to read while eavesdropping on conversations about end-of-year exams, mean bosses, new girlfriends, old boyfriends and mother-in-law disputes.

In the middle of the night, I'd ease down from my berth for a trip to the loo, invariably putting a socked foot on a stranger's blanket-covered back,
25 mumble my apologies and hope they'd be gone by morning. On other days, I'd board at the opposite end, squeezing on to wooden slats with farmers and fruit sellers who would place guavas in my palm, while joking with their friends through paan*-stained teeth. They'd count their money, touching it

Exam-style questions

to their foreheads with thanks, before sloping off the train and crossing the
30 tracks to find the next customer.

On arrival in Londa, I paced the platform munching on hot, fresh vadas and enquired when the return train would arrive, and was dismayed to discover it wasn't due until 2 a.m. It was barely 6 p.m. Gradually the crowds thinned, the skies turned indigo and there was nothing but the chirp of crickets
35 for company. A lone passenger watched me from a doorway. And he wouldn't leave.

At the other end of the platform I spotted a sweeper and beelined for the elderly man, who led me to a nearby guesthouse where I could stay for a few hours before the train arrived – it was always the kindness of strangers.

40 Just before 2 a.m. I crossed the road to the station as the train was rolling in. With no reservation, I boarded the women's compartment, a dimly lit dormitory of bundled bodies and bare feet. Finding me an unoccupied berth, the ticket inspector gestured for me to climb up. The train sailed out of the station and I wriggled down under the blanket before turning over to see my
45 neighbour watching me. She winked and her diamond nose stud shone in the milky light from the moving platform. I was back in my safe place, back at home.

betel-nut: *nut commonly chewed as a stimulant in India*
livery: *painted symbols indicating ownership*
sari: *traditional outfit worn by Indian women*
'locals': *local trains*
microcosm: *a little world*
paan: *betel nut rolled in a betel leaf*

Source 7B: 'Baghdad to Basra, On the Wrong Side of the Tracks' by Cesar G. Soriano

This extract is taken from Cesar G. Soriano's essay 'Baghdad to Basra, On the Wrong Side of the Tracks' from *Best of Lonely Planet Travel Writing*. The writer describes a long train journey in Iraq.

Jabar, Sabah and most of the male passengers passed the time on the long train ride by chain-smoking. It wasn't long before the carriages were thick with smoke. For non-smokers like me, relief could only be found by sticking our heads out of the cracked windows or putting our noses to one
5 of the many bullet holes. Despite all this, across the aisle from me, Abdul Yaseen, his wife and their four children were ecstatic about their first-ever train adventure. They were returning home to Basra after attending a wedding near Baghdad. 'I like the train because it's more comfortable, slow and lets the kids have a chance to see the countryside,' he said. His wide-
10 eyed children were peering from the windows, wearing their best clothes, reminiscent of a time when travelling was actually an occasion for dressing up. Abdul's nine-year-old daughter, Haba, surprised to see an American on board, latched onto us and peppered me with questions in broken English: 'Mister, where you from? You married? You have children? You like Arabian
15 music? You like Jennifer Lopez? Mister, buy me Pepsi!'

Practice EXAM

Exam-style questions

Around 4pm the train pulled into the station in Nasiriyah, one of the largest cities in southern Iraq. But, unlike our stops at other cities, the train did not immediately pull out but sat at the platform. And sat. And sat. There was no announcement or explanation for our delay. The thermometer
20 on the platform read 100°F. Inside, the train was becoming a steel oven, baking us alive. Within minutes, we were drenched in sweat. The stench of body odour, dirty baby diapers and the raw sewage on the tracks became unbearable. An old woman fainted and was carried outside into the shade and doused with water, and many more of us followed her out into the air.
25 Angry passengers took out their rage on the conductor, who explained that the station manager had refused to give clearance for the train to proceed. Apparently there was only one working track between Nasiriyah and Basra, and a northbound cargo train already had dibs*. An hour later, without a whistle or warning, the train began pulling out of the station. Of course, most
30 of us were still out on the platform and had to run and jump back onto the moving train.

South of Nasiriyah, we reached the most scenic point of the journey. The endless monochrome images of brown, dusty villages were replaced by lush, green landscape, fields of corn, alfalfa and date palms. This was the Arab
35 Marshland, a fertile region between the Tigris and Euphrates Rivers that is the legendary location of the Garden of Eden. The setting sun blazed into the windows of the right side of the train. There were no curtains or shades to pull down, so passengers took chewing gum from their mouths and used it to stick newspapers onto the windows to shield their heads from the sun. Ah,
40 so that was why there was gum stuck all over the windows.

dibs: *priority*

P2/Q7(b)

7(b).3

Q7(b) Compare how the writers present ideas and perspectives about wild swimming.

You should write about:
- the ideas and perspectives
- how they are presented
- how they are similar/different.

Support your answer with detailed references to the texts. **[14 marks]**

> **LINK**
>
> This question refers to the whole text of Source 8A: 'RIP wild swimming! Nature's "cure all" has thrown in the towel' by Eva Wiseman, and the whole text of Source 8B: 'When wild swimming is deeply dangerous' by Helen Carroll. These sources can also be found on pages 230–232.

Source 8A: 'RIP wild swimming! Nature's "cure all" has thrown in the towel' by Eva Wiseman

> This is an opinion piece from the *Guardian* newspaper by a regular columnist.

Farewell, wild swimming, it's been fun. Well, not fun. Not 'fun' in the traditional sense of the word. More, it's been baffling, sometimes blood-curdling and, eventually, a banal cliché* flattened by over-use, but this is an obituary of sorts, so we will be kind.

5 Much in the same way Lucozade rebranded itself from medicine to energy drink, in the past decade this hobby pivoted to wellness, adding the 'wild' having spent many years known simply as 'swimming'. Led in no small part by this newspaper, it became a trend, elevated by its health-giving properties and photos of nice ladies grinning in swimwear. It was not for me. No, I am
10 a person quite tied to dry land, and cosiness, and a lack of eels scraping my shins, but I applaud those who did it. Those brave enough to jump straight into lakes, whether for exercise, their mental health, their headaches or their Instagrams. You always knew who was a wild swimmer, because they would tell you, frequently. And I'd applaud until my palms stung, because this was
15 a feat of endurance and bravery so far beyond my own pathetic limits that they might as well have jumped into an active volcano rather than the local pond. But.

But but but. When something becomes a trend, its clock starts ticking. Wild swimming is no different. The first nail in its coffin came with the blunt force
20 of marketing: it was presented as a cure for everything. Feeling sad, feeling a low ache in your temples, feeling burned out, grim from too long online, feeling an unravelling guilt about contributing to the climate crisis, feeling disconnected from your body, disconnected from your community, feeling too many feelings or too few – take your clothes off and jump in the lake.
25 There, nature will cleanse you quickly of all your human agonies and sins. Cured.

It has long bothered me, this idea that nature exists as a wellness product, like a scented candle or very green tea, rather than a system that persists in spite of our many-pronged attempts to control it or, of course, profit from
30 it. The popularity of wild swimming led to an increased interest in similar nature therapies, like 'forest bathing', said to counter illnesses including

Practice

Practice EXAM

Exam-style questions

'cancer, strokes, gastric ulcers, depression, anxiety and stress'. This morning I received an email advertising a restorative forest bathing retreat with overnight prices starting at £599 – a light lunch is included. Without wanting
35 to sound too much like a red-faced management consultant shouting in a beer garden, that is a lot of money to spend on going for a walk. Isn't it?

I have no doubt these moments of slowness and fresh air do help, but their ability to cure a person of all their pains surely also relies on serious structural support and a little bit of medicine, too. But the nail had been
40 banged: these spiritual experiences had been packaged and given price tags, and the magical sheen was dulled.

The second nail was, well, the sewage. Last year, the images of blissy swimmers we'd become accustomed to were replaced by pictures of floating faeces and stories about people falling horribly ill after ingesting raw sewage.
45 According to the Labour Party's analysis of Environment Agency data, since 2016 water companies have pumped raw sewage into our seas and rivers for more than 9m hours. And last week it was reported that hundreds of landfill dumps containing 'plastics, chemicals and other waste are a ticking timebomb threatening to leach pollution' on to beaches and into the sea.

banal cliché: *something that has become boring by repetition*

Source 8B: 'When wild swimming is deeply dangerous' by Helen Carroll

This extract is from an article published in the *Daily Mail*: 'When wild swimming is deeply dangerous' by Helen Carroll (July 2021).

When Sophie Skellern lost her grandma, whom she had nursed through her dying days during the first lockdown, the one thing that helped ease her grief was open-water swimming. Whatever the weather, three times a week, Sophie would pull on her swimming costume and head to the lake at Sale
5 Water Park, near her home in Manchester, where, front crawling through the chilly waters, she would briefly forget her sadness. In fact, wild swimming left Sophie, 29, feeling so exhilarated that it had never occurred to her what a risky form of exercise it can be. But last month — if she hadn't had a float and her boyfriend on hand — she could have died while swimming in a lake near
10 Mount Snowdon during a holiday.

'I was half a mile from the water's edge when both my calves cramped up and I couldn't move or kick them, the pain was so intense,' recalls Sophie, shuddering at the memory of what happened in Llyn Gwynant. 'I felt almost paralysed from the waist down as I lay on my back trying to float. Luckily
15 I knew to immediately lie on my back and put the tow float I was pulling across my chest. Someone new to this may not have had a float with them and I dread to think what would have happened if I'd panicked. That's when people drown. However, the 30 minutes it took for the cramping to pass were

among the scariest of my life. Fortunately, my partner, Jack, was also in the lake, in a kayak about 100 metres away. He noticed I'd stopped swimming and was on my back and I was able to raise my arm and beckon him over.

'It was a tiny one-person kayak, so there was no way he could have pulled me in, or even towed me back to shore, but he stayed beside me, giving me sips of water, while I tried to point my toes to stretch out the muscles, until the cramping finally eased enough for normal sensations to return to my legs. It would have been so easy to start hyperventilating. However, thankfully, I forced myself to keep taking deep breaths and stay calm, because getting stressed and anxious in water is the very worst thing you can do. After half an hour, my legs felt strong enough for Jack to escort me back to the shore.'

Sophie, who organises art exhibitions and is studying for a PhD, believes her legs cramped because she had not drunk enough water and had become dehydrated in the heat, nor had she left enough of a gap between eating lunch and getting into the water — mistakes she will not repeat.

She's one of many women who enjoy so-called 'wild swimming', which has caught on like wildfire in recent years. Barely a day goes by without someone in the public eye — supermodel Helena Christensen, TV presenters Fearne Cotton and Susannah Constantine and even former Prime Minister David Cameron are all fans — espousing its virtues. From improving sleep, boosting immunity and metabolism, to 'significantly reducing' symptoms of anxiety and depression, outdoor swimming is seen by many as a cure-all.

Yet despite its benefits, there is no denying that swimming in open water is far riskier than a trip to your local pool. Since the heatwave began on July 14, at least 40 people have lost their lives in open water — rivers, lakes, natural pools and the sea — treble the usual rate of water deaths, which average 19 a year.

But wild swimming poses risks whatever the weather, with dangers including near freezing temperatures, water-born contaminants and hidden obstructions.

Knowledge EXAM

Paper 2: Questions 8 and 9

Questions 8 and 9: Overview

Focus	Marks	Time	AO
Write for a form, audience, and purpose	40 marks	45 minutes	AO5, AO6

Questions 8 and 9 are writing tasks that ask you to write in a particular form, and for a particular audience and purpose. You may be given an opinion statement and be asked to give your own opinion on it. You could be asked to write a letter, an article, text for a leaflet, a review, an essay, or a speech. You may have to persuade, explain, inform, or explore. These are known collectively as '**transactional** writing'. You only have to choose *one* of the two questions.

Whichever question you answer, it is important to plan your response before you start writing. Aim to plan one clear point per paragraph. Use the planning box on the exam paper for this.

LINK

The language features you could talk about for this question are covered in the Concept Knowledge sections on pages 2–62. Look at the sections on texts and their meaning, rhetoric, attitudes and perspectives, and structuring an argument.

Questions 8 and 9: Strategy

Follow the steps below to respond to a Question 8 or 9 task.

Step 1: Read both questions carefully. Think about:
- what the statement or instruction says
- the text type, audience, and purpose (TAP).

Step 2: Jot down one or two ideas that you could use for each question.

Step 3: Bearing in mind your ideas for each question, decide which one to answer.

Step 4: Write a simple plan for structuring your writing.

Step 5: Write your response.

Step 6: Proofread and make corrections for spelling, punctuation, and grammar.

P2/Q8-Q9

Questions 8 and 9: Example

Here is an example Question 8 or 9 asking you to argue your point of view:

Section B: Transactional Writing

You should spend about **45 minutes** on this section.

Q8/9 A newspaper editorial has said: **'Young people are dangerously addicted to mobile phones and other smart devices.'**

Write a **letter to the editor** in which you argue your point of view on this statement.

In your letter, you could include:

- how young people use phones and devices
- the positives of phone and device use
- the negatives of phone and device use

as well as any other ideas you might have.

Your response will be marked for the accurate and appropriate use of vocabulary, spelling, punctuation, and grammar.

[40 marks]

Questions 8 and 9 are both worth 40 marks out of a total of 96 marks, so it's important to make sure you leave enough time to tackle one of them in detail.

In an opinion-based question, the statement will give a strong view about something to help you form an opinion. You don't *have* to say whether you agree or disagree with it, but you will probably write more effectively if you lead up to a conclusion supporting one side or the other.

You will be given the text type and purpose, and sometimes a clear audience, so you can decide the **tone** and level of formality of your writing. Here, it is a letter to an editor arguing your point of view, so you should write in an engaging but firm tone. Remember to begin with 'Dear Editor' and end with 'Yours sincerely...'. You don't need to include an address.

Each question will include some bullet points that you might want to include in your answer. These can be the basis of your planning and writing. However, you are not required to use these suggestions.

Out of the 40 marks available, up to 16 marks are for spelling, punctuation, grammar, and vocabulary choice (AO6), so it's really important that you allow time to proofread and don't miss out on easy marks getting the basics right. The other 24 marks are for how clearly you communicate and organise your ideas, considering form, purpose, and audience (AO5).

LINK

All the language features and structural devices from the Concept Knowledge section on pages 2–62, and the Writing Knowledge you will explore in the rest of this section, can be used in your writing for Questions 8 and 9.

Knowledge **201**

Knowledge

EXAM

Paper 2: Questions 8 and 9

Questions 8 and 9: Structure

The purpose of your writing could be to argue, persuade, explain, inform, advise, or review. These are all possible purposes, but it is highly likely that the purpose of at least one question will be to argue or persuade. This could be in various text types, such as a letter or speech.

Whatever topic you are writing about or form you are writing in, there are many possible approaches. Here is one way you could structure a response to a question asking you to argue or explain your opinion:

Four-part structure

1 Opening: give a clear outline of the issue you are discussing and your views on it. You could write a balanced, neutral response which discusses the merits of both sides, but it is usually easier to write expressing a strong opinion. Depending on the audience and purpose, you might use emotive language or imagery in your opening.

2 Counter-argument: explain why other people might disagree with you, or how some people feel differently, but show why those opinions aren't as strong as yours.

3 Develop your argument in three ways. Aim to write at least three paragraphs for this main part of your response:

  a   An emotive argument: Explore the *emotional* reasons why your reader should agree with you, e.g., how it might impact people who are vulnerable.

  b   An anecdote: Give a *specific* example of how the issue has affected a real person, e.g., *My cousin had this exact issue when...*

  c   Consequences: Show that *if* this problem doesn't change, *then this* will be the consequence. Describe what will happen in the worst-case scenario to show how serious the problem is.

4 Finish your argument with a solution to the problem:
e.g., *Change the law now and end this injustice...*
If we make this positive change in our daily lives, we can make the world a better place...

❶ Your purpose is key here: consider, what does your writing need to achieve? Your opening should make this clear.

❷ Argumentative writing may be more challenging and less accepting of alternative viewpoints than persuasive writing, which aims to change a reader's mind rather than simply challenge it. Explorative writing may consider the different aspects of an issue without reaching a clear conclusion.

❸ Each of these approaches can be used for different purposes. For example, an emotive argument can be persuasive when it creates sympathy, or explanatory when it supports a point, or argumentative when it creates outrage.

❹ A persuasive ending may try to connect with the reader, whereas an argument could be more forceful in its demand for change.

> **REMEMBER**
> The opening and closing of your writing will be slightly different if you are writing a letter – see the example on pages 206–207.

P2/Q8-Q9

Expressing a point of view

Follow these tips when writing to express a point of view:

- Repetition and groups of three – use lists of ideas, repeated phrases, and sentences in groups of three to create impact and show you can craft language.
- Consider tone – A letter to an MP needs to be more formal than a persuasive speech for teenagers. Always write in Standard English, but adjust your use of humour and dramatic language to suit the task and audience.
- Choose vocabulary carefully – a range of interesting word choices including **rhetorical** and emotive language will create tone and help build a sophisticated argument. Offensive language is never appropriate, however strongly you wish to make a point.
- Sentence structure – if every sentence starts the same way and is roughly the same length, your writing will feel dull. Vary sentence length and structure for interest.

Even if there is no audience defined in the question, it is helpful to think in terms of what readers you are aiming at. This is especially important with letters and speeches. For any writing to persuade, it is effective to end with a 'call to action', telling your audience what you think they should do, or what should be done – for example, by your school or the local council.

Knowledge

Knowledge — EXAM

Paper 2: Questions 8 and 9

Questions 8 and 9: Writing a letter – planning

A letter is one of the most common forms used in Questions 8 and 9. Here is an example:

> **Q8/9** A newspaper editorial has said: 'Young people are dangerously addicted to mobile phones and other smart devices.'
>
> Write a letter to the editor in which you argue your point of view on this statement.
>
> In your letter, you could include:
> - how young people use phones and devices
> - the positives of phone and device use
> - the negatives of phone and device use
>
> as well as any other ideas you might have. **[40 marks]**

Every writing task is different and could be answered in many ways. It is important that your own style and voice shine through. The example below is just one approach to planning a response for the above question. Look at how it works and consider how you might use similar ideas and techniques yourself.

For your plan, you could use five sections to quickly jot down ideas for your four key argument areas, plus some key vocabulary you might be able to use as you write. As a general rule, each section of your plan could become a separate paragraph in your answer. A simple alternative is to follow the bullet prompts in the question, and then add a conclusion.

Letter – purpose: to argue for the statement, 'mobile phones are a dangerous addiction for teenagers'

- **OPENING** Key vocabulary: maze, false, plague, fear
- **DEVELOP** Key phrases: children and young people, social media danger
- **COUNTER-ARGUMENTS** Counter-argument: usefulness of phones in sharing ideas. Key vocabulary: yes, we might…, however…, but…, it is clear that…,
- **FINISH** Key phrases: take smart phones away now
- **VOCABULARY** toxicity, addiction, unfortunately

P2/Q8-Q9

Questions 8 and 9: Writing an article – planning

A magazine article is also a common form used in Questions 8 and 9. This type of text may invite you to explore or inform, rather than argue or persuade. Here is an example:

> **Q8/9** Write an article for a magazine about the perfect holiday.
>
> In your article, you could include:
> - what people look for in a holiday
> - different types of holidays
> - advice for having the perfect holiday
>
> as well as any other ideas you might have. **[40 marks]**

The following approach also uses five sections for your four key ideas, plus some useful vocabulary. Each section in your plan can form the basis of a paragraph

EXAMPLE PLAN:

Opening	{ What is a 'holiday'?
Options	{ Some people like to...
Develop	{ purpose, fun, industry, romance
	anecdote: when it goes wrong
Finish	{ Tips on how to have a perfect holiday
Vocabulary	{ perspective, dwindle, adrenalin

Knowledge

Knowledge

Paper 2: Questions 8 and 9

Questions 8 and 9: Letter – sample answer

Here is an example response to the question on page 201, using the four-part structure outlined earlier.

Dear Editor

I am writing in response to your article last week about young people's addiction to smart devices. I agree that mobile addiction is a plague on our society. Generation Z are locked into a virtual maze where we value ourselves by 'likes' and strangers can contact us with false identities. I fear that, unless we act soon, we will become slaves to tech. **❶**

It is true, of course, that smart phones and tablets have their uses. We need to communicate, and the internet is an incredibly helpful tool. However, this doesn't mean we need it all day, every day, everywhere. Yes, we might use an app to communicate with our loved ones when we are outside the house, but that quickly turns into late night scrolling and sending GIFs to each other at 2 a.m. Yes, we might use Google maps to help us find our way, but when do we explore the world as it really is? Yes, we might find new ideas posted online, but that can quickly turn into hate and doom-scrolling. These devices offer more harm than good. **❷**

We know that everyone wants to keep children and vulnerable people safe from harm. We would never allow a 13-year-old to roam the streets alone at night, so why do we let them roam social media? There are dangerous people and extreme groups lurking in the shadows. In between the videos of cats playing the piano and people jumping into really cold water, there are messages of hate. Unfortunately, there is nothing we can do to clean up platforms like TikTok and Instagram.

❶ OPENING: The student introduces the key issue and gives a strong opinion. This is emotive and uses a metaphor (phones are a *plague*), which creates a compelling argument.

❷ COUNTER-ARGUMENT: Phrases like 'some might argue…, but…' and 'it might be true that… however…' enable you to acknowledge other ideas while still developing your own. Notice that the second part of this paragraph includes three sentences which use the structure: 'Yes… but…'. Using the same device, word, or structure three times is an effective way of crafting persuasive language.

206   Paper 2: Question 8 and 9

P2/Q8-Q9

❸ DEVELOP: Emotional argument about children and vulnerable people. Notice the final two sentences in the paragraph: 'Unfortunately… Fortunately…' This is an effective way to connect sentences and show that there can be a solution to a problem.

❺ This list of three rhetorical questions is an effective way to make the reader think, and to show how urgent the problem is.

Fortunately, there is one certain way to keep young people safe: stop them using social media. ❸

We have all heard of characters who are making millions from their content and extreme views online. Recently in Leeds, a teenage boy was arrested for sharing hatespeech online and he was suspended from school. It turned out he'd been approached on social media by someone who claimed to be his own age, and over time he'd been brainwashed. Thankfully, this young man could be helped. It will take time, but he will come through this. ❹ But what about all those who don't? What about those who are pulled further and further into the black hole of the internet? Who will save them? ❺

These devices are a blight on society and a threat to our safety and mental health. Childhood innocence has become a shadow of what it was. Young people are chained to a constantly updated feed, and we must cut it off at the source. Take smart phones away now, or risk losing a whole generation. ❻

Yours sincerely…

TIP
Look at the sophisticated vocabulary selections in this sample answer: 'addiction', 'virtual maze', 'vulnerable', 'blight', etc. These words enhance the quality of writing – vocabulary is weighted very heavily on the mark scheme, so think carefully about your vocabulary choices!

❹ DEVELOP: Anecdote makes case come to life using an example.

❻ FINISH: This use of emotive imagery – 'shadow', 'chained' – is an effective persuasive technique. The student concludes with a solution to the problem.

Examiner's comments
This is a well-structured and sophisticated response, sticking to the focus of the question, and bearing in mind the counter-arguments. The argument flows point by point, helped by vocabulary choices and sparing use of rhetorical devices, including emotive language.

Key terms Make sure you can write a definition for these key terms.

rhetorical language   transactional

Knowledge   207

Knowledge EXAM

Paper 2: Questions 8 and 9

Questions 8 and 9: Article – sample answer

Here is an example response to the question on page 205 which makes use of the bullet prompts in the question.

> **Sun, sea, and sand? What's your perfect holiday?**
>
> What do the words 'perfect holiday' say to you? An oasis of waving palm trees, a tranquil blue sea, a little light reading on the beach? Or would you rather be hiking to Base Camp Everest or para-gliding in the Pyrenees? Maybe you'd be happier cruising up a canal on the Norfolk Broads — or even staying in your own back garden. ❶
>
> Once a holiday was just that — a 'holy day', just one special day when you could down tools and mill around in the town centre, or enjoy some maypole-dancing. Then a few wealthy Victorians invented foreign travel as a mind-broadening pastime. Nowadays, a multi-million pound holiday industry presents a many-tentacled octopus of options. Just deciding is exhausting. It's enough to make you need — well, a holiday! ❷
>
> When it comes to holidays, there's no one-size-fits-all, and of course your budget is a big factor. Some people look forward to camping in the Lake District, come rain or shine, and swear that outdoor cooking tastes twice as good. Others abandon the UK's unpredictable weather for somewhere more reliable or exotic. If you like culture, how about a Nile cruise? Gliding down this ancient waterway is like time-travelling a thousand years back, and there's always a tomb or temple to explore. Others would rather just sprawl on a beach by day, and take in the buzz of night-life in the evening. ❸
>
> If you're trying to choose, ask yourself what you want to get out of a holiday. Most people

❶ The student begins by engaging the reader with a rhetorical question, and giving a range of possible answers that incorporate a tricolon (list of three).

❷ Compares old- and new-style holidays, ending with an engaging, appropriate, and appropriately light-hearted metaphor. Humour establishes a light-hearted tone.

❸ Takes one option and expands it, and offers alternatives.

P2/Q8–Q9

agree that a change of scene provides a new perspective. Problems dwindle viewed through the other end of the telescope. And if we're wound up on deadline adrenalin, a breather can be a live-saver — perhaps literally. On the other hand, some people say the whole point is to make you glad to get home. In that case, the most effective holiday might be the non-stop disaster. Someone I know had her passport stolen in Morocco, spent a week trying to report it, and eventually missed her flight home. She was pretty relieved when she got back! ❹

So, how to achieve that ever-elusive perfect holiday? Well, you first need to choose who you go with. I, for example, wouldn't go with my grandparents. They love cruises. They claim they see the world, but they mostly see the sea — which for me would be as much fun as a month of wet Mondays. However, most of us have partners or families, so we need something for everyone. The trick here is to research what a holiday offers and discuss with the family in advance. Maybe not everyone has to go for the camel ride! And remember, if you cram in too much, it's like a suitcase that just won't shut. ❺

Above all, just have fun. That's more important than being able to upload the perfect holiday video to social media just to show off to your friends! ❻

TIP

Try to use some sophisticated vocabulary – like 'tranquil', 'dwindle', and 'ever-elusive' in this response, and one or two examples of figurative language, such as 'many-tentacled octopus'.

❹ The paragraph opens with a topic sentence and signals a slight change of direction – to offering practical advice. The paragraph explores the topic, then develops this with an anecdote to illustrate a point.

❺ General advice in the form of a metaphor. A powerful and appropriate simile with which to end the paragraph.

❻ Finishes with a final instruction and a humorous twist.

Examiner's comments

The response is well shaped, moving from a question-based exploration of options, to some history, and on to holiday preferences and advice. The light-hearted tone is maintained, yet there are genuinely helpful tips. The student has used a wide range of vocabulary, sentence types, and punctuation, accurately and creatively.

REMEMBER

- Allow 45 minutes to complete this writing task.
- Planning is essential. Spend 5 minutes planning the structure of your response before you begin writing.
- Write for the specific form, purpose, and audience specified in the exam question.
- Use a range of interesting vocabulary and sentence structures.
- Spend 5 minutes at the end proofreading and correcting your work.

Knowledge

Retrieval EXAM

Paper 2: Questions 8 and 9

Use the following questions to check your understanding of the knowledge covered in this section. Then cover the answers column with a piece of paper and write down as many as you can. Check and repeat.

Questions | Answers

#	Questions	Answers
1	How long should you spend on Question 8 or 9?	45 minutes
2	How many marks are available for Questions 8 or 9?	40 marks
3	What is the focus of Questions 8 and 9?	Write for a form, audience, and purpose.
4	How many marks are available for clear, effective, and imaginative communication (AO5), and how many for range of vocabulary and sentences, with accurate spelling and punctuation (AO6)?	AO5: 24 marks AO6: 16 marks
5	How many of the two questions do you have to answer?	One
6	Name one possible purpose for which you may be asked to write.	Choose from: argue; persuade; explain; inform; advise; review; or explore.
7	Name one possible text type you may be asked to write.	Choose from: letter; article; text for a leaflet; review; essay; or speech.
8	Summarise the six steps for tackling Question 8 or 9.	**Step 1**: read both questions carefully. Think about: the statement, text type, audience, and purpose (TAP). **Step 2**: jot down ideas for each question. **Step 3**: decide which one to answer. **Step 4**: write a simple plan. **Step 5**: write your response. **Step 6**: proofread and make corrections.

Previous questions

Now go back and use these questions to check your knowledge of previous topics.

Questions | Answers

#	Questions	Answers
1	What is meant by the 'register' of a text?	The type of language used – especially its level of formality.
2	What is meant by the 'tone' of a text?	A writer's attitude towards a subject, and the relationship they want with the reader.
3	What is meant by the 'perspective' of a text?	The view that the writer has taken on a topic.

Practice

EXAM — **P2/Q8–Q9**

Exam-style questions

Answer the exam-style questions on pages 211–213. Remember, you have a choice of tasks. You must answer only one question.

8.1/9.1

Q8 A university has given this prompt for their essay competition for teenagers.

'Shakespeare is outdated and irrelevant and should be taken off the school curriculum.'

Write an essay for the competition in which you argue your point of view on this statement.

In your essay, you could include

- your views about Shakespeare's relevance
- your views about why it might be worth studying Shakespeare
- arguments for studying other things instead

as well as any other ideas you might have.

[40 marks]

> **EXAM TIP**
>
> In your answer, you should:
>
> - read Questions 8 and 9 carefully again before you begin, even if you read them when you started the exam
> - spend about five minutes planning your answer. It is time well spent as it will help you focus and give your answer a structure
> - spend 35 minutes writing your answer
> - spend the final five minutes proofreading and correcting your answer.

OR

Q9 Write a review of a performance you have seen.

In your review, you could include:

- details of the performance
- your view on what was successful or less so
- how other audience members responded to the performance

as well as any other ideas you might have.

[40 marks]

Practice EXAM

Exam-style questions

8.2/9.2

Q8 'Playing video games is a waste of time that could be spent in the real world.'

Write the text for a leaflet for secondary school pupils in which you explain your point of view on this statement.

In your leaflet, you could include:

- why people find video games appealing
- the advantages and disadvantages of playing video games
- what teenagers could be doing instead

as well as any other ideas you might have.

[40 marks]

OR

Q9 A local newspaper has published a reader's letter stating that 'Young people today have a much easier life than ever before.'

Write a letter to the editor giving your views on this comment.

In your letter, you could include

- your views on what things might have become easier for young people
- your views on what is difficult for young people nowadays
- what things young people will have to face in coming years

as well as any other ideas you might have.

[40 marks]

P2/Q8-Q9

8.3/9.3

Q8 'Nurses are poorly paid, while footballers are paid millions. This is a ridiculous imbalance that should be redressed.'

Write a speech for your school podcast in which you argue your point of view on this statement.

In your speech, you could include:

- your views about nurses' pay
- your views about footballers' pay
- what you think should be done about this

as well as any other ideas you might have.

[40 marks]

OR

Q9 'Developments in science and technology will transform the world for the better in years to come.'

Write a magazine article in which you explore this statement.

In your article, you could include:

- what developments are taking place now
- what you expect the world's future to be like
- how far you think the statement will prove true

as well as any other ideas you might have.

[40 marks]

Knowledge

Paper 1: Source bank

Source 1

Source 1: *Far from the Madding Crowd* by Thomas Hardy

This extract is taken from the novel *Far from the Madding Crowd* by Thomas Hardy, written in 1874. A farmer, Bathsheba, is working with Gabriel Oak trying to save her harvest from a coming storm, because her husband has got all her workers drunk.

Before Oak had laid his hands upon his tools again out leapt the fifth flash, with the spring of a serpent and the shout of a fiend. It was green as an emerald, and the reverberation was stunning. What was this the light revealed to him? In the open ground before him, as he looked over the ridge
5 of the rick, was a dark and apparently female form. Could it be that of the only venturesome woman in the parish – Bathsheba? The form moved on a step: then he could see no more.

'Is that you, ma'am?' said Gabriel to the darkness.

'Who is there?' said the voice of Bathsheba.

10 'Gabriel. I am on the rick, thatching.'

'O, Gabriel! – and are you? I have come about them. The weather awoke me, and I thought of the corn. I am so distressed about it – can we save it anyhow? I cannot find my husband. Is he with you?'

'He is not here.'

15 'Do you know where he is?'

'Asleep in the barn.'

'He promised that the stacks should be seen to, and now they are all neglected! Can I do anything to help? Liddy is afraid to come out. Fancy finding you here at such an hour! Surely I can do something?'

20 'You can bring up some reed-sheaves to me, one by one, ma'am; if you are not afraid to come up the ladder in the dark,' said Gabriel. 'Every moment is precious now, and that would save a good deal of time. It is not very dark when the lightning has been gone a bit.'

'I'll do anything!' she said, resolutely. She instantly took a sheaf upon her
25 shoulder, clambered up close to his heels, placed it behind the rod, and descended for another. At her third ascent the rick suddenly brightened with

LINK

Source 1 is used for the questions on pages 67, 73, 80, and 90.

the brazen glare of shining majolica* – every knot in every straw was visible. On the slope in front of him appeared two human shapes, black as jet. The rick lost its sheen – the shapes vanished. Gabriel turned his head. It had been the sixth flash which had come from the east behind him, and the two dark forms on the slope had been the shadows of himself and Bathsheba. Then came the peal. It hardly was credible that such a heavenly light could be the parent of such a diabolical sound.

'How terrible!' she exclaimed, and clutched him by the sleeve. Gabriel turned, and steadied her on her aerial perch by holding her arm. At the same moment, while he was still reversed in his attitude, there was more light, and he saw, as it were, a copy of the tall poplar tree on the hill drawn in black on the wall of the barn. It was the shadow of that tree, thrown across by a secondary flash in the west.

The next flare came. Bathsheba was on the ground now, shouldering another sheaf, and she bore its dazzle without flinching – thunder and all – and again ascended with the load.

There was then a silence everywhere for four or five minutes, and the crunch of the spars*, as Gabriel hastily drove them in, could again be distinctly heard. He thought the crisis of the storm had passed. But there came a burst of light.

'Hold on!' said Gabriel, taking the sheaf from her shoulder, and grasping her arm again.

Heaven opened then, indeed. The flash was almost too novel for its inexpressibly dangerous nature to be at once realised, and they could only comprehend the magnificence of its beauty. It sprang from east, west, north, south, and was a perfect dance of death. The forms of skeletons appeared in the air, shaped with blue fire for bones – dancing, leaping, striding, racing around, and mingling altogether in unparalleled confusion. With these were intertwined undulating snakes of green, and behind these was a broad mass of lesser light. Simultaneously came from every part of the tumbling sky what may be called a shout; since, though no shout ever came near it, it was more of the nature of a shout than of anything else earthly.

majolica: *shiny, brightly coloured pottery*

spar: *a sharpened wooden rod*

Knowledge

EXAM

Paper 1: Source bank

Source 2

Source 2: *Wuthering Heights* by Emily Brontë

This extract is taken from the 1847 novel *Wuthering Heights*, by Emily Brontë. The 'mistress' of the house, Catherine, has been talking to her childhood friend Heathcliff, with whom she is very close, against the wishes of her husband Edgar Linton. This part of the story is narrated by a servant, Nelly.

'Have you been listening at the door, Edgar?' asked the mistress, in a tone particularly calculated to provoke her husband, implying both carelessness and contempt of his irritation. Heathcliff, who had raised his eyes at the former speech, gave a sneering laugh at the latter; on purpose, it seemed, to
5 draw Mr Linton's attention to him. He succeeded; but Edgar did not mean to entertain him with any high flights of passion.

'I've been so far forbearing with you, sir,' he said quietly; 'not that I was ignorant of your miserable, degraded character, but I felt you were only partly responsible for that; and Catherine wishing to keep up your
10 acquaintance, I acquiesced – foolishly. Your presence is a moral poison that would contaminate the most virtuous: for that cause, and to prevent worse consequences, I shall deny you hereafter admission into this house, and give notice now that I require your instant departure. Three minutes' delay will render it involuntary and ignominious.'

15 Heathcliff measured the height and breadth of the speaker with an eye full of derision.

'Cathy, this lamb of yours threatens like a bull!' he said. 'It is in danger of splitting its skull against my knuckles. By God! Mr Linton, I'm mortally sorry that you are not worth knocking down!'

20 My master glanced towards the passage, and signed me to fetch the men: he had no intention of hazarding a personal encounter. I obeyed the hint; but Mrs Linton, suspecting something, followed; and when I attempted to call them, she pulled me back, slammed the door to, and locked it.

'Fair means!' she said, in answer to her husband's look of angry surprise. 'If
25 you have not courage to attack him, make an apology, or allow yourself to be beaten. It will correct you of feigning more valour than you possess. No,

LINK

Source 2 is used for the questions on pages 70, 76, 86, and 97.

I'll swallow the key before you shall get it! I'm delightfully rewarded for my kindness to each! After constant indulgence of one's weak nature, and the other's bad one, I earn for thanks two samples of blind ingratitude, stupid to absurdity! Edgar, I was defending you and yours; and I wish Heathcliff may flog you sick, for daring to think an evil thought of me!'

It did not need the medium of a flogging to produce that effect on the master. He tried to wrest the key from Catherine's grasp, and for safety she flung it into the hottest part of the fire; whereupon Mr Edgar was taken with a nervous trembling, and his countenance grew deadly pale. For his life he could not avert that excess of emotion: mingled anguish and humiliation overcame him completely. He leant on the back of a chair, and covered his face.

'Oh, heavens! In old days this would win you knighthood!' exclaimed Mrs Linton. 'We are vanquished! we are vanquished! Heathcliff would as soon lift a finger at you as the king would march his army against a colony of mice. Cheer up! you sha'n't be hurt! Your type is not a lamb, it's a sucking leveret*.'

'I wish you joy of the milk-blooded coward, Cathy!' said her friend. 'I compliment you on your taste. And that is the slavering*, shivering thing you preferred to me! I would not strike him with my fist, but I'd kick him with my foot, and experience considerable satisfaction. Is he weeping, or is he going to faint for fear?'

The fellow approached and gave the chair on which Linton rested a push. He'd better have kept his distance: my master quickly sprang erect, and struck him full on the throat a blow that would have levelled a slighter man. It took his breath for a minute; and while he choked, Mr Linton walked out by the back door into the yard, and from thence to the front entrance.

---

sucking leveret: *a young hare still being fed by its mother*
slavering: *dribbling from the mouth, often in hunger or anticipation*

Knowledge

Paper 1: Source bank

Source 3

Source 3: *Frankenstein* by Mary Shelley

This extract is taken from the 1818 novel *Frankenstein* by Mary Shelley. A monstrous 'creature' tells his creator, Victor Frankenstein, that he wants a mate. The story is narrated by Frankenstein.

What I ask of you is reasonable and moderate; I demand a creature of another sex, but as hideous as myself; the gratification is small, but it is all that I can receive, and it shall content me. It is true, we shall be monsters, cut off from all the world; but on that account we shall be more attached to one
5 another. Our lives will not be happy, but they will be harmless and free from the misery I now feel. Oh! My creator, make me happy; let me feel gratitude towards you for one benefit! Let me see that I excite the sympathy of some existing thing; do not deny me my request!'

I was moved. I shuddered when I thought of the possible consequences
10 of my consent, but I felt that there was some justice in his argument. His tale and the feelings he now expressed proved him to be a creature of fine sensations, and did I not as his maker owe him all the portion of happiness that it was in my power to bestow? He saw my change of feeling and continued,

15 'If you consent, neither you nor any other human being shall ever see us again; I will go to the vast wilds of South America. My food is not that of man; I do not destroy the lamb and the kid to glut my appetite; acorns and berries afford me sufficient nourishment. My companion will be of the same nature as myself and will be content with the same fare. We shall make our bed of
20 dried leaves; the sun will shine on us as on man and will ripen our food. The picture I present to you is peaceful and human, and you must feel that you could deny it only in the wantonness* of power and cruelty. Pitiless as you have been towards me, I now see compassion in your eyes; let me seize the favourable moment and persuade you to promise what I so ardently desire.'

LINK

Source 3 is used for the questions on pages 70, 76, 86, and 98.

25 'You propose,' replied I, 'to fly from the habitations of man, to dwell in those wilds where the beasts of the field will be your only companions. How can you, who long for the love and sympathy of man, persevere in this exile? You will return and again seek their kindness, and you will meet with their detestation; your evil passions will be renewed, and you will then have a
30 companion to aid you in the task of destruction. This may not be; cease to argue the point, for I cannot consent.'

'How inconstant are your feelings! But a moment ago you were moved by my representations, and why do you again harden yourself to my complaints? I swear to you, by the earth which I inhabit, and by you that made me, that
35 with the companion you bestow I will quit the neighbourhood of man and dwell, as it may chance, in the most savage of places. My evil passions will have fled, for I shall meet with sympathy! My life will flow quietly away, and in my dying moments I shall not curse my maker.'

His words had a strange effect upon me. I compassionated him* and sometimes
40 felt a wish to console him, but when I looked upon him, when I saw the filthy mass that moved and talked, my heart sickened and my feelings were altered to those of horror and hatred. I tried to stifle these sensations; I thought that as I could not sympathize with him, I had no right to withhold from him the small portion of happiness which was yet in my power to bestow*.

wantonness: *wickedness*
compassionated him: *felt sorry for him*
bestow: *give*

Knowledge

Paper 1: Source bank

Source 4

Source 4: *Great Expectations* by Charles Dickens

This extract is taken from the 1861 novel by Charles Dickens, *Great Expectations*. A young boy, Pip, has been told that he has to visit a strange, rich old woman, Miss Havisham, who is the guardian of a girl, Estella. Miss Havisham wants to see Pip play with Estella. The story is narrated by Pip as an adult.

'Call Estella,' she repeated, flashing a look at me. 'You can do that. Call Estella. At the door.'

To stand in the dark in a mysterious passage of an unknown house, bawling Estella to a scornful young lady neither visible nor responsive, and feeling it
5 a dreadful liberty so to roar out her name, was almost as bad as playing to order. But she answered at last, and her light came along the dark passage like a star.

Miss Havisham beckoned her to come close, and took up a jewel from the table, and tried its effect upon her fair young bosom and against her pretty
10 brown hair. 'Your own, one day, my dear, and you will use it well. Let me see you play cards with this boy.'

'With this boy? Why, he is a common labouring boy!'

I thought I overheard Miss Havisham answer – only it seemed so unlikely, 'Well? You can break his heart.'

15 'What do you play, boy?' asked Estella of myself, with the greatest disdain.

'Nothing but beggar my neighbour, miss.'

'Beggar him,' said Miss Havisham to Estella. So we sat down to cards.

It was then I began to understand that everything in the room had stopped, like the watch and the clock, a long time ago. I noticed that Miss Havisham
20 put down the jewel exactly on the spot from which she had taken it up. As Estella dealt the cards, I glanced at the dressing-table again, and saw that the shoe upon it, once white, now yellow, had never been worn. I glanced down at the foot from which the shoe was absent, and saw that the silk stocking on it, once white, now yellow, had been trodden ragged. Without
25 this arrest of everything, this standing still of all the pale decayed objects, not even the withered bridal dress on the collapsed form could have looked so like grave-clothes, or the long veil so like a shroud.

LINK

Source 4 is used for the questions on pages 71, 77, 87, and 100.

So she sat, corpse-like, as we played at cards; the frillings and trimmings on her bridal dress, looking like earthy paper. I knew nothing then of the discoveries that are occasionally made of bodies buried in ancient times, which fall to powder in the moment of being distinctly seen; but, I have often thought since, that she must have looked as if the admission of the natural light of day would have struck her to dust.

'He calls the knaves Jacks, this boy!' said Estella with disdain, before our first game was out. 'And what coarse hands he has! And what thick boots!'

I had never thought of being ashamed of my hands before; but I began to consider them a very indifferent pair. Her contempt for me was so strong, that it became infectious, and I caught it.

She won the game, and I dealt. I misdealt, as was only natural, when I knew she was lying in wait for me to do wrong; and she denounced me for a stupid, clumsy labouring-boy.

'You say nothing of her,' remarked Miss Havisham to me, as she looked on. 'She says many hard things of you, but you say nothing of her. What do you think of her?'

'I don't like to say,' I stammered.

'Tell me in my ear,' said Miss Havisham, bending down.

'I think she is very proud,' I replied, in a whisper.

'Anything else?'

'I think she is very pretty.'

'Anything else?'

'I think she is very insulting.' (She was looking at me then with a look of supreme aversion.)

'Anything else?'

'I think I should like to go home.'

'And never see her again, though she is so pretty?'

'I am not sure that I shouldn't like to see her again, but I should like to go home now.'

'You shall go soon,' said Miss Havisham, aloud. 'Play the game out.'

Paper 2: Source bank

Source 5A

Source 5A: 'Bah humbug to all of you who just hate Christmas' by David Mitchell

> This text is taken from 'Bah humbug to all of you who just hate Christmas' by David Mitchell, a newspaper article published in 2008. David Mitchell is a comedian who is giving his opinion about people who don't like Christmas.

My official policy on Christmas is that I like it. That says a lot more about me than that I'm partial to a day spent watching TV and stuffing my face. More fundamentally, it shows that I can't stand the thought of our most public and celebratory festival being a lie. It is a happy and magical time, I'm insisting,
5 for deeper and more sinister reasons than a liking for Brazil nuts and *Shrek 3*.

Other people – my enemies – love to hate Christmas. They rejoice in looking at the sparkle, the bustle, the drinking and the queues and muttering: 'Christmas is a nightmare'; 'We're going to Jane's parents – it's going to be a living hell'; 'The sooner we can forget all the expense and false jollity, this
10 great capitalist hypocrisy dance, the better, I say,' as if commerce* were as exclusive to this time of year as mince pies.

As they grumble and sneer their way through the season – seek each other out for affirmation that it's all just a sick joke and that participating is as joyous as diarrhoea and as prudent as a pyramid scheme* I stand shocked
15 and afraid. To the boy I once was, heart buoyed* by the air of magic, and expectation of an acquisitive* nature about to be satisfied, this is a colossal slap in the face: it has finally all ended in tears.

So I must sustain my policy. It's vulnerable, I know. I'm not at a good time of life for liking Christmas. The childhood enchantment has long gone, as has
20 the excitement about presents, and I have no children to help me rediscover it vicariously*. Meanwhile, shopping is stressful, tree lights never work, turkey's not the best meat in the world and Christmas pudding is weird. If I'm not careful, I'll realise I'm only in it for the booze.

But I'm still too tribal to accept this conclusion. We of the Christmas-liking
25 tribe will keep the Christmas-cynic tribe in perpetual subjugation – they will be made to join in whether they like it or not and particularly if not. They will never, if we can help it, be permitted to 'get away somewhere hot' but, if they do, we can be confident that our allies overseas will besiege them with spray-on snow and piped-in Slade even as they sweat round the pool.

30 This is a time when we all come together to disagree about how Christmas is supposed to be done. It's not so much 'love thy neighbour' as 'mock the neon Santa on thy neighbour's roof'. I think these divisions might be

LINK

Source 5A is used for the questions on pages 123, 129, 135, 166, and 184.

what saves my pro-Christmas policy because I love asserting my way of celebrating it over everyone else's. In another life, I could have been a great
35 witchfinder general, paranoid anti-communist or warrior ant. I will root out people who slightly differ from me in their Christmas traditions and blow them away with the twin barrels of my British disdain gun, which are, of course, snobbery and inverse snobbery.

To test your suitability for this fight, consider your reaction to the phrase:
40 'We actually had goose this year.' It's not the nature of your reaction that's important, but its strength. I'm hoping for a strong one. Either: 'Yes of course, goose is a much tastier meat and an older tradition. I can't believe those turkey-eating scum are suffered to live. They should be locked up in the same hell sheds where the bland objects of their culinary affection are
45 chemically spawned.' Or, and this is the one I favour: '[Get] back to Borough Market with your talk of goose deliciousness. We're supposed to eat turkey – that's now the tradition.'

commerce: *buying and selling*
pyramid scheme: *a sales scheme: people pay to join and only make money by recruiting others*
buoyed: *lifted up*
acquisitive: *wanting possessions*
vicariously: *through someone else*

Source 5B

Source 5B: 'Why I skipped Christmas – and why you might like to try it too' by Sandy Summons

This extract is from an article, 'Why I skipped Christmas – and why you might like to try it too', by Sandy Summons, in the *Guardian* (December 2022).

Christmas is the most magical time of the year. But is it really? Now I'm no grinch*. In fact, I absolutely love Christmas. Yet there was a stage when I needed to have a holiday from this popular holiday. So one year we decided to 'skip Christmas' to simplify our Christmas Day.

5 The festive season is overwhelming for many, especially with increased financial pressures and family obligations. A recent report revealed one in six people believe Christmas is the most stressful time of the year. Family conflict is often rife, with some sort of bickering over presents or food. And then there's the family member who has too much to drink and thinks it
10 is their duty to sing a 'special' rendition of Mariah Carey's 'All I Want for Christmas'. Unlike friends, we can't choose our relatives!

LINK

Source 5B is used for the questions on pages 147, 154, 166, and 184.

Knowledge

Paper 2: Source bank

When I was younger, Christmas Day seemed so much simpler. With only my parents and siblings, it was fun and uncomplicated. We spent time playing with our new toys and wearing the clothing items we received. I still remember getting green knickerbockers one Christmas (for those that don't know, a style of shorts that were very hip back then), and I was utterly delighted. We didn't need anything more.

These days are quite different. My husband and I usually celebrate with our extended families. However, over the years it has become more demanding. It's not that we didn't want to spend time with family. But traipsing all over the countryside to catch up with relatives and visiting, on average, four to five homes in one day became too much. Yes, at one stage we did that exhausting amount.

One year after being inspired by the movie *Christmas with the Kranks*, we thought we'd change it up. In the movie Tim Allen and Jamie Lee Curtis, who play Luther and Nora Krank, boycott their traditional family Christmas. They choose not to partake in anything Christmas-related including presents, family gatherings, parties, or decorations.

Similarly, we chose to skip the 30C heat, not put up a Christmas tree or to attend our family Christmas festivities. And even though this may seem drastic, to escape the obligations of Christmas we jetted off on an overseas holiday to New York.

While most of our Christmases have been jam-packed, we were able to spend the day how we wanted to. After a lazy breakfast at the hotel, we watched a basketball game at Madison Square Garden, then finished the day walking through a snow-laden Central Park. Spending the time together with our little core family was memorable. It was relaxed and enjoyable.

Funnily enough, skipping our traditional Christmas that year gave us clarity on how we wanted to spend future Christmases. It made us look forward to a simpler Christmas with our extended family. Previously, we had bought presents for our parents, siblings and their partners, plus all their children. It was exhausting, not to mention all the presents destined for either the regifting pile or for landfill. These days only the nieces and nephews aged under 21 receive gifts. In the past, the host would have a meltdown from cooking up a storm, but now we all bring food to share. We realised we enjoyed being with the family but we also wanted to do what makes us happy. To slow down and enjoy stress free, quality time with each other.

grinch: *someone who spoils the enjoyment of others*

Source 6A

Source 6A: 'I left my job in London to grow food' by Claire Ratinon

This extract is taken from a *Guardian* newspaper article by Claire Ratinon, published in 2022. She explains how she left her life in London to move to the countryside and grow organic food.

In July 2016, I was sitting on the rooftop of a building in central London, listening to the gentle rumble of a nearby beehive, when I realised that my life had changed entirely. I didn't intend to quit – quitting crept up on me. After eight years of working in the media, I was on a path to becoming an
5   organic food grower, with a temporary side hustle of city beekeeping.

Not long before that point, I was just like the people in the office building below me. My work days were spent behind a desk or lugging around camera equipment, but now I am devoted to a life of nurturing the soil and growing the plants that end up on our plates. [...]

10 I was growing tired of my life in London and I wanted to explore somewhere new, and it was in New York that a seed was (literally and figuratively) sown for my unexpected change of profession. I encountered the alchemy of food growing for the first time at Brooklyn Grange – a rooftop farm that sits above New York's busy streets and overlooks Manhattan. Dusky leaves of Tuscan
15 kale*, peppers and tomatoes in unexpected shapes and colours, striped aubergines wearing spiked sepal* hats – chaos of abundance in the most unlikely of places. I was captivated.

From that day, all I could think about was getting through each week of working in documentary production so that, come the weekend, I could join
20 the other farm workers at Brooklyn Grange while they harvested, planted out and raked the earth to a fine tilth, ready for the next sowing of seeds. After two seasons of volunteering there, I was determined to make growing food a bigger part of my life. So, as the city I'd come to love was celebrating Halloween, I boarded a plane headed for London.

25 By the time I'd moved back to Hackney, I had a job working in the evenings – and occasionally nights – which left my days free to seek out the unlikely spaces where edible plants could be found growing in the city. After a year, I quit that role and tried to take on any job – each day a different one – that meant I could spend my days outside, my hands in the soil. I stepped into all
30 kinds of roles and every one taught me something precious.

Working as a school gardener showed me how little room there is in the school day and national curriculum for children to learn about how food arrives on their plate; training as a beekeeper taught me that growing nectar-rich flowers is a far better way of supporting pollinators than keeping hives;
35 and growing organic salad leaves to supply a veg box that filled the plates of people in Hackney made me realise there is nothing quite so ordinary and yet somehow remarkable than the act of feeding people.

LINK

Source 6A is used for the questions on pages 126, 132, 140, 173, and 191.

Knowledge EXAM

Paper 2: Source bank

> Leaving London in 2019 to move to a more rural location changed the shape of my life. Now, in a garden of my own, I grow vegetables and fruit of my own choosing […]
>
> I'm probably too romantic in the way I speak about working the land. The fact that it is a difficult and arduous way to make a living is worth stating – if only not to seem delusional. It is work that is backbreaking, exhausting and painfully underpaid. I have sacrificed my bodily wellbeing at its altar many times, yet it remains the most important thing I've ever done.
>
> **kale:** *a leafy vegetable*
> **sepal:** *the outer leaves that protect a flower*

(line numbers: 40, 45)

Source 6B

Source 6B: *Deep Country* by Neil Ansell

> This extract is taken from *Deep Country* by Neil Ansell, who left a life in London, living communally and working with teenagers in care, to live alone in a remote cottage in Wales, where he managed to grow his own food on previously uncultivated land.
>
> Without the sheep coming in to trim it, the grass grew in rank tussocks that I had to hack back with a sickle. Besides the fruit tree, the jackdaw ash and the cotoneaster next to the porch, there was one small rhododendron and a clump of blackthorn by the gate. Once, before my time, a solitary pine had stood guard over the house from above the quarry wall, but it had been unlucky…. I planted out a larch to stand in for the lonesome pine, and in the southwest corner of the garden a beech, which will one day afford the cottage a little shelter from the prevailing wind. Then a couple of rowans, for berries for the birds, and a buddleia for the butterflies. Apart from a row of poppies and wild flowers along the fence, I didn't trouble with flowers. I needed the land for food.
>
> Although I planted a patch of herbs – coriander, dill and parsley, which were unavailable locally – my priority was the heavy vegetables. I didn't want to be hauling sackfuls of potatoes up the mountainside when I could be growing them myself. Preparing the land was hard work; the roots of the grass grew deep and tangled. Then I had to pick out all the rocks, carefully lift any daffodil bulbs for transplantation elsewhere, and lime the soil. Each year I would dig an extra patch, and prepare another for the next year by pegging down a sheet of tarpaulin with bricks to kill off the grass. I didn't want to use any pesticides, and besides the lime I bought no fertilizer. Each

(line numbers: 5, 10, 15, 20)

LINK
Source 6B is used for the questions on pages 150, 160, 173, and 191.

winter, when the bats were long gone to their hibernation roost, I would clamber up into the loft and shovel up bagfuls of guano*. It was dry and powdery and odourless, and it seemed somehow appropriate that the bats who shared my home with me should help me grow my food.

25 I had never grown anything before, I had never stayed in one place long enough to even think about it, and had no idea what would grow well at this altitude, and in a location so exposed to the elements, so it was a process of trial and error. Each year I would try a few new things; if they grew well they would become a fixture; if they failed I would abandon them and try
30 something else. I had a small patch of early potatoes, and a larger patch of main crops. I got a metal dustbin which I kept in the pantry and would fill it to the top with these, enough to last the whole year. Onions and garlic I hung on strings on the woodshed wall, as the mice didn't ever bother them. Garlic was the only thing I planted in autumn; growing garlic seems magical in its
35 simplicity. Take a head of garlic, break it into cloves and plant them in a row. By the next year each clove will have turned into a new head.

Carrots and parsnips I stored in the ground and lifted when I needed them. The carrots in particular were a revelation; they are hard to grow in most places because of the depredations of the carrot fly, but the altitude here
40 kept my crop pest-free. They grew to over a pound in weight without becoming woody, were such a deep orange they were almost red, and tasted better than any others I have had before or since.

guano: *droppings from bats or seabirds*

Source 7A

Source 7A: *Around India in 80 Trains* by Monisha Rajesh

This extract is from a book of travel writing called *Around India in 80 Trains* by Monisha Rajesh. This extract describes her experience of train travel in India.

LINK

Source 7A is used for the questions on pages 126, 142, 176, and 194.

Six-people deep, and growing by the second, the crowd tensed. A single knuckle pressed into my back and betel-nut* breath filled my nostrils as a steady beat rose above the din. Against the peach pink of Mumbai's evening skies, the commuter service curled into view, passengers hanging from
5 the sides like moving livery*. Braking with a wail and grind of metal, the train slowed into the station and I braced against the surge of bodies from behind. Like relay runners, they began to move before the train had stopped, reaching over my head at the same time as a torrent of polyester shirts and satchels thundered down from the open doorways.

10 A slice of papaya in one hand my bag gripped with the other, I battled through elbows, meaty shoulders and thick plaits slicked with coconut oil.

Knowledge

Knowledge

Paper 2: Source bank

In the crush the papaya was knocked to the ground and my sandal came off, but I made it on board and fell sideways into a seat as the train jerked away from the platform. Wiping someone else's sweat from my arm, I watched fellow travellers scrabble for handholds, adjust saris* and pull out phones before relaxing into the ride with a mix of relief and pride. I'd survived my first experience on the infamous Mumbai 'locals'*.

Inside the carriages, a microcosm* of Indian society spanned the train from one end to the other. With my earphones plugged in and my music turned off, I'd pretend to read while eavesdropping on conversations about end-of-year exams, mean bosses, new girlfriends, old boyfriends and mother-in-law disputes.

In the middle of the night, I'd ease down from my berth for a trip to the loo, invariably putting a socked foot on a stranger's blanket-covered back, mumble my apologies and hope they'd be gone by morning. On other days, I'd board at the opposite end, squeezing on to wooden slats with farmers and fruit sellers who would place guavas in my palm, while joking with their friends through paan*-stained teeth. They'd count their money, touching it to their foreheads with thanks, before sloping off the train and crossing the tracks to find the next customer.

On arrival in Londa, I paced the platform munching on hot, fresh vadas and enquired when the return train would arrive, and was dismayed to discover it wasn't due until 2 a.m. It was barely 6 p.m. Gradually the crowds thinned, the skies turned indigo and there was nothing but the chirp of crickets for company. A lone passenger watched me from a doorway. And he wouldn't leave.

At the other end of the platform I spotted a sweeper and beelined for the elderly man, who led me to a nearby guesthouse where I could stay for a few hours before the train arrived – it was always the kindness of strangers.

Just before 2 a.m. I crossed the road to the station as the train was rolling in. With no reservation, I boarded the women's compartment, a dimly lit dormitory of bundled bodies and bare feet. Finding me an unoccupied berth, the ticket inspector gestured for me to climb up. The train sailed out of the station and I wriggled down under the blanket before turning over to see my neighbour watching me. She winked and her diamond nose stud shone in the milky light from the moving platform. I was back in my safe place, back at home.

---

betel-nut: *nut commonly chewed as a stimulant in India*
livery: *painted symbols indicating ownership*
sari: *traditional outfit worn by Indian women*
'locals': *local trains*
microcosm: *a little world*
paan: *betel nut rolled in a betel leaf*

Source 7B

Source 7B: 'Baghdad to Basra, On the Wrong Side of the Tracks' by Cesar G. Soriano

This extract is taken from Cesar G. Soriano's essay 'Baghdad to Basra, On the Wrong Side of the Tracks' from *Best of Lonely Planet Travel Writing*. The writer describes a long train journey in Iraq.

Jabar, Sabah and most of the male passengers passed the time on the long train ride by chain-smoking. It wasn't long before the carriages were thick with smoke. For non-smokers like me, relief could only be found by sticking our heads out of the cracked windows or putting our noses to one
5 of the many bullet holes. Despite all this, across the aisle from me, Abdul Yaseen, his wife and their four children were ecstatic about their first-ever train adventure. They were returning home to Basra after attending a wedding near Baghdad. 'I like the train because it's more comfortable, slow and lets the kids have a chance to see the countryside,' he said. His wide-
10 eyed children were peering from the windows, wearing their best clothes, reminiscent of a time when travelling was actually an occasion for dressing up. Abdul's nine-year-old daughter, Haba, surprised to see an American on board, latched onto us and peppered me with questions in broken English: 'Mister, where you from? You married? You have children? You like Arabian
15 music? You like Jennifer Lopez? Mister, buy me Pepsi!'

Around 4pm the train pulled into the station in Nasiriyah, one of the largest cities in southern Iraq. But, unlike our stops at other cities, the train did not immediately pull out but sat at the platform. And sat. And sat. There was no announcement or explanation for our delay. The thermometer
20 on the platform read 100°F. Inside, the train was becoming a steel oven, baking us alive. Within minutes, we were drenched in sweat. The stench of body odour, dirty baby diapers and the raw sewage on the tracks became unbearable. An old woman fainted and was carried outside into the shade and doused with water, and many more of us followed her out into the air.
25 Angry passengers took out their rage on the conductor, who explained that the station manager had refused to give clearance for the train to proceed. Apparently there was only one working track between Nasiriyah and Basra, and a northbound cargo train already had dibs*. An hour later, without a whistle or warning, the train began pulling out of the station. Of course, most
30 of us were still out on the platform and had to run and jump back onto the moving train.

South of Nasiriyah, we reached the most scenic point of the journey. The endless monochrome images of brown, dusty villages were replaced by lush, green landscape, fields of corn, alfalfa and date palms. This was the Arab
35 Marshland, a fertile region between the Tigris and Euphrates Rivers that is the legendary location of the Garden of Eden. The setting sun blazed into the windows of the right side of the train. There were no curtains or shades to

LINK

Source 7B is used for the questions on pages 150, 151, 161, 176, and 194.

Knowledge

EXAM

Paper 2: Source bank

pull down, so passengers took chewing gum from their mouths and used it to stick newspapers onto the windows to shield their heads from the sun. Ah, so that was why there was gum stuck all over the windows.

dibs: *priority*

Source 8A

Source 8A: 'RIP wild swimming! Nature's "cure all" has thrown in the towel' by Eva Wiseman

This is an opinion piece from The *Guardian* newspaper by a regular columnist.

Farewell, wild swimming, it's been fun. Well, not fun. Not 'fun' in the traditional sense of the word. More, it's been baffling, sometimes blood-curdling and, eventually, a banal cliché* flattened by over-use, but this is an obituary of sorts, so we will be kind.

5 Much in the same way Lucozade rebranded itself from medicine to energy drink, in the past decade this hobby pivoted to wellness, adding the 'wild' having spent many years known simply as 'swimming'. Led in no small part by this newspaper, it became a trend, elevated by its health-giving properties and photos of nice ladies grinning in swimwear. It was not for me. No, I am
10 a person quite tied to dry land, and cosiness, and a lack of eels scraping my shins, but I applaud those who did it. Those brave enough to jump straight into lakes, whether for exercise, their mental health, their headaches or their Instagrams. You always knew who was a wild swimmer, because they would tell you, frequently. And I'd applaud until my palms stung, because this was
15 a feat of endurance and bravery so far beyond my own pathetic limits that they might as well have jumped into an active volcano rather than the local pond. But.

But but but. When something becomes a trend, its clock starts ticking. Wild swimming is no different. The first nail in its coffin came with the blunt force
20 of marketing: it was presented as a cure for everything. Feeling sad, feeling a low ache in your temples, feeling burned out, grim from too long online, feeling an unravelling guilt about contributing to the climate crisis, feeling disconnected from your body, disconnected from your community, feeling too many feelings or too few – take your clothes off and jump in the lake.
25 There, nature will cleanse you quickly of all your human agonies and sins. Cured.

It has long bothered me, this idea that nature exists as a wellness product, like a scented candle or very green tea, rather than a system that persists in

> **LINK**
> Source 8A is used for the questions on pages 127, 133, 144, 179, and 197.

230 Paper 2: Source bank

spite of our many-pronged attempts to control it or, of course, profit from
it. The popularity of wild swimming led to an increased interest in similar
nature therapies, like 'forest bathing', said to counter illnesses including
'cancer, strokes, gastric ulcers, depression, anxiety and stress'. This morning
I received an email advertising a restorative forest bathing retreat with
overnight prices starting at £599 – a light lunch is included. Without wanting
to sound too much like a red-faced management consultant shouting in a
beer garden, that is a lot of money to spend on going for a walk. Isn't it?

I have no doubt these moments of slowness and fresh air do help, but
their ability to cure a person of all their pains surely also relies on serious
structural support and a little bit of medicine, too. But the nail had been
banged: these spiritual experiences had been packaged and given price tags,
and the magical sheen was dulled.

The second nail was, well, the sewage. Last year, the images of blissy
swimmers we'd become accustomed to were replaced by pictures of floating
faeces and stories about people falling horribly ill after ingesting raw sewage.
According to the Labour Party's analysis of Environment Agency data, since
2016 water companies have pumped raw sewage into our seas and rivers
for more than 9m hours. And last week it was reported that hundreds of
landfill dumps containing 'plastics, chemicals and other waste are a ticking
timebomb threatening to leach pollution' on to beaches and into the sea.

banal cliché: *something that has become boring by repetition*

Source 8B

Source 8B: 'When wild swimming is deeply dangerous' by Helen Carroll

This extract is from an article published in the *Daily Mail*: 'When wild swimming is deeply dangerous' by Helen Carroll (July 2021).

> **LINK**
> Source 8B is used for the questions on pages 151, 162, 179, and 197.

When Sophie Skellern lost her grandma, whom she had nursed through her dying days during the first lockdown, the one thing that helped ease her grief was open-water swimming. Whatever the weather, three times a week, Sophie would pull on her swimming costume and head to the lake at Sale Water Park, near her home in Manchester, where, front crawling through the chilly waters, she would briefly forget her sadness. In fact, wild swimming left Sophie, 29, feeling so exhilarated that it had never occurred to her what a risky form of exercise it can be. But last month — if she hadn't had a float and her boyfriend on hand — she could have died while swimming in a lake near Mount Snowdon during a holiday.

'I was half a mile from the water's edge when both my calves cramped up and I couldn't move or kick them, the pain was so intense,' recalls Sophie, shuddering at the memory of what happened in Llyn Gwynant. 'I felt almost paralysed from the waist down as I lay on my back trying to float. Luckily I knew to immediately lie on my back and put the tow float I was pulling across my chest. Someone new to this may not have had a float with them and I dread to think what would have happened if I'd panicked. That's when people drown. However, the 30 minutes it took for the cramping to pass were among the scariest of my life. Fortunately, my partner, Jack, was also in the lake, in a kayak about 100 metres away. He noticed I'd stopped swimming and was on my back and I was able to raise my arm and beckon him over.

'It was a tiny one-person kayak, so there was no way he could have pulled me in, or even towed me back to shore, but he stayed beside me, giving me sips of water, while I tried to point my toes to stretch out the muscles, until the cramping finally eased enough for normal sensations to return to my legs. It would have been so easy to start hyperventilating. However, thankfully, I forced myself to keep taking deep breaths and stay calm, because getting stressed and anxious in water is the very worst thing you can do. After half an hour, my legs felt strong enough for Jack to escort me back to the shore.'

Sophie, who organises art exhibitions and is studying for a PhD, believes her legs cramped because she had not drunk enough water and had become dehydrated in the heat, nor had she left enough of a gap between eating lunch and getting into the water — mistakes she will not repeat.

She's one of many women who enjoy so-called 'wild swimming', which has caught on like wildfire in recent years. Barely a day goes by without someone in the public eye — supermodel Helena Christensen, TV presenters Fearne Cotton and Susannah Constantine and even former Prime Minister David Cameron are all fans — espousing its virtues. From improving sleep, boosting immunity and metabolism, to 'significantly reducing' symptoms of anxiety and depression, outdoor swimming is seen by many as a cure-all.

Yet despite its benefits, there is no denying that swimming in open water is far riskier than a trip to your local pool. Since the heatwave began on July 14, at least 40 people have lost their lives in open water — rivers, lakes, natural pools and the sea — treble the usual rate of water deaths, which average 19 a year.

But wild swimming poses risks whatever the weather, with dangers including near freezing temperatures, water-born contaminants and hidden obstructions.